HR
Competencies

HR
Competencies

Mastery at the Intersection of People and Business

By
Dave Ulrich
Wayne Brockbank
Dani Johnson
Kurt Sandholtz
Jon Younger

The Society for Human Resource Management (SHRM) is the world's largest professional association devoted to human resource management. Our mission is to serve the needs of HR professionals by providing the most current and comprehensive resources, and to advance the profession by promoting HR's essential, strategic role. Founded in 1948, SHRM represents members in over 125 countries, and has a network of more than 575 affiliated chapters in the United States, as well as offices in China and India. Visit SHRM at www.shrm.org.

The RBL Institute is a leadership forum for thoughtful engagement on Strategic Human Resources. The goal of the Institute is to advance HR practice through participative education, joint research, and networking among senior HR Executives.

Library of Congress Cataloging-in-Publication Data
HR competencies : mastery at the intersection of people and business /
by Dave Ulrich ... [et al.].
    p. cm.
  Includes index.
  ISBN 978-1-58644-113-5
  1. Personnel management. I. Ulrich, David, 1953-

HF5549.H6538 2008
658.3--dc22

                          2007047977

Interior design by: Shirley E.M. Raybuck

Printed in the United States of America.
10 9 8 7 6 5   10-0278

Table of Contents

HR Competencies

For the last 20 years, we have been active observers of the human resources (HR) profession and HR professionals. At times, we have championed the HR profession as a source of competitive advantage that offers unique value to customers, particularly in emerging service and knowledge economies. At other times, we have challenged HR professionals to focus on what they deliver more than what they do, and to deliver value to multiple stakeholders inside and outside their organization. At other times, we have been cheerleaders convincing line managers to invite HR professionals to contribute and cajoling HR professionals to accept the opportunities that await them. And, at other times, we have tried to provide a blueprint for how HR practices, professionals, and departments can create and deliver value.

In all of these observations, we have tried to help define and deliver a new set of expectations for HR professionals. These expectations have been rooted in the competencies that HR professionals must master to deliver value over time. When we began our study of HR competencies, the norm was to look at a handful of successful and less successful HR professionals within a firm, to identify critical incidents where their success was magnified, then to build an HR competence model for HR professionals in that organization. Little systematic research was done on the broad set of HR competencies for HR professionals in small or large firms, junior or senior positions, specialists or generalist roles, or global settings.

In addition, the field of HR was filled (some would say plagued) with the latest fads based on well-intended hopes, but with little research. Twenty years ago when we decided to systematically observe HR professionals, we wanted to couple our field work inside companies with rigorous research across companies. We recall the first round of the Human Resource Competency Study (HRCS). We filled a room with piles of participant surveys, associate surveys, and cover letters from us and the corporate sponsor. Over many evenings, we stuffed envelopes and sent thousands of surveys to HR professionals around the world, hoping we could discern patterns of HR competencies that distinguished effective HR professionals.

We were pleasantly surprised by our findings and realized that such rigorous research could inform opinion and help shape the profession, so we decided to replicate our study every five years. This work has resulted in doctoral dissertations, dozens of papers and chapters, assessments, an on-line learning HR toolkit, learning workshops as well as thousands of speeches. It has been acknowledged by leading HR professional associations as the standard for HR competencies. We are pleased that this research can motivate HR professionals to contribute into a roadmap for how to do so.

We have continued the research, doing waves of data collection and analysis, about every five years. Each time, we wonder what we will discover that is new, but we know that relying on data is better than using hunches and that broad-based data sets offer more insightful conclusions about the state of the HR professionals than isolated studies within single companies.

We have promised ourselves after each round of data collection and analysis that we should pull the research together into a book. In 2002, we prepared a workbook, *Competencies for the New HR*, which synthesized the results and offered guidelines on how to interpret the data. In this round of data collection, we committed to finally prepare a book that lays out in some detail the research we have done, our findings and the implications of those findings.

This book is not for everyone. It is not *HR for Dummies*. It is not for those who are afraid of lots of data. It is not for those who want a quick dip in the fountain of HR knowledge so they can catch the next wave. We have chosen to write a comprehensive and empirical book focused on the Round 5 research and findings. We are not ashamed of the data we present and we have tried to present it and our interpretations of it in ways that will inform and guide the profession. We believe that facts and data have more sustainable impact that perceptions and beliefs.

We have tried to organize the book so that readers can confidently answer key questions that face the evolving HR profession:

- **What makes a successful HR professional?** We want to state with clarity and evidence the knowledge, skills, and values that successful HR professionals demonstrate in all types of positions, companies, and geographies.
- **Which HR competencies have the most impact on the performance of the HR professional?** We want to prioritize what HR professionals should know and do as they try to deliver value. Being equally good at all things generally means being excellent at nothing. Being average is the enemy of great, and we want to identify where HR professionals should be great.
- **How do HR competencies affect business performance?** We believe that in knowledge and service economics, organization and people issues become key to long-term success. HR professionals who have competencies to architect, coach, design, and facilitate organization and people issues will help their organization succeed.
- **How much do HR departments affect business vs. individuals who work in HR?** In this round of study, we wanted to not only identify competencies for HR professionals, but governance of HR departments.

We think that these are interesting questions for anyone in HR who wants to be better. For those entering the profession, we chart what will be required to get started. For those in mid career in HR, we lay out challenges to move forward. For those running HR departments, we raise the bar on what should be expected from those in HR. For line managers, we clarify expectations of what HR can and should deliver.

We are indebted to many people who have made this work possible. In the early studies, we had the privilege of working with Dale Lake who helped shape the research; Arthur Yeung who handled thousands of details and set the foundation for excellent analysis; Connie James who brought academic rigor to the data; and Dave Yakonich who helped translate the 2002 data into HR implications.

Since 1982 Dave and Wayne have been privileged to be on the faculty of the Ross School of Business at the University of Michigan. For the majority of that time, we have worked in the Executive Programs. Michigan has been an incredible platform from which to work, learn, and contribute. We are surrounded by outstanding colleagues who continually inform our thinking. Administrators have been supportive and encouraging. Participants in executive programs are inquisitive as well as open to learning and sharing. Our university colleagues have become our friends. We are forever indebted to the University for its support. In particular, we owe a huge debt of both financial and emotional support to Ron Bendersky, who has been our primary contact at the University of Michigan. When we approached Ron with our grand ideas and budget, he was and has been upbeat, encouraging and forthcoming. We are enormously indebted to Michigan's support and Ron's sponsorship and friendship.

We are also grateful for our HR colleagues who have informed our thinking. This list clearly includes writers such as Dick Beatty, Michael Beer, John Boudreau, Peter Cappelli, Wayne Cascio, Ram Charan, Lee Dyer, Bob Eichinger, Jac Fitz-enz, Fred Foulkes, Bob Gandossy, Jay Galbaith, Marshall Goldsmith, Lynda Gratton, Mark Huselid, Bill Joyce, Tom Kochan, Steve Kerr, Ed Lawler, Mike Losey, Sue Meisinger, Henry Mintzberg, Jeffrey Pfeffer, Bonner Ritchie, Libby Sartain, and Patrick Wright.

In this round of the study, to attain a global sample, we have drawn on colleagues from around the world who have partnered with us.

In Latin America, Alejandro Sioli has been instrumental in our study since the 1997 study, the data of which he used as a base for his dissertation, and has shaped our thinking not only in Latin America, but in HR worldwide. With Michel Hermans, they have adapted this work throughout Latin America. We have found superb sponsorship and colleagueship in Europe with the Irish Management Institute and Martin Farrelly, who has a charming and unique mix of insight and energy. Professors Xiaoming Zheng and Felicia Deng opened our eyes and project to the emerging China Market and spent countless hours devising and executing a separate data collection strategy when the first failed to obtain the desired result. Together, they were able to translate ideas and words into the Chinese context. Paul Dainty and Anne-Marie Dolan helped us adapt ideas to Australia and the southeast. Their academic and practical work is much appreciated. In the United States, we have had ongoing support and help from key people at SHRM, namely, Evren Esen and Jessica Collison, who we thank as much for their patience with us as for their attention to detail in recruiting and helping U.S. companies participate; Deb Cohen for her insight into the initial survey and support throughout the process; and Martin Schuebel and Steve Williams for helping us turn this data into tools that will help companies in the future.

We have been privileged to work at The RBL Group (www.rbl.net), which has also sponsored this work and offered extensive insights into its implications. We are particularly indebted to Norm Smallwood, the managing partner, and Warren Wilhelm, who has been a colleague for over a decade. Many of the members of the RBL Institute have been instrumental in shaping our thinking and ideas.

We have been blessed to learn from thought leaders in leading firms who have taught us by their creation and application of ideas. There are too many to mention, but our industry thought leaders include Chris Altizer, Dick Antoine, Katy Barclay, Bob Berman, Svali Björgvinsson, Ken Carig, Bill Conaty, Ralph Christensen, Frank Doyle, Bob Gandossy, John Hofmeister, Paul Humphries, Tony McCarthy, Randy MacDonald, Hallstein Moerck, Paul McKinnon, Patty Murray, Chuck Nielson, Mike Peel, Satish Pradhan, Neil Rhoden, Tony Rucci, Mike Rude, Matt Schuyler, Mike Tucker, Kathleen Wilson-Thompson, and Dean Weatherford.

Finally, we acknowledge over 40,000 people who have filled out surveys and participated in the process of shaping a profession.

We have written this book to synthesize our research and combine insights in one place that might be a starting point for dialogue about HR. As observers of the HR profession, we have enormous faith for the future. We envision HR continuing to be center stage as organizations face greater business changes than they have ever faced. We see HR professionals not only invited to business discussions, but contributing to those discussions. We are advocates for the profession and the professionals who make it happen. We hope this work will help make HR professional more professional.

- Dave Ulrich, Alpine, Utah
- Wayne Brockbank, Accra, Ghana
- Dani Johnson, Salt Lake City, Utah
- Kurt Sandholtz, Stanford, California
- Jon Younger, Short Hills, New Jersey

We are deeply indebted to our regional partnering organizations, who spent countless hours and much expense to help us create the database for the fifth round of HRCS.

Society for Human Resource Management (SHRM)

The Society for Human Resource Management (SHRM) is the world's largest association devoted to human resource management. Representing more than 225,000 individual members, the Society's mission is to serve the needs of HR professionals by providing the most essential and comprehensive resources available.

As an influential voice, the Society's mission is also to advance the human resource profession to ensure that HR is recognized as an essential partner in developing and executing organizational strategy. Founded in 1948, SHRM currently has more than 575 affiliated chapters and members in more than 125 countries.

We have been pleased to have SHRM's cooperation in both the study and resulting tools tools since 2002.

IAE School of Business

IAE is the Management and Business School of the Universidad Austral, with 25 years of experience in the education of business executives in South America. Its mission is "to contribute to the development of knowledge and the training of business people, not only on management skills but also on the human values required for management." Throughout its programs, it provides a service to society in general and to the business world in particular. Its rigorous and qualified teaching is based on solid research of the problems affecting business. As every school of the Universidad Austral, IAE entrusts the prelacy of the Opus Dei with the religious, ethical, and anthropological aspects of its academic activity.

IAE has been an active partner with HRCS since 1997 and has been instrumental in extending the study throughout Latin America. In 1999, IAE also partnered with the Ross School of Business at the University of Michigan to form a research center called Latin American Human Resource Partnership (LAHRP). The center focuses on regional HR issues and includes a group of companies like Unilever, IBM, Pan American Energy (British Petroleum), Techint Group, Standard Bank, and RepsolYPF. Wayne Brockbank and Alejandro Sioli act as academic co-directors.

Irish Management Institute

Since its foundation in 1952, Irish Management Institute (IMI) has been at the forefront of management and organizational development in Ireland. IMI has built an international reputation in the field of adult learning and has contributed to Irish economic and social development.

IMI's mission is to work with individuals and organizations to improve the practice of management. This mission is delivered by providing a forum for practicing managers to exchange leading-edge experience by providing access to international thinkers in the field of management and by operating a world class management training center.

The Champion for HRCS in Europe is Martin Farrelly.

Australian Human Resources Institute (AHRI)

The Australian Human Resources Institute (AHRI) is the national association representing human resource and people management professionals in Australia. AHRI leads the direction and fosters the growth of the HR profession through actively setting standards and building the capability of the profession. Through its international affiliations and its close association with industry and academia, AHRI ensures that its members are given access to a soundly-based professional recognition framework.

AHRI recognizes the changing requirements of Australian business against a background of considerable economic challenge. It also acknowledges the continuing opportunity for the HR profession to actively contribute specialist knowledge for the delivery of people management solutions to business.

Tsinghua University

In 1984, The School of Economics and Management, Tsinghua University was established by Professor Zhu Rongji, the Founding Dean, who later became the fifth Premier of the People's Republic of China. Over the ensuing years, Tsinghua SEM has emerged as the leading business school in China and one of the foremost in Asia. The integration of the School of Economics and Management with the other outstanding faculties at Tsinghua University provides an extraordinarily strong foundation for its future. That foundation will enable the University as a whole, in addition to the School of Economics and Management, to play a major role in helping continue the economic development of China.

Tsinghua SEM has long been cooperating with the best international business schools and institutions. They promote the spirit of TSEM: Always Pursuing Excellence, Always Valuing Actions over Words.

National HRD Network

National HRD Network is a non-profit organization formed on 2 March 1985 with headquarters at Hyderabad, Andhra Pradesh State, India. NHRD has 35 chapters across India with a membership of around 6,000 professionals. The main objectives of the National HRD Network are:

- Humanize systems and organizations positively.
- Build a rigorous, scientific store-house of knowledge and skills.
- Develop and maintain standards of professional excellence.
- Disseminate knowledge and skills among HRD practitioners.
- Break new ground for the HRD movement.

CHAPTER 1

The Journey of HR

For more than 20 years, we have been participants in and observers of the human resources (HR) journey. Along the way, we have tracked the evolution of HR in response to increasing demands. This journey has more of a direction than a destination. HR wants to add value, to contribute in meaningful ways to employees and line managers inside the company and to customers, communities, partners, and investors outside the company. At times, those on the journey have been the target of snipers who discount HR's value and want to send it back to its administrative beginnings. At other times, progress has been slowed by cynics who doubt that HR can overcome its legacy and fully contribute. For the most part, the journey has been forward-looking, with growing momentum toward true value creation.

The following examples illustrate how the journey affects many in and out of the HR profession:

- Robert is a 52-year-old career HR employee. He started in compensation analysis, but has worked through many HR positions, including plant HR director, labor relations specialist, and corporate compensation director. Now he is an HR generalist in a large business unit. He finds himself under increasing pressure to know the business, to talk with senior managers about how to deliver on their results, and to participate in business strategy discussions. While he likes the increased attention and salary, he secretly wonders if he knows enough about business to really make a difference.

- Judy studied psychology because she likes people, but when she looked for a job in business, organizational development was the closest match to her background. She enjoys working with teams to help individuals work through their differences and become focused on a common goal or agenda. Lately, the teams she coaches have become more globally diverse with team members from varied backgrounds, and these teams have enormous business pressure for results. Her manufacturing teams have to reduce inventory, increase turns, and increase quality. Her marketing and customer teams have to build customer share with demanding customers. Her corporate staff teams have to justify their existence at the risk of outsourcing. She worries that her team-building skills are not sufficient to help these teams have good relationships and deliver results.
- Harvey moved from a line manager role to the head of HR. The previous HR leader held the job for many years and had enormous personal credibility. People liked him and enjoyed working with him. Harvey, who is biased toward sales and marketing, has found that the HR team focuses mostly on activities, not deliverables. When he asked for HR metrics, his direct reports prepared activity grids of things they did; for example: number of people with so many hours in training, number of people hired, percent of people with pay-for-performance goals, days lost to benefits, etc. He learned from sales that the key is not activities, such as making sales calls, but results such as making sales. He worries that his charter is not to do more, but to deliver value—which means helping the business succeed. He wonders if his HR staff is up to the task.
- Helen is excited to be the general manager of her company's largest division. She knows that, in this job, she has the responsibility to transform the business. She has created a plan with a new product mix, go-to-market strategy and financial controls. But she finds that her organization, the culture and the people in the division are not moving fast enough. She feels that ultimate transformation will require a change in her mindset, so she turns to the head of HR for advice.
- Daniel is the HR director of a small but rapidly growing bank in India, which is hiring thousands of people every month to keep up with demand, and losing thousands of people every month to other entrepreneurial companies. Daniel is concerned that his relentless focus on recruiting and retention prevents him from helping the business in other ways.

Each of these individuals is somewhere along the HR journey. Robert is feeling the pressure to respond to increasing business demands. It is not enough for him to be technically competent in the latest compensation, labor, or staffing practices; he now needs to engage in defining and delivering business results. Judy cannot rely on her personal reputation and high emotional intelligence to help people work together; she has to help teams respond to real business pressures. Harvey has been charged with upgrading an HR function that is slow to change. Helen knows that her business objectives depend on the quality of talent and organization she has. She hopes HR can help her deliver on her ambitious goals. Daniel is so focused on selecting, hiring, and retaining talent that he has no time to invest in or build better capability for the business in other strategic areas.

On their respective HR journeys, each requires a fresh look at what it takes to be successful. They each live in an organizational world where the demands have increased and more is expected from HR. Responding to these demands will require dramatic shifts in what they know and do.

We have spent the last 20 years doing empirical research and field practice to learn specific ways in which HR can respond to current organizational challenges. We now have a longitudinal database of some 40,000 data points—the most comprehensive empirical study of the HR profession available. The richness of these data allows us to zoom in on specific issues and compelling features of HR's journey. This book will be devoted to exploring and illuminating these issues.

What Is Human Resources?

The term "human resources" may refer to five different subjects, each of which we hope to inform through the research and recommendations in this book.

The HR Profession

The HR profession is growing dramatically in numbers, global reach and scientific sophistication. Consider the record membership in many HR-oriented professional associations around the world:

- Society for Human Resource Management (SHRM): more than 225,000 members.
- Chartered Institute for Personnel Development (England and Europe): 127,000 members.
- Canada Council of Human Resources: 24,000 members.
- Australian Human Resource Institute: 15,000 members.

- National Institute of Personnel Management, India: 11,000 members.
- Association of Brazil for Human Resources: 8,000 members.
- Institute of People Management, South Africa: 8,000 members.

In addition, there are literally hundreds of national and local HR associations worldwide attempting to offer insight and advice on the changing HR profession. Many universities have established HR centers which focus research, teaching, and students on HR challenges; for example: Cornell, University of Illinois, Rutgers, and University of Southern California in the United States; London Business School, Henley, and Rotterdam School of Management in Europe; IAE in Argentina; and Tsinghua University in China. This book offers a long-term empirical view of what is required for HR professionals and HR departments to deliver value. Often, the HR profession is influenced by fads and clever ideas that are not grounded in research. As the HR profession becomes more of a discipline and science[1], fads will be replaced by decision rules grounded in research. These decision rules will guide the profession to have the impact it desires.

The HR Department

HR often refers to the department or function. As start-up organizations grow, business leaders realize that they need functional expertise to meet changing business needs. Finance, IT, marketing, and HR-functional areas become separate departments or functions that bring their expertise and knowledge to solve business problems. In larger organizations, HR departments may be very complex, with HR professionals working in embedded organization units (business, functional, or geography units), in centers of expertise where they offer specific technical advice, or in corporations wherethey oversee all HR work within a company. The HR department may be thought of as a "business within a business," as these departments have strategies, goals, and the challenge of allocating resources to deliver value. This book will propose specific ways that HR departments can be focused and organized to operate more efficiently and effectively.

HR Practices

HR is the label we put on a specific set of practices, policies, procedures, and programs that manage people and organizations. There are dozens of HR practices that may be created.[2] We have clustered this array into four categories:

People

Many HR practices deal with the flow of people within an organization. These practices include recruitment, staffing, orientation, training, development, retention, outsourcing, and other programs related to the movement of people within an organization.

Performance

HR practices may deal with measurement, performance appraisal, compensation, rewards, and benefits. These practices deal with ensuring accountability through managing performance from individuals, teams, and organization units.

Information

HR practices increasingly focus on communication processes within a company, such as external public relations and internal employee communications. Communication practices need to be aligned with other HR practices to send signals to people both inside and outside the organization.

Work

HR practices related to the workflow include how to work in teams, how to design and deliver administrative policies, how to manage terms and conditions of work (e.g., labor relations), how to facilitate work processes redesign, how to design physical facilities and space, and how to structure a company to align with strategy. These HR practices also affect both talent and organization capability.

In this book, we will agree with others who argue that these practices need to be both aligned and integrated.[3] Alignment means that these practices should help deliver strategic goals; integration means that they should work together. We also want to identify which HR practices are emerging and which ones will have the most impact on business results.

HR Professionals

For many people, HR refers to the group of people who make up the profession, who work in HR departments, and who design and deliver the HR practices. As suggested in the introduction, demands on HR continue to increase, and the expectations on HR professionals have changed dramatically over the 100 years since the National Cash Register Company established the first personnel department after a particularly rancorous strike in 1901.

Originally, HR professionals were expected to be administrative experts who facilitated transactions related to people and handled workforce grievances. Then, HR professionals argued that they should become partners and have a place at the management table. Today, HR professionals in leading firms sit at the table and have opportunities to participate fully in business discussions. In our research, 66% of the people who answered our survey said that their vice president of HR reported directly to the CEO. To contribute and add value to these discussions, HR professionals must not only ensure smooth administrative systems, but consider the strategic implications of talent and organization choices. HR professionals are the primary audience for this book. We want to identify the competencies required to be an effective HR professional and suggest specific ways to assess and build the competencies that really count.

HR Issues

Finally, HR is often used as the label for a broad category of issues related to people management (talent, human capital, workforce) and organizations (teams, organization capability, culture), not just those issues within the HR department. The workforce and workplace are increasingly a critical part of a firm's ability to deliver on its goals. Line managers are the ultimate owners with responsibility to ensure that an organization has both the right talent in place to deliver on expectations to customers, shareholders, communities, and employees, and the right organization capabilities in place to sustain a culture and reputation. Numerous efforts like the war for talent, balanced scorecards, and lists of top companies to work for have prescribed how line managers can better manage their people and organization. This book will suggest not only what line managers can expect from HR professionals, but also what they must value, know, and do to ensure that people and organizations deliver value.

Each of these five views of HR is driven by a common agenda: to deliver value. When HR departments, practices, professionals, and people focus more on what they deliver than on what they do, value is created. This value might come from people being more competent or committed and/or organizations having the capabilities required to meet customer and investor expectations. Thus, the HR journey has a definite direction (to create value) and growing ranks of travelers who are committed to follow through on this promise.

By targeting each of these five dimensions of HR (profession, department, practices, professionals, and broader issues of people/organization), we want to ensure that the new HR will exceed the expectations of employees and line managers inside an organizations and investors, customers, and communities outside. To deliver value, the new HR needs to understand the challenges contained in a changing business context as shown in Figure 1.1.

Figure 1.1. **The New HR**

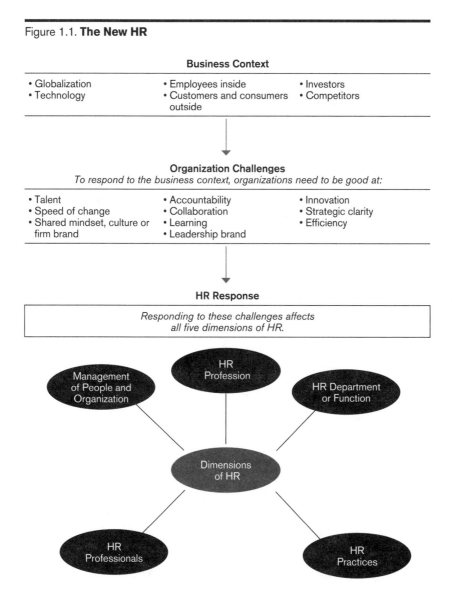

Business Context

• Globalization • Technology	• Employees inside • Customers and consumers outside	• Investors • Competitors

Organization Challenges
To respond to the business context, organizations need to be good at:

• Talent • Speed of change • Shared mindset, culture or firm brand	• Accountability • Collaboration • Learning • Leadership brand	• Innovation • Strategic clarity • Efficiency

HR Response

*Responding to these challenges affects
all five dimensions of HR.*

Management of People and Organization

HR Profession

HR Department or Function

Dimensions of HR

HR Professionals

HR Practices

Changing Business Context

Similar themes surface in conferences focused on the world of business. Globalization has made the world a global village with new markets offering new challenges and opportunities, especially in China, India, Brazil, and Russia. Global issues like trade barriers, exchange rates, tariffs, and distribution havev become important elements of managerial choice. Technology has increased access, accessibility, visibility, and connection. The connected world is smaller, rapidly changing, and has more open information. Employees represent increasingly diverse demographic backgrounds including not only race and gender, but personal preferences, global or cultural backgrounds, and orientation to work. In some parts of the world, employees are aging more than in others. Employee expectations are constantly rising as they gain in education and skills. Customers have become increasingly segmented, literate, and demanding. As they have greater choice, they become more selective about with whom they work. Investors have become increasingly attuned to and actively concerned about not only financial results, but intangibles. Competitors come from both traditional, large global players and increasingly smaller innovators.

Many spend enormous amounts of time specifying these trends and their implications on business in general and HR in particular.[4] Most of these trends are outside the control of any one individual or any one company. They occur in both predictable and unpredictable ways. They affect all aspects of business, including how to fund a firm, how to position the firm in customers' minds, and how to engineer and deliver products. They also affect human resources. HR's legacy was to monitor terms and conditions of work through industrial relations, then to design systems and practices that shape how people are treated in an organization. With this orientation, HR professionals had little reason to be more than casual observers of business trends. Now, the HR profession is being asked to help businesses compete, and to do so, HR must not only observe, but understand and adapt to these business trends.

Organization Responses

The business context offers challenges to which organizations must respond. When organizations are defined through their capabilities more than their hierarchies, managers have to learn to create capabilities to respond to these business challenges. These capabilities represent what the organization is known for, what it is good at doing, and how it patterns activities to deliver value. The capabilities define many of the intangibles that investors pay attention to and the firm brand to which customers can relate. These capabilities also become the middle ground between line managers who build strategies and HR professionals who implement strategies.

Line managers take primary responsibility for shaping strategy, and HR professionals take primary responsibility for crafting HR practices to support the strategy. But line managers and HR professionals share in the diagnosis and investment in organization capabilities. For line managers, these capabilities become the culture that drives sustainable business success. For HR professionals, these capabilities become the deliverables or outcomes of their work. These capabilities can be tracked and measured so that they are taken seriously within the organization. In Figure 1.2, we have identified 10 possible capabilities, each of which define an organization capability and specify expectations for HR professionals. Understanding and delivering against these capabilities raises the bar for HR.

Talent

We are good at attracting, motivating, and retaining competent and committed people. Assuring talent means going beyond the platitudes such as "people are our most important asset" and "strategy follows people" and investing time and resources to secure superior talent. Employees must be both competent and committed. Competent employees have the skills for today's and tomorrow's business requirements. Committed employees deploy those skills regularly and predictably. HR professionals may assess the extent to which their organization regularly attracts and keeps top talent and the extent to which that talent is productive and focused. Assuring competent employees comes as organizations buy (bring in new talent), build (develop existing talent), bound (move the right talent into increasingly responsible positions), borrow (access thought leaders through alliances or partnerships), bounce (remove poor talent), and bind (keep the best talent). See Chapter 5 for more information on the "six Bs."

Speed

We are good at making important changes happen fast. Gaining speed goes beyond change to fast change. Speed means that the organization has an ability to identify and move quickly into new markets, new products, new employee contracts, and new business processes. Leaders embed this capability into the organization by being focused on making decisions rigorously,

Figure 1.2. **Organization Capabilities and their Implications for HR Professionals**

Principle We are good at …	Capability Our organization is successful if …	Implication HR professionals should be able to …
Talent: Ensuring competent and committed people	It attracts, motivates, retains, and engages competent employees	• Do talent audit of what is and what is not necessary • Build an employee value proposition that engages talented employees
Speed: Making important changes happen fast	It is able to change quickly to align with customer needs	• Build and enact a disciplined change process • Assimilate change into a new identity
Shared Mindset: Turning customer reputation and identity into employee actions	It is able to build a culture that reflects customer expectations and turns them into employee actions	• Perform a cultural audit • Make customer reputation real to employees
Accountability: Implementing disciplines that result in high performance	It is able to meet commitments and do what it says it will do	• Build and implement a disciplined performance management system • Follow up to ensure consequences
Collaboration: Working across boundaries to ensure leverage and efficiency	It is able to make the whole more than the sum of the parts	• Increase efficiency through productivity improvement efforts • Increase leverage by sharing ideas, people, products, services
Learning: Generating and generalizing ideas with impact	It is able to generate new ideas and then generalize those ideas across boundaries	• Generate new ideas by experimenting, acquiring skills, continuous improvement, benchmarking • Generalize ideas across boundaries
Leadership Brand: Embedding leaders throughout the organization who embody the leadership brand	It is able to identity a leadership brand that connects customer reputation and employee behaviors	• Ensure that leaders demonstrate the leadership code • Prepare a statement of leadership brand and invest in it
Innovation: Doing something new in both content and process	It is able to innovate and create new ways to do things	• Establish an innovation protocol that helps shape new ideas • Instill a spirit of innovation among all employees
Strategic Clarity: Articulating and sharing a point of view about the future	It is able to envision a future state and ensure that employees and practices are aligned to it	• Establish a process to ensure strategic clarity • Align organization actions to make the strategy happen
Efficiency: Managing the costs of operation	It is able to work to reduce costs	• Increase productivity • Manage processes efficiently • Allocate resources on key projects

by implementing change processes throughout their organization, by removing bureaucratic barriers to change, and by eliminating organizational viruses. Building the capacity to change takes time because the laws of inertia keep change from happening, but when large firms can act like small, nimble firms, they have mastered the speed capability.

Shared Mindset

We are good at ensuring that customers and employees have positive images of and experiences with our organization. Gaining a shared mindset, or firm brand identity, becomes a vital capability. Many firms have moved from individual product brands to firm brands. The Marriott name on a hotel adds value because it gives the traveler confidence in the product. Being affiliated with the Olympics brand is worth millions to companies that want to be associated with the positive image of the Olympics tradition. HR professionals help identify and shape their shared mindset, or firm brand, by building a consensus among their management team of what they want the firm to be "known for" by its best customers in the future. Once a consensus is reached on this identity, they may invest in a series of actions to make the identity real to both customers and employees.

Accountability

We are good at the disciplines that result in high performance. Some firms have developed accountability habits. It is not acceptable to miss goals. Performance accountability becomes a firm capability when employees realize that they must meet their performance expectations. Accountability comes when strategies translate into measurable standards of performance, and then when rewards are linked to meeting or missing standards. When there is a line of sight between rewards, appraisals, and strategies, accountability is more likely to follow. When an HR professional designs an employee performance appraisal form, it should reflect the strategy the employee is attempting to accomplish and what specific actions the employee should take to help accomplish the strategy. Financial and non-financial rewards reinforce the strategy and enable the employee to receive clear and definitive feedback on his performance.

Collaboration

We are good at working across boundaries to ensure both efficiency and leverage. The whole needs to be greater than the sum of the parts. Some organizations have more value when broken in pieces, rather than held together.

These organizations do not understand that collaboration is a capability. Collaboration may come when the combined organization gains efficiencies of operation through shared services, technology, or economies of scale.

Collaboration also may come when the combined organization accomplishes more together than it could separately through learning and sharing ideas across boundaries, allocating resources to key areas, and creating strategies that leverage products and customers. HR professionals build collaboration by seeking both efficiencies and leverage throughout the organization.

Learning
We are good at generating and generalizing ideas with impact. Generating new ideas comes from benchmarking (seeing what others have done and adapting it), experimentation (trying new things to see if and how they work), competence acquisition (hiring or developing people with new skills and ideas), and continuous improvement (improving on what was done through suggestion systems and process analysis). Generalizing ideas means that the ideas move across a boundary of time (from one leader to his or her successor), space (from one geography to another), or structure (from one business unit to another). Sharing ideas across boundaries may be done through leveraging technology, creating communities of practice, or moving people. HR professionals who encourage individual and team learning also can create organization learning through these practices.

Leadership
We are good at embedding leaders throughout the organization who deliver the right results in the right way by carrying our leadership brand. Some organizations produce leaders. These organizations generally have a leadership brand, or clear statement of what leaders should know, be and do. A leadership brand exists when the leaders from top to bottom of an organization have a unique identity. These leaders are identifiable. They are focused. They possess attributes of success and deliver results. HR professionals have the responsibility to produce the next generation of leaders by helping establish the leadership brand, assessing the gaps in the present leadership against this brand, then investing in future leaders.

Customer Connection
We are good at building enduring relationships of trust with targeted customers. Many firms have discovered through customer value analysis

that 20% of customers account for 80% of business performance. These targeted customers become absolutely critical for a firm to compete and win. Customer connectivity originates in a variety of practices. It may start with databases that identify and track each individual customer preference. Customer connectivity may also come from dedicated account teams who build long-term relationships with targeted accounts.

Customer connection may also come from involving a customer in the firm's HR practices. To leverage such opportunities, many firms are including customers in staffing, training, compensation, and communication practices. The net result of these activities is customer intimacy and the resultant sales. Customer connection may also be enhanced when large proportions of the employee population have meaningful exposure to or interaction with external customers. All of these result in an information and mindset convergence between employees and customers.

Innovation

We are good at doing something new in both content and process. Innovation focuses on creating opportunities for the future rather than relying on past successes. Innovation fosters growth. It excites employees by focusing on what can be, anticipates customer requests and delights customers with what they did not expect, and builds confidence with investors by creating intangible value. HR professionals who focus on innovation constantly ask, "What's next?" in all domains of their business. Innovative product offerings include revolutionary new products or product extensions (that is, added features, performance, or functionality). Business strategy innovation changes how the enterprise makes money (as with the current emphasis on services), where the enterprise does business (opening up new geographies), how the enterprise goes to market (via new channels), how the customers experience the firm (its brand identity), or how the firm serves customers (as when eBay discovered it could grow by helping customers sell things to each other). Administrative innovation occurs when new processes are introduced in finance, IT, marketing, HR, manufacturing, or other staff systems.

Strategic Unity

We are good at articulating and sharing a strategic point of view. More organizations have strategies than accomplish them. Often this comes because there is not a unity of shared understanding of the desired strategy. Three agendas go into creating strategic unity. An intellectual agenda assures that employees from top to bottom share both what the strategy is and why it is important. This agenda is delivered through simple messages repeated constantly. A behavioral agenda assures that the strategy shapes how employees behave by telling employees what to do and by asking employees what they will do based on the strategy. By allowing employees to define their behaviors relative to strategy, they become committed to it. A process agenda ensures that the organization's processes, such as budgeting, hiring, and decision making, align with strategy. These processes may be reengineered to ensure that they create unity. When all three agendas are in place, strategic unity follows.

Efficiency
We are good at managing the costs of operation. In competitive markets, managing costs efficiently increases flexibility. HR professionals may reduce costs through process, people, and projects. Process improvements come through kaizen or other productivity improvement efforts that reduce variance, remove steps in getting work done, reduce inventories and work space, and ensure a flow of products and services. People improvements come from doing more with less through technology, teams, and more efficient processes. Project investments come from managing capital spending to allocate money wisely for future investments. HR professionals who pay attention only to costs and ignore growth fail because no company can save its way to prosperity, but HR professionals who avoid costs and efficiency improvements will not likely have the opportunity to grow the top line.

Clearly, these are not the only capabilities that HR professionals working with leaders may instill into an organization. But they are indicative of the types of capabilities that make intangibles tangible. They delight customers, engage employees, establish reputations among investors, and provide long-term sustainable value. These capabilities become the intangibles that investors value and the deliverables that HR departments must offer.

HR Responses
The response of HR to the business context and organization capabilities requires change in all five dimensions of HR: the HR profession, the HR department or function, HR practices, HR professionals, and HR issues.

HR Profession

The HR profession is moving toward being more aligned with business outcomes. In HR conferences sponsored by HR professional associations, presentations are increasingly focused on business topics and building organization capabilities. While it is imperative that the technical aspects of HR practices remain current, mastery of the technical elements of HR is increasingly only the ticket of admission. For example, SHRM's monthly publication recently has featured headlines and articles that reflect the changing HR profession, such as "HR and the Board," "HR Outsourcing" and "HR Measurement and Analytics." HR professional associations will both lead and respond to the new expectations on HR.

HR Department or Function

To respond to the business context and create requisite capabilities, HR departments are evolving in how they deliver HR. Increasingly, HR departments are being split in half, with one half focusing on HR transactions and operations and the other half on HR transformation and strategic work. Both parts add value: the transaction work ensures efficiency, cost control, and error-free work; the transformation work enables strategies to be executed.[5]

HR transactions must be done to ensure that employees' administrative concerns are treated quickly and accurately. But they should also be done to minimize costs while maintaining parity levels of quality and service. The production of administrative efficiency comes through establishment of service centers where HR work is consolidated, through e-HR where employees become self-reliant and connected through technology, and through outsourcing HR to a service provider who can ensure consistency and efficiency. This mix of processes helps streamline and reduce the cost of HR operations. It also reduces the number of people who work in HR by automating, standardizing, and reengineering HR processes. We have also observed that HR professionals can't do the transformational work until they find a way to manage the transactional. There's simply no time. Transactional work is short term, urgent, and concrete. Transformational work is longer term, conceptual, and ambiguous. When faced with both sets of tasks simultaneously, the transactional work wins. Transactional work pushes out the time to do strategic work.

HR transformational or strategic work requires collaboration among embedded HR professionals and those working in centers of expertise. Embedded HR professionals may be called generalists, partners, relationship managers, or business-based HR. Regardless of their title, they are assigned to work with organization units (business, geography, or functional unit). Their task is to participate in the strategic planning process and ensure that strategies happen through organization capabilities. They sit on the management team of their unit, they conduct organization and intangibles audits, they set organization priorities, and they source HR expertise from centers of expertise. They are measured by the extent to which they can help make strategies happen.

HR professionals in centers of expertise are known for their technical acumen. They keep current in their specialty area, but are also able to tailor and adapt ideas to the requirements of the business units. They contract their knowledge to the embedded HR professionals to help solve problems. They create menus of choices for delivering state-of-the-art HR. They share knowledge from one unit to another. They also represent some of the corporate initiatives sponsored by the executives. They are measured by the application of innovative HR practices throughout the company and the extent to which the company shares experiences across units.

HR professionals engaged in operational execution work become consultants and solution providers within the business. These are talented HR professionals who bridge the knowledge from centers of expertise with the strategic requirements defined by the embedded HR generalists. These are the people who make the analytical, operational, and tactical processes of HR happen. They take strategic advice from the embedded HR strategist and couple it with HR insight from the centers of expertise, then define and implement projects. They enable the HR generalists to focus on strategy and the centers of expertise to focus on technical depth.

Corporate HR professionals have responsibility for the HR philosophies that permeate the entire organization. They represent the firm to external stakeholders (regulators, investors, and communities) and need to help establish a corporate brand or reputation. They also help senior executives select HR initiatives that will permeate the entire organization. They work with boards to ensure effective governance and with senior executive leaders as coaches and team facilitators.

The culmination of embedded HR, centers of expertise, operational HR, and corporate HR professionals ensures that the HR organization operates as a unified team that creates value through transformation.

HR Practices

The practices of HR (people, performance, information, and work) are evolving to deliver value. While innovations are occurring within each specific practice (e.g., innovations in executive compensation through performance shares rather than stock options), some patterns are evident across practices. First, the HR practices are being aligned and managed through an external customer and investor lens. In staffing, it is no longer sufficient to be the "employer of choice." It is important to be the "employer of choice of employees our customers would choose."

In training, it is no longer enough to offer action learning, case studies, and skill-based training. This training needs to prepare employees who will respond to customer expectations. In communications, it is not enough to share messages with employees, but with customers and investors as well. The practices may be built around customer and investor expectations, such as "Let's train our employees in what the customer expects them to know." The HR practices may involve the customer in the design and delivery of this practice; for example: involve customers in designing, participating in, and delivering training activities.

Second, HR practices are increasingly being aligned to deliver strategy through capabilities. The firm's strategy defines how it allocates resources to respond to the challenges of the business context. The capabilities represent the organization's unique identity and characteristics that enable it to respond to business context. HR practices that deliver capabilities are much better aligned to strategy.

Third, HR practices are becoming more integrated. A firm might hire people with skills A, B, and C, and then train employees in skills D, E, and F, and pay people to do G, H, and I. The firm then wonders why employees don't have a shared focus. Integration of HR practices means that they all focus on the same expectations. These expectations are governed by the capabilities the organization is attempting to generate.

Finally, HR practices are evolving to include more practices. Originally, HR practices focused on bringing in good people. HR practices have evolved to include performance management and are continuing to evolve to include communications and work design. Any action within a company that sends signals to employees, customers or investors about what is important and what matters most should be aligned with other HR practices.

Work space is one interesting example. Anyone who has walked into an office building or an office can attest to the signal sent by the work space. The office layout, placement of the desks and chairs, colors, lighting, symbols, and pictures all create an impression of the organization and the individuals working there. When HR professionals participate in conceiving and designing work spaces, they help shape the organization's capabilities.

HR Professionals

The business context and organization capabilities required to succeed have raised the bar for HR professionals. Those who succeeded 30, 20, or even 10 years ago likely would not succeed today. HR professionals are expected to play new roles. HR roles play a large part in the identity and reputation of HR professionals. As evidenced in the cases at the beginning of the chapter, HR professionals need to learn how to play roles that require technical expertise and apply that expertise to business performance. HR professionals need new competencies to play such roles. The bulk of this book focuses on the competencies required for HR professionals to play these roles and deliver value.

HR Issues

HR issues encompass the management of people and the organization. We would be remiss if we did not highlight the importance of the line manager in managing both people and the organization. HR is not just for HR. It affects the quality of individual talent and organization capabilities that must exist within an organization. We believe the line manager is the ultimate owner of both the workforce and the workplace. When playing the right roles with the right competencies, HR professionals become activists, executors, allies, architects, stewards, and designers of managing both people and organizations. Line managers retain responsibility, however, for building capabilities that respond to business conditions.

Organization of this Book

As we have traveled on this HR journey for the past 20 years, we have continually studied how HR can respond to the business context and organization challenges synthesized in this chapter. This book reports that research, with a focus on how the data can be turned into actions that shape the HR profession and departments, as well as its practices and professionals. Chapter 2 provides a "big picture" view of the Human Resource Competency Study (HRCS). We lay out the research design, provide a brief history of HR competency models, and report on findings of past iterations of this research. We also summarize the overall results of the most recent (2007) HRCS. In this survey, we found that HR professionals need to master six competency domains: Credible Activist, Culture & Change Steward, Talent Manager/Organization Designer, Strategy Architect, Operational Executor, and Business Ally. The research creating these domains and the overall impact of these domains will be reported.

Chapters 3 through 8 dive deep into each of the six domains, presenting research that articulates the factors that define excellence in each:

- Chapter 3 explores how to be a Credible Activist by simultaneously building relationships of trust and delivering business results.
- Chapter 4 treats the interrelated topics of culture and change, focusing on how to make changes happen while weaving them together into a cultural story.
- Chapter 5 discusses how HR professionals can ensure that their companies have both talented individuals with the ability to compete, and dynamic organizations with the capabilities to sustain new strategies.
- Chapter 6 outlines the role of HR in not only helping execute strategy, but in actively participating in its creation by staying close to external customers.
- Chapter 7 examines the Operational Executor who is responsible for ensuring that crucial administrative matters and day-to-day tasks are efficiently and flawlessly delivered.
- Chapter 8 shows why HR professionals must know how companies make money, and the broader societal context in which they compete.

We also share case studies of individuals and companies who excel at the skills required by each domain, and suggest specific development activities to increase HR competence in these skills.

Chapter 9 takes a research-based look at the HR department. We identify how the department should connect with key stakeholders, where it should focus attention, and which HR practices should be prioritized to deliver business success. This chapter suggests that it is not just competent HR professionals who make a difference, but also high-performing HR departments.

Chapter 10 highlights implications of this work for the HR profession and for line managers who have ultimate responsibility for people and organizations. This chapter also suggests that the research we have done may be a model for staff leadership and suggests ways that other functions might engage in similar research to deliver value.

Collectively, we hope that this research and its implications will help HR live up to the increased demands and expectations placed on it. There has never been a more exciting time to be on the HR journey!

CHAPTER 2

The State of the HR Profession

In Chapter 1, we introduced the metaphor of the HR journey—a continuing quest among committed HR professionals for greater value-added in their respective organizations. We pointed out that the journey has a direction, though perhaps not a specific destination, and argued that the goal of HR's journey is both important and elusive. We may never be able to state with finality that HR has arrived. Because the target will continue to move, the bar will always be raised. But can we measure our progress? Are there check-points or milestones along the way?

Our answer is an unequivocal "Yes!" At five-year intervals since 1988, we have surveyed the increasingly global HR community in an attempt to docu-ment "how we're doing." These pulse checks constitute a history of HR's milestones along the HR journey. Over the 20-year trajectory of this research, we have seen the definition of "value added" evolve and broaden. The fifth iteration of the survey, concluded in 2007, provides a comprehensive portrait of HR's role in today's fast-changing world. As such, it represents the current state of the HR profession.

This chapter presents a high-level overview of Round 5 of the HRCS. Our presentation of the findings will be guided by the following five questions:
- How have people understood and studied competencies for HR profes-sionals, both in general and in our research?
- What are the scope, demographic makeup, and methodological approach for Round 5 of the HRCS?

- What is the new model of HR competence, based on Round 5 of the HRCS, and how does the global HR community stack up against this model?
- Which of the HR competencies are most important for predicting the performance of the individual HR professional?
- Which of the HR competencies are most important for predicting business performance?

Our approach is unabashedly quantitative; in this and the chapters that follow, be prepared for a boatload of statistics. Unlike true data wonks, however, our goal is always to tell the story behind the stats rather than numb you with the numbers. If you find the density of data figures not to your liking, we recommend skimming the explanatory paragraphs for key insights, while focusing more on the accompanying case studies and tools.

How Have People Understood And Studied Competencies For HR Professionals, both In General and in Our Research?

While competency modeling became a fad during the 1990s, its roots go much deeper. During World War II, a young psychologist named John Flanagan joined the Army Air Corps and helped developed aptitude tests to select successful pilots. Competencies have since become important not only in recruiting, but in a variety of HR applications. Well-defined competencies can be taught, learned, measured, and monitored. They are the antecedent signals that individuals will deliver results. They can be used to match an individual to a particular job, integrate diverse HR practices, measure individual contribution and performance, and add value to customers.

Throughout this book, we will use two distinct terms that are often confused with one another: *competencies* and *capabilities*. In our usage, these are not interchangeable terms. Competencies refer to the knowledge, skills, and behaviors demonstrated by individuals in the course of getting their work done. Competencies may be technical in nature (such as specific engineering expertise or financial know-how), or more socially oriented (such as relationship building or leadership). Capabilities, in our parlance and as outlined in Chapter 1, are the collective abilities of an *organization*. Here again, they may be technical in nature, such as Sony's famed expertise in miniaturization or Apple's genius in product design, or more socially defined, such as Pepsico's emphasis on accountability, or Southwest Airlines' legendary efficiency. They permeate an organization's culture (its unquestioned way of doing things—its DNA), and are demonstrated in various ways by the organization's members, though not dependent on any one individual. They become what the organization is known for, and are enormously difficult for competitors to imitate.

Figure 2.1 sharpens the division between competencies and capabilities. This distinction and need for alignment between technical and social skills was articulated in the late 1950s and early 1960s by theorists advocating the "sociotechnical" approach to organization design.

The goal of our research has been to identify the requisite technical and social competencies at the level of the individual HR professional. As mentioned, one of the crucial competencies for HR professionals is to be able to understand and help create organization capabilities. This topic will be explored in much greater depth in Chapter 6.

Figure 2.1. **Individual Competencies vs. Organization Capabilities**

		Unit of Analysis	
		The Individual	The Organization
Nature of the Knowledge, Skill, or Behavior	Technical	Technical or functional competencies (often called "hard skills")	Technical or business competencies (sometimes called "core competence")
	Social	Interpersonal or leadership competencies (often called "soft skills")	Organization capabilities (often embodied in the culture)

Our efforts certainly were not the first attempts to define competencies specific to HR. As early as the mid-1980s, the American Society for Training & Development (ASTD) sponsored Patricia McLagan in her efforts to identify competencies for HR development professionals. Her work subsequently broadened to include all HR professionals.[1] Around the same time, a number of large companies began creating their own internal HR competency models. Out of these independent efforts grew many frameworks for HR competencies, but there were relatively few efforts to document professional HR competencies across firms, industries, or geographies. The profession needed a competency model a set of expectations for those who work in HR and a basis for assessment and improvement in the quality of HR professionals.

We began our research on competencies in 1988 with the desire to answer three questions:

- What are the competencies that are required of HR professionals if they are to add greater value to their key stakeholders?
- How can HR professionals develop these competencies in the fastest and most effective ways?
- How can HR competencies and HR practices align to business performance?

We knew we needed lots of data to answer these questions for the HR profession, so we designed and administered a large-scale survey of HR professionals and their HR and non-HR associates. This work has resulted in five rounds of data collection in 1988, 1992, 1997, 2002 and 2007, and

Figure 2.2. **Miles Along the Journey: Competency Models, 1987 to 2007**

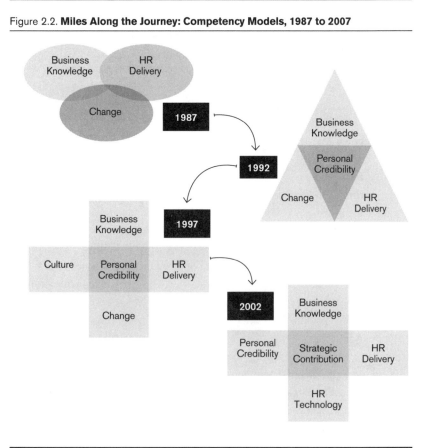

a total of more than 40,000 responses over the study's course. As illustrated in Figure 2.2, the resulting competency models have grown more complex with each round of the study, suggesting that HR is coming of age as a true profession with a consistent and identifiable body of knowledge, skills, and behaviors. For a more complete history of our previous rounds of research and the resulting models, please refer to Appendix 1.

What Are The Scope, Demographic Makeup, And Methodological Approach for Round 5 of the HRCS?

For each round of data collection and analysis, we used the same basic methodology. This methodology will be briefly described here with respect to Round 5 of the research. A comprehensive discussion on this methodology can be found in Appendix 2.

Round 5 of HRCS was jointly sponsored by The RBL Group and the Ross Business School of the University of Michigan. We chose to partner with leading HR institutions in regions around the world to have a broader representation of non-U.S. participants. These regional partners identified firms in their geographies and were instrumental in facilitating data collection and analysis. This study would have been impossible without the collaboration of the:

- Society for Human Resource Management (SHRM), a partner in 2002 and 2007, which represented North America.
- IAE, the Management and Business School of Universidad in Argentina (a partner in 2002 and 2007), headed by Professor Alejandro Sioli and Michel Hermans, which represented Latin America.
- Irish Management Institute (IMI, headed by Martin Farrelly with the assistance of Grace Kearns, representing Europe.
- National HRD Network in India, headed by Jagdeep Khandur.
- Tsinghua University in Beijing, China, headed by Dr. Xiaoming Zheng and Dr. Felicia Deng.
- Australian Human Resource Institute (AHRI), headed by Paul Dainty with Anne Marie Dolan who worked in Australia and Asia Pacific.

Following a standard 360-degree approach, we sent invitations to HR professionals to participate in the survey. These participants completed the survey and sent it to their peers, subordinates, supervisor, and clients (associates), some of whom were in HR and some of whom were not. Most of the data were collected on-line. The sample for Round 5 includes the categories and numbers of participants indicated in Figure 2.3. These respondents belong to 413 separate business units in 6 distinct geographic regions.

Figure 2.3. **Profile of Respondents in Round 5 of HRCS**

Respondent type	Definition	N
HR Participants	HR participants who completed the self-assessment and nominated associates to complete on their behalf	1,669
HR Associates	All associate raters who work in HR and who completed the survey on behalf of an HR participant	5,048
Non-HR Associates	All associate raters who work outside of HR and who completed the survey on behalf of an HR participant	3,346
All Respondents	Total of all participants, HR associates, and non-HR associates	10,063

Before administering the surveys, however, we met with the regional partners to identify major trends that were affecting business in general and the organization capabilities required to respond. (See Chapter 1 for a summary of these discussions). Based on this input, we modified the core set of questions—keeping in mind we wanted to balance historical questions that appeared in previous rounds of research with questions that reflected the unique challenges facing HR professionals today. This resulted in modification to approximately 50% of the survey questions from Round 4 in 2002.

Competency questions generally focused on the knowledge and abilities of the HR professional and the extent to which he or she could use HR practices to build business success. One of the survey questions, and the corresponding response scale, are shown below.

Sample Survey Question and Response Scale
For each of the human resource practices listed below, please indicate the extent to which the participant is capable of using the practice to build success in the participant's business?
* Promotes appropriate people.
* Retains appropriate people.
* Outplaces appropriate people.
* Designs development programs that facilitate change.

Response Scale:
1 = to a very little extent
2 = to a little extent
3 = to some extent
4 = to a large extent
5 = to a very large extent
NA = don't know/not applicable

In an attempt to provide some linkage between an HR professional's competence and his or her impact, we devised two dependent variables, one focused on the performance of the individual HR professional and the other on the performance of the business. First, we asked about the overall effectiveness of the HR professional as perceived by his or her associates with the question: Overall, compared with the other human resource professionals that you have known, how does the participant compare? The response scale ranged from 0% to 100% in 5% increments. In other words, if the respondent believed that the participant was better than 80% of the other HR professionals he or she had known, the response would reflect this "percentile" comparison. As shown in Figure 2.4, the Round 5 sample is a high-performing group of HR professionals—or, alternatively, their respondents were a bit on the generous side.

Second, we wanted to understand the connection between HR and the size of the business. This is a complicated and difficult relationship to measure. We were not able to use publicly reported corporate data because we were examining results at the business-unit level. For example, in large companies, we might have data from two or three out of 10 business units; aggregating the HR data from two or three businesses and then comparing to corporate financial results would introduce a high probability of distortion and inaccuracy. For small companies with one business, the "corporate" and "business" data would be identical. We opted in this round to use multiple measures of business performance, anchored by the following four perceptions:

- How well does your business unit meet its customer requirements?
- How well does your business unit meet its owner/stakeholder requirements?
- How competitive is your business unit in the marketplace?
- How well managed is your business unit financially?

For each of these areas, we asked participants to rate their businesses on a five-point scale, from low (1) to high (5). Since we had about 10,000 respondents and 400 businesses, we had an average of 25 respondents per business unit. We believe that this multi-dimension and multi-rater approach offers a reasonable (if perceptual) indicator of business performance. Figure 2.5 shows a fairly normal distribution of perceived business performance across the four quartiles, using the multi-dimension and multi-rater methodology.

Figure 2.4. **Individual Performance**

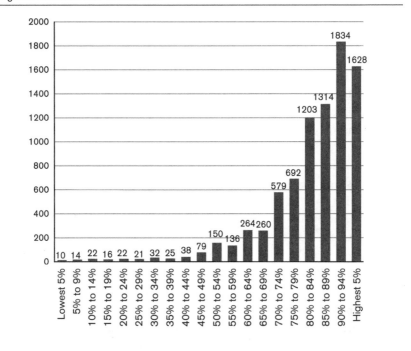

Figure 2.5. **Business Performance Aggregated to Business Unit**

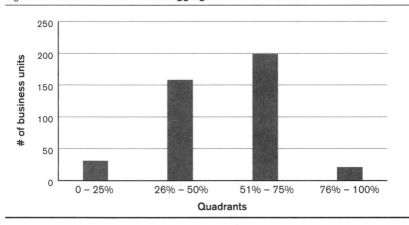

Figure 2.6 offers a fascinating view of the HR journey over the years of the HRCS. Since the data represent a large cross section of the HR profession, we can make some general observations about the evolving profession.[2]

Gender

There has been an explosive growth of women in the profession since 1987. Since we last collected our data five years ago, this profession underwent a dramatic change from being male-dominated to being female-dominated. However, some of this may be accounted for by sampling more global and smaller companies. Gender scholars who study organizations tell us that this change has real consequences, both positive and negative, for the profession and the future of HR.[3] On the positive side, the historical bias against women in the profession has shifted. A more equal representation of men and women in a profession often reflects less tolerance for underperforming men in a profession, and thus indicates an increase in quality standards. On the other hand, the feminization of an occupation sometimes also leads to "male flight" from the occupation, which can again lower the standards and quality of employees. In addition, male flight from an occupation is also typically related to decreasing prestige and wages. However, much of what is known about gender in occupations is based on data from the late 1990s. The next round of our own data will be very important to see whether these trends continue. The gender trends over the next five years in this profession are extremely consequential, not just on the future of our profession but on research and information about gender in occupations in a more broad way.

We are optimistic. We believe that the increasing percentage of women in this occupation reflects an ongoing commitment to high quality.

Education

Most of the HR professionals in this sample have a college education (78% in Round 5 of HRCS). While this number has dropped somewhat compared to previous rounds of the study (87% in 2002; 90% in 1997), the study continues to draw on HR professionals with higher education. This may explain the high performance ratings of HR professionals in this round, shown in Figure 2.2. Perhaps our sample is drawn from the upper end of the

Figure 2.6. **Characteristics of the Human Resource Competency Data Set, Rounds 1-5**

Round	Round 1	Round 2	Round 3	Round 4	Round 5
Year Conducted	1987	1992	1997	2002	2007
Number of Total Respondents	10,291	4,556	3,229	7,082	10,063
Number of Business Units	1,200	441	678	692	413
Respondent					
Associate Raters	8,884	3,805	2,565	5,890	8,394
HR Participant	1,407	751	664	1,192	1,669
Gender					
Male	77%	78%	70%	57%	46%
Female	23%	22%	30%	43%	54%
Relationship of Associate to					
Participant	12%	12%	10%	16%	19%
Supervisor	42%	41%	46%	28%	30%
Peer	28%	26%	11%	25%	27%
Subordinate (direct report)	18%	21%	33%	28%	24%
Client				3%	
Other					
Education of HR Participant					
High school degree	3%	7%	4%	4%	9%
Associate college degree	5%	7%	6%	9%	12%
Bachelor degree	48%	43%	42%	42%	37%
Graduate degree	44%	43%	48%	45%	41%
Level of the HR Participant					
Individual contributor	20%	24%	29%	24%	28%
Manager of individual contributors	36%	41%	34%	34%	30%
Director of managers	36%	29%	30%	31%	20%
Top manager	8%	6%	7%	11%	21%
Size of HR Participant's Company					
1-499	15%	17%	22%	25%	31%
500-999	10%	9%	13%	15%	14%
1,000-4,999	25%	22%	34%	33%	28%
5,000-9,999	11%	12%	11%	9%	6%
Over 10,000	39%	40%	20%	18%	20%

distribution of HR professionals, both in terms of education and performance. But it also reflects the trend of HR becoming a profession.

Management Level of Participant

We arrayed HR professionals into 4 levels (loosely consistent with four stages of careers[4]). In Round 5 HRCS data, we had a larger portion (21%) of the sample identifying themselves as the top manager of HR. This may be because the Round 5 data set has more small-size firms with fewer HR professionals, but those in place doing more director-level work.

Figure 2.6. **Characteristics of the Human Resource Competency Data Set, Rounds 1-5**

Round	Round 1	Round 2	Round 3	Round 4	Round 5
Year Conducted	1987	1992	1997	2002	2007
Years in HR Profession for					
Participant	10%	14%	13%	25%	24%
5 years or less	14%	19%	15%	18%	20%
6-9 years	26%	24%	21%	22%	23%
10-14 years	50%	43%	51%	35%	32%
15 or more years					
Industry of HR Participant					
Agriculture	0%	0%	0%	10%	6%
Petroleum and mining	6%	5%	3%	7%	17%
Chemicals, allied products,	11%	9%	7%	15%	12%
pharmaceutical	28%	14%	20%	5%	20%
General manufacturing	4%	3%	1%	6%	0%
Automotive	14%	14%	11%	16%	7%
Communications and high	14%	14%	11%	8%	5%
technology	11%	7%	27%	11%	7%
Retail and wholesale	8%	15%	14%	16%	20%
Financial services	4%	19%	6%	3%	4%
Utilities	0%	0%	0%	3%	3%
Public administration					
Primary Role of HR Participant					
Benefits/medical/safety	6%	5%	5%	4%	3%
Compensation	5%	4%	4%	6%	6%
HR planning/strategy/affirmative	6%	8%	5%	8%	14%
action	6%	8%	5%	6%	5%
Labor relations	2%	5%	3%	13%	7%
Org. development/research/	3%	6%	4%	4%	6%
effectiveness	7%	14%	6%	12%	9%
Recruiting	61%	45%	60%	48%	49%
Training/communication					
Generalist					

Size of Firm

We started the research focused on larger firms (Rounds 1 and 2 had 39% and 40% of respondents in firms over 10,000 employees), but in the Round 5 data, we wanted to include greater representation of smaller firms (20% of respondents in firms with over 10,000 employees and 31% of respondents in firms with fewer than 500 employees).

Primary Role of the HR Participant

In the Round 5 data, more HR professionals (14%) have titles related to HR strategy or planning. In the last 20 years, more resources have gone into this role as HR has worked to be more aligned with business results. The number of HR professionals doing work in benefits has declined as E-HR and Service Centers have streamlined benefits operations.

Figure 2.7 reports the geographic mix of the sample, comparing Round 5 with Round 4. This shows that the study is becoming more global (especially with respondents from China and India). Overall, the Round 5 data reflect a broad cross section of the HR profession. This is the largest data set of its kind describing the HR profession as it exists today.

Figure 2.7. **Geographic Distribution of Round 5 Data**

	U.S. and Canada	Latin America	Europe	China	Australia/ Asia Pacific	India
2007 # of Respondents	2,773	2,127	1,553	2,110	1,235	263
2007 % of Total Respondents	28%	21%	15%	21%	12%	3%
2002 % of Total Respondents	42%	36%	10%	0%	12%	0%

A Method to Our Madness

As mentioned in Chapter 1, careful statistical analysis for the Round 5 data led to the creation of a new model with six domains of HR competence. If you want to cut to the chase and begin learning about these domains, skip ahead to the next section in this chapter. Before you do so, however, allow us to reiterate: These six domains were not pulled out of thin air, nor dreamed up in someone's office one morning after too much coffee. They are the result of hundreds of hours of number crunching and interpretation. To give you a feel for this process, we will present a grossly simplified overview of our methodology—in effect, to tell the "detective story" behind the final model. (For a comprehensive discussion on data analysis, please see Appendix 2.) And to those who want to skip the methodology altogether, we'll see you in the next section.

The HRCS was made up of 130 survey items.[5] Using a technique called factor analysis, we asked the computer to identify patterns of relationship among respondents' answers to these 130 items. Six major factors (or groups of responses) emerged (see below). We called these six factors *competency domains*. This is one of the "cleanest" factor analyses we have ever seen, meaning that individual survey items grouped together very consistently and did not double or triple factor. This factor analysis can be seen in Appendix 2.

Each of the six competency domains contained between 8 and 45 individual items. Because of the complexity of these competency domains, we conducted a subsequent factor analysis on each domain. This resulted in the identification of *competency factors* within each competency domain. These factors are detailed in Chapters 3 through 8.

For each competency domain and its related competency factors, we calculated the average or mean score. The mean scores show how effectively HR participants exhibit the competency domains and factors. We looked for differences in these average scores in a number of areas:
- **HR vs. non-HR respondents:** Is the HR community more competent in its own eyes, or in the eyes of its colleagues outside of HR?
- **Participants vs. associates:** Do HR professionals demonstrate a collective "blind spot," seeing themselves as more (or less) competent than their colleagues perceive them to be?
- **Geography:** Are competency strengths and weaknesses consistent across the regions where the HR professionals work?
- **Industry:** Is the pattern of relative strengths and weaknesses different for HR professionals in different industries?
- **HR channel:** Are strengths and weaknesses different depending on the type of HR work the professional does (e.g., corporate, Embedded HR, Center of Expertise)?
- **Size of company:** Do different patterns emerge based on the size of the company?

The next step in the analysis was to employ regression analysis to determine the relative impact of the six domains on an HR professional's individual performance and his or her business unit's overall performance.[6] Regression answers the question, "How much of an individual's professional competence is explained by the six domains together? By each? Separately? By each of the factors within each domain?"[7]

We performed a similar regression to business results. We wanted to determine if HR competencies had an impact on business outcomes and if so, the relative impact of each of the HR competency domains on those outcomes.

That, in a nutshell, is the methodology that resulted in the HR Competency model, competency domains, and statistical comparisons discussed in the rest of this book.

What Is the New Model of HR Competence, Based on Round 5 of the HRCS, and How Does the Global HR Community Stack Up Against this Model?

Computers are excellent at crunching numbers. They are not so good at interpreting or putting a name on the numbers. These tasks were left to mere mortals, and posed a significant challenge. The data suggested that we focus not just on the knowledge and ability of the HR professional, but on what the HR professional *becomes* through the use of that knowledge and ability. Hence, the six domains sound almost like the roles played by a fully competent HR professional. For example, in the past we referred to the domain regarding knowledge of the business simply as Business Knowledge because an HR professional needs to have business knowledge. This time, we chose to call this domain Business Ally because an HR professional needs to become a business ally by using his or her knowledge of the business. We see HR professionals as needing to know, but more important, needing to act on what they know.

Here, then, are quick definitions of the six competency domains from Round 5 of the HR Competency Study:

Credible Activist

The HR professional is both credible (respected, admired, listened to) and active (offers a point of view, takes a position, challenges assumptions). Some have called this "HR with an attitude."[8] HR professionals who are credible but not activists are admired but have little impact. Activists who are not credible have ideas that no one implements.

Culture & Change Steward

The HR professional appreciates, articulates, and helps shape a company's culture. Culture is a pattern of activities more than a single event. Ideally this culture starts with clarity around external customer expectations (firm identity or brand) and then translates these expectations into internal employee and organization behaviors. As stewards of culture, HR professionals respect the past culture and also can help to shape a new culture. They coach managers in how their actions reflect and drive culture, they weave the cultural standards into HR practices and processes, and they make culture real to employees. Additionally, successful HR professionals facilitate change in two ways. First, they help make culture happen. Second, they develop disciplines to make changes happen throughout the organization. This may include implementation of strategy, projects, or initiatives. They help turn what is known into what is done.

Talent Manager/Organization Designer

The HR professional masters theory, research, and practice in both talent management and organization design. Talent management focuses on competency requirements and how individuals enter and move up, across, or out of the organization. Organization design focuses on how a company embeds capability (for example, collaboration) into the structure, processes, and policies that shape how an organization works. HR professionals ensure that the company's means of talent management and organization capabilities are aligned with customer requirements and strategy, integrated with each other, and working effectively and efficiently. HR is not just about talent or organization, but also about the two of them together. Good talent without a supporting organization will not be sustained, and a good organization will not deliver results without talented individuals with the right competencies in critical roles.

Strategy Architect

The HR professional has a vision for how the organization can "win" in the marketplace, now and in the future. He or she plays an active part in the establishment of the overall strategy to deliver on this vision. This means recognizing business trends and their impact on the business, forecasting potential obstacles to success, and facilitating the process of gaining strategic clarity. The HR professional also contributes to the building of the overall strategy by linking the internal organization to external customer expectations. This linkage helps make customer-driven business strategies real to the employees of the company.

Operational Executor

The HR professional executes the operational aspects of managing people and organization. Policies need to be drafted, adapted, and implemented. Employees also have many administrative needs (e.g., to be paid, relocated, hired, and trained). HR professionals ensure that these basic needs are efficiently dealt with through technology, shared services, and/or outsourcing. This operational work of HR ensures credibility if executed flawlessly and grounded in the consistent application of policies.

Business Ally

Businesses succeed by setting goals and objectives that respond to external opportunities and threats. HR professionals contribute to the success of a business by knowing the social context or setting in which their business operates. They also know how the business makes money, which we call the value chain of the business: who customers are, why they buy the company's products or services. Finally, they have a good understanding of the parts of the business (finance, marketing, research and development, engineering), what they must accomplish and how they work together, so that they can help the business organize to make money.

The six competency domains lend themselves naturally to a new graphical representation, seen in Figure 2.8 The graphic captures a number of the model's important implications. HR professionals play a unique role at the intersection of people and business issues. This is represented by the large arrows or vectors bordering the model. In the midst of constant change and upheaval, HR professionals serve the organization's people, communicating care, concern, and compassion for employees. Some have called this "keeping the human in human resources."[9] But marketplace dynamics also require that HR professionals be attuned to customer and investor expectations by making sure that strategies are designed and delivered.

Following only one of these two arrows independent of the other will lead to failure. HR professionals who emphasize the people side at the exclusion of the business side may be well liked and popular, but they will not succeed because their work does not further business goals. HR professionals who focus on the business side without sensitivity to the human element also will struggle, because while the business may prosper in the short term, people will not sustain the success in the longer term.

Bordered by the people and business arrows, the six competency domains are arrayed according to our research findings. Credible Activist is at the crux. Credibility enables the HR professional to relate to people, but being an activist means that the HR professional has a point of view about the business and actively participates in furthering strategic goals. Being a Credible Activist ensures that HR professionals can both build relationships and deliver on business performance.

Moving up the people arrow, HR professionals must master the basic systems and processes related to people—the HR fundamentals. We discover most of

Figure 2.8. **The Round 5 HR Competency Model**

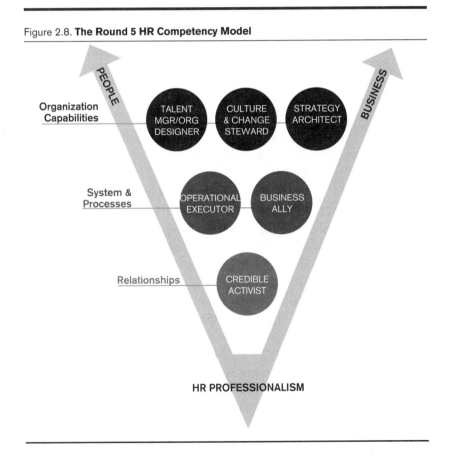

these processes in the Operational Executor role. HR professionals who master such processes as payroll, benefits, relocation, retirement, and so forth, help ensure that employees' needs are met. HR professionals who become Talent Managers/Organization Designers ensure that the right people with the right skills are in the right jobs—now and in the future. At the same time, they focus on building crucial organization capabilities. Thus the people axis begins with relationships, creates systems or processes to sustain those relationships, then builds capabilities that become embedded in the organization.

Along the business arrow of the model, HR professionals must start with "Business 101" in order to become Business Allies. HR professionals simply have to be business literate, or able to talk knowledgeably about competitors, customers, business context, financial performance, and how the business makes money. Then, they can move into the role of the Strategy Architect who helps align all HR practices with the company's business strategy. Strategy Architects ensure that the organization has a clear view about the future, its strategies are formulated consistent with customer expectations, and these strategies are executed through HR practices and leadership behaviors.

Bridging the two arrows is the role of Culture & Change Steward. This domain connects business demands and employee expectations. HR professionals who turn customer and business requirements into employee behaviors create cultures that endure.

HR Competence by the Numbers
Earlier in this chapter, we made no apology for the abundance of data that we would share. Too often, HR is seen as a "soft and fuzzy" profession, based more on common sense and conventional wisdom than hard data. By the end of this chapter—and throughout the chapters that follow—we will have sorted through more data than most of us have seen since our introductory stats course in college. Hopefully, a deeper understanding of the multifaceted HR profession will emerge.

Descriptive Statistics: A Report Card on the Global HR Community
To fully capture how HR professionals demonstrate their competence, we looked at the mean scores for each competence by a number of sub-groupings in the data. We were looking for differences in how these six competency domains were demonstrated by HR professionals. We should note that we are

not reporting *statistical significance* in the data, since with an overall sample size of 10,000, very minor differences are *statistically* significant. Rather, we are interested in *meaningful differences*, which might show up as variations in scores or as patterns in the data.

We start in Figure 2.9 by showing how HR participants (those doing self reports), HR associates, and non-HR associates scored the six competencies. The pattern is much the same within each respondent group, with the six competencies grouping roughly into three levels of proficiency or report-card "grades":
Grade A: Credible Activist is the highest-rated competency domain, scoring on average above a four ("to a large extent") on the five-point response scale.

Grade B: Culture & Change Steward and Talent Manager/Organization Designer are next, and roughly equally rated.

Grade C: Strategy Architect, Operational Executor and Business Ally trail somewhat in terms of HR proficiency.

Figure 2.9 also shows the trends between Round 4 and Round 5. Since we changed some of the questions from Round 4 to Round 5, it is not possible to do a direct comparison, but we can compare the domains somewhat over time.

Figure 2.9. **Mean Scores on Major Competency Domains by Respondent Type for Round 5 (and Round 4) Data (Round 4 data are in parentheses)**

Round 5 Domains *(Round 4 domains)*	HR Participants	HR Associates	Non-HR Associates
Credible Activist (personal credibility)	4.16 *(4.34)*	4.23 *(4.16)*	4.14 *(4.18)*
Culture & Change Steward (strategic contribution)	3.80 *(3.83)*	3.84 *(3.57)*	3.75 *(3.61)*
Talent Manager/Organization Designer (HR delivery)	3.73 *(3.82)*	3.80 *(3.62)*	3.76 *(3.57)*
Strategy Architect (strategic contribution)	3.49 *(3.83)*	3.67 *(3.57)*	3.58 *(3.61)*
Operational Executor (HR delivery/HR technology)	3.47 *(3.26)*	3.58 *(3.17)*	3.63 *(3.35)*
Business Ally (Know the business)	3.39 *(3.46)*	3.55 *(3.42)*	3.48 *(3.53)*

Credible Activist is the highest-scoring competency domain in both Round 4 and Round 5 by HR participants, HR associates, and non-HR associates. But the score drops in the Round 5 data. HR professionals in Round

5 are seemingly less credible than they were in Round 4. This may be because the Round 5 sample includes more data from emerging markets (e.g., China, where Credible Activist scores are lower), but also may suggest that while expectations and opportunities for HR professionals have increased, many practitioners are not keeping pace.

Both HR and non-HR associates rated HR professionals higher in Culture & Change Steward and Strategy Architect in Round 5 than in Round 4. In the changing business context we described in Chapter 1, HR professionals have become more engaged in helping make culture change happen. It is no longer enough to know and/or do a specific HR practice; it is important to put it into the context of a culture or pattern of events.

Both HR and non-HR associates rate HR higher in the traditional HR skill areas of Talent Manager/Organization Designer. HR professionals have increased in their technical acumen. The body of knowledge that makes up HR is becoming both known and deployed.

In terms of Operational Executor, HR professionals have increased their scores dramatically. Perhaps the E-HR systems and other administrative changes (e.g., shared services or outsourcing) have helped HR professionals execute their day-to-day operations more effectively. Unfortunately, Business Ally skills have not improved dramatically. Even with all the talk about HR "knowing the business," HR professionals are not yet seen as mastering the basics of the business. It's still more rhetoric than results. This lack of business acumen may become a rate-limiting factor on increased HR contribution to the business.

To further understand the state of the profession, Figure 2.10 examines how the six competency domains differ by geography. The pattern of the six domains is much the same for most regions except for a few differences.

North America
The domains fall into three categories: Credible Activist ("A" grade); Culture & Change Steward, Talent Manager/Organization Designer, and Strategy Architect ("B grade); and Operational Executor and Business Ally ("C" grade).

Latin America
HR professionals are stronger at Operational Executor work.

Europe

HR professionals are stronger at Talent Manager/Organization Designer, but less effective at Operational Executor.

China

All six domains are about equal in terms of proficiency, but as noted, the Chinese HR profession lags the rest of the world in Credible Activist, Talent Manager/Organization Designer, and Culture & Change Steward. China is the only region where Operational Executor is rated higher than Culture & Change Steward, Talent Manager/Organization Designer, and Strategy Architect.

Australia/Asia Pacific

HR professionals in Australia/Asia Pacific have much the same profile as those in Europe and North America.

India

HR professionals in India score between China and the rest of the world on most of the competencies, except that they have higher scores in Talent Management/Organization Development.[10]

Figure 2.10. **Mean Scores on Six Major Competency Domains by Region**

	U.S. and Canada	Latin America	Europe	China	Australia/ Asia Pacific	India
Credible Activist	4.38	4.15	4.22	3.96	4.23	4.14
Culture & Change Steward	3.94	3.84	3.81	3.55	3.81	3.76
Talent Manager/ Organization Designer	3.89	3.80	3.83	3.59	3.76	3.85
Strategy Architect	3.73	3.59	3.67	3.53	3.58	3.67
Operational Executor	3.59	3.71	3.48	3.63	3.52	3.66
Business Ally	3.55	3.54	3.51	3.47	3.47	3.69
Note: Overall Item Average	3.87	3.78	3.78	3.60	3.75	3.80

Overall scores differ for China, according to Figure 2.10. Perhaps the HR profession there has not made as much progress in the more strategic areas. This is an emerging economy, and the HR profession is lagging. These lower scores may also reflect the Chinese culture, where there is more respect for authority and less willingness to openly confront one's superior. The low scores in China may also explain some of the lower overall scores in 2007 than in 2002. Another explanation of this is that when an economy is expanding as fast as India's and China's, the transactional work takes precedence because it's more important. Hiring, compliance, etc., are the critical (though tactical) business challenges.

One of the inevitable questions for HR professionals is to what extent competency expectations should be universal vs. unique to each region. This data set suggests more universality than uniqueness. The HR profession has common platforms on which to build success.

Figure 2.11 examines the different competencies by industry. There are unique results within some industries (e.g., construction industry scores lower in all six domains; utilities, communications, and services generally score higher). In general, service-oriented industries have HR professionals who score higher in the six domains than capital-intensive industries.

Figure 2.11. **Mean Scores on Major Competency Domains by Industry**

	Credible Activist	Culture & Change Steward	Talent Manager/ Organization Design	Strategy Architect	Operational Executor	Business Ally
Agriculture	3.97	3.61	3.68	3.55	3.57	3.50
Mining	4.06	3.67	3.69	3.60	3.63	3.52
Construction	*3.96*	*3.49*	*3.55*	*3.41*	*3.57*	3.45
Food	4.11	3.73	3.71	3.59	3.48	*3.44*
Pharmaceuticals / Chemicals	4.27	**3.89**	**3.91**	**3.70**	3.62	3.57
Manufacturing	4.20	3.78	3.79	3.60	3.60	3.51
Wholesale / Retail Trade	**4.26**	3.83	3.78	3.61	3.57	3.48
Utilities & Communications	4.31	**3.94**	**3.89**	3.71	**3.66**	3.52
Banking & Real Estate	4.30	3.87	3.80	3.59	3.59	3.47
Services	**4.33**	3.93	3.87	**3.73**	**3.66**	**3.60**
Public Administration	4.25	3.84	3.81	3.65	3.58	3.52

Bold=high; *Italics=low*

This makes sense because service industries where labor is a larger part of the competitive equation would require HR professionals who have more competence to deal with workforce and workplace issues.

However, regardless of industry, the pattern of results is similar. Credible Activist is consistently the highest score, followed by Culture & Change Steward, Talent Manager/Organization Designer, Strategy Architect, Operational Executor, and Business Ally.

Figure 2.12 shows that the pattern of HR competency scores is similar regardless of which part of HR the person works in. "Channel" refers to the type of role or organization through which the HR professional delivers his or her expertise. Embedded HR professionals (those who work as generalists, partners, or relationship managers within a business) score highest on all six of the domains. This may indicate that those who assume the HR generalist roles are seen as more talented than those in other channels of distribution. Often more senior HR professionals are assigned to the embedded roles, while those working in Service Centers and E-HR tend to be newer to the profession and thus have lower overall competency scores.

Figure 2.12. **Mean Scores on Six Major Competency Domains by HR Channel**

	Credible Activist	Culture & Change Steward	Talent Manager/ Organization Designer	Strategy Architect	Operational Executor	Business Ally
Functional HR	4.10	3.65	3.64	3.53	3.60	3.48
Centers of Expertise	4.18	3.82	3.79	3.67	3.63	3.56
Embedded HR	4.29	3.87	3.87	3.66	3.59	3.52
Service Center	4.07	3.65	3.63	3.54	3.68	3.46
E-HR	4.06	3.69	3.67	3.72	3.73	3.61
Corporate HR	4.19	3.82	3.80	3.65	3.57	3.53

Figure 2.13 shows the relative weighting of HR competencies by size of business. The Figure shows that in general, larger companies have HR professionals with greater competence than do smaller companies. Perhaps in larger companies, more resources are invested in HR development than in small companies. In particular, larger firms generally have HR professionals who have more competence as Credible Activists, Culture & Change

Stewards, Talent Managers/Organization Designers, and Strategy Architects. These more strategic HR competencies seem to reside more in HR professionals in larger firms. In the smallest companies (0 to 99 employees), HR professionals are more competent in the Operational Executor role, indicating that the HR work in these smaller firms requires more attention to day-to-day issues.

Figure 2.13. **Mean Scores for Six Major Competency Domains by Size of Business**

Mean Scores, Raters only	0 to 99	100 to 499	500 to 999	1,000 to 4,999	5,000 to 9,999	10,000 to 24,999	25,000+
Number of Associate Raters	314	1,032	1,051	2,112	1,607	838	1,412
Credible Activist	4.00	4.09	4.15	4.19	4.19	4.33	4.26
Culture & Change Steward	3.67	3.67	3.76	3.78	3.81	3.89	3.88
Talent Manager/ Organization Designer	3.67	3.64	3.75	3.75	3.83	3.85	3.89
Strategy Architect	3.60	3.47	3.57	3.58	3.69	3.74	3.75
Operational Executor	3.64	3.54	3.67	3.60	3.58	3.56	3.61
Business Ally	3.53	3.41	3.50	3.49	3.56	3.54	3.59

Figure 2.14 shows the competency scores by gender. It reveals that women generally score higher in the Credible Activist domain, which may indicate that women build relationships of trust more readily than men. Women and men score about the same on Culture & Change Steward and Talent Manager/Organization Designer. Men generally score higher than women at Strategy Architect, Operational Executor, and Business Ally, some of the more administrative and business-focused areas. But again, note the same general pattern for the six domains.

Figure 2.14. **Mean Scores for Six Major Competency Domains by Gender**

Domain	Male	Female
Credible Activist	4.15	4.24
Culture & Change Steward	3.79	3.80
Talent Manager/Organization Designer	3.80	3.78
Strategy Architect	3.67	3.60
Operational Executor	3.64	3.56
Business Ally	3.60	3.45

The overall takeaway from these descriptive statistics is that the pattern of HR competence is much the same regardless of geography, industry, channel of distribution, size of business, or gender. While there are some subtle differences within each of these sub-groups, we can begin to summarize with confidence the strengths and development needs of the global HR community. Credible Activist is a strength; Culture & Change Steward and Talent Manager/Organization Designer are near-strengths; Strategy Architect, Operational Executor, and (especially) Business Ally are development needs. We find it hard to overlook that two of the profession's three overall development needs are along the "business" arrow of the model.

Which of the HR Competencies Are Most Important for Predicting the Performance of the Individual HR Professional?

Correlations to Individual Performance

The above section offers a descriptive view of the HR profession. This section offers a more prescriptive presentation. In this section, we attempt to show not only what is, but what *should be* in terms of HR competencies. To define what should be, we performed a regression analysis that allowed us to determine the relative impact of the various HR competency domains on perceived individual performance as gauged by the question: "On a scale from 0-100, how does this individual compare to other HR professionals you have known?"

Figure 2.15 indicates that competence in any one of the domains has a halo effect on overall individual HR performance. This requires a short digression into mechanics of statistical regressions. As discussed above, regression analysis attempts to explain an individual's performance score (say 90 out of 100). A regression may be done by finding out how much each of the six domains explains the individual's overall performance (percent of 90 points). For example, if an HR professional is a gifted Credible Activist, how much does competence in that single domain explain the overall performance of the HR professional? We can ask this question about each of the six competency domains. The percent remaining of individual performance after the first domain is considered may then be calculated.[11]

As Figure 2.15 indicates, if the effect of Credible Activist is calculated first, it explains 93% of the individual performance, and the other five domains explain 7%. Culture & Change Steward explains 79%, with the other five domains explaining 21%, and so forth. One of the takeaways from this chart is that when an HR professional is perceived as excellent in one of the first four domains, that HR professional is seen as effective overall. Excellence in a particular domain will have a halo effect.

This finding is consistent with much of the recent research on strengths-based development.The implication is that if someone has a predisposition to Credible Activist, Culture & Change Steward, Talent Manager/Organization Designer, or Strategy Architect, then the HR professional should pursue those strengths and move from proficiency to mastery. A similar pattern is less likely to hold if the HR professional is excellent as an Operational Executor or Business Ally.

Figure 2.15. **Impact of Each of the Six Major Competency Domains on Perception of Individual Performance**

(The column represents how much each domain explains individual performance if that domain were used exclusively.)

	Credible Activist	Culture & Change Steward	Talent Manager/ Organization Designer	Strategy Architect	Operational Executor	Business Ally
Credible Activist	**93%**	16%	20%	30%	**47%**	**53%**
Culture & Change Steward	6%	**79%**	1%	2%	4%	4%
Talent Mgr./ Org. Designer	1%	4%	**76%**	1%	1%	1%
Strategy Architect	0%	0%	4%	**66%**	0%	0%
Operational Executor	0%	0%	0%	1%	37%	0%
Business Ally	0%	0%	0%	0%	11%	42%
Total	100%	100%	100%	100%	100%	100%

To further understand the impact of these six competency domains on individual performance, we did two types of regression analysis. First, we wanted to find out how much an HR professional's individual performance is determined by the HR professional's overall competence. For example, if a participant scored 90 (out of 100) on the survey's individual performance measure, multiple regressions would tell us how much of that 90% was explained by the competencies we are studying. Second, we wanted to find out the relative impact of each of the independent variables on the dependent variable. For example, we wanted to find out how much of the 90% that each of the six domains explained. This analysis will tell us the relative impact and weighting of each of the six competency domains.

As shown in Figure 2.16, the basic pattern of results is the same. Competence as a Credible Activist explains more individual HR performance than any of the other competency domains, followed by Culture & Change Steward, Talent Manager/Organization Designer, and Strategy Architect, followed by Operational Executor and Business Ally. This same pattern holds regardless of the sub-sample in the data: HR professionals who rate themselves; HR professionals who rate others; and non-HR professionals. Each sub-group has much the same pattern, according to the columns in Figure 2.16. This suggests that for an HR professional to be seen as individually competent, all six domains have some impact, but being an effective Credible Activist is the most important. The good news is that Credible Activist is also the highest rated in the descriptive data above.

The bottom row of Figure 2.16 shows that the six competency domains collectively explain 39.1% of the individual's performance (the 90 points in the above example) when using all respondents, but only 18.6% when looking only at HR participants' self-assessment data. What this suggests is that HR professionals' own perception of their strengths and weaknesses does not correlate very closely with their overall performance as judged by others. Self-insight is not as good as it should (or could) be—a common finding with 360-degree feedback. Perhaps even more significant is the strength of the correlation between non-HR raters and an HR professional's performance (47.3%). This explains why we have paid close attention to the non-HR feedback throughout our analysis.

Figure 2.16. **Relative Impact of Six Major Competency Domains on Individual Performance**

	HR Participants	HR Associates	Non-HR Associates
Credible Activist	23%	24%	23%
Culture & Change Steward	19%	20%	20%
Talent Manager/Organization Designer	23%	19%	19%
Strategy Architect	17%	17%	16%
Operational Executor	7%	9%	11%
Business Ally	10%	11%	10%
Multiple Regression R²	*.186*	*.419*	*.473*

Figure 2.17 compares the Round 5 results with the Round 4 results. The comparisons are not exact since the competency domains have evolved somewhat. The largest change is that the domain "Strategic Contribution" from Round 4 was divided into two domains in Round 5 (Culture & Change Steward and Strategy Architect). Even with this change, Credible Activist (the Round 4 domain "Personal Credibility") continues to be the most important competency for HR professionals. However, with this change, an HR professional's ability to contribute to culture, change, and strategy explain more of the HR professional's performance (37% in Round 5 vs. 25% in Round 4). This may be an indicator of the new expectations of HR professionals, who must contribute to the business through shaping the culture and helping architect the strategy.

Figure 2.17. **Relative Impact of Each of the Six Major Competency Domains Comparing Round 4 and Round 5 Data**

New Domain	Old Domain	Round 4 data	Round 5 data
Credible Activist	Personal credibility	33%	24%
Culture & Change Steward	Strategic contribution	25%	20%
Strategy Architect			17%
Talent Manager/ Organization Designer	HR delivery	22%	20%
Operational Executor	HR delivery/HR technology	8%	9%
Business Ally	Business knowledge	12%	11%

Figure 2.18 reports the relative impact of the six competency domains according to geographic region. The data show an amazingly similar pattern regardless of geography. The major exception is China. China requires more Operational Executor work than other geographies. As previously mentioned, the Chinese HR profession may be requiring more administrative and day-to-day work than other regions since the HR profession in China is still emerging. The administrative tasks associated with HR are the basics that enable HR professionals to participate in future business results.

Figure 2.18. **Relative Impact of Six Major Competency Domains on Individual Performance by Region**

	U.S. and Canada	Latin America	Europe	China	Australia/ Asia Pacific	India
Credible Activist	25%	23%	27%	18%	24%	16%
Culture & Change Steward	21%	18%	21%	18%	20%	18%
Talent Manager/ Organization Designer	19%	19%	19%	18%	19%	20%
Strategy Architect	17%	16%	18%	17%	17%	21%
Operational Executor	9%	13%	5%	16%	10%	13%
Business Ally	9%	11%	10%	14%	12%	12%

A question that is often raised is whether the impact of the HR competencies would differ by career stage or job level. We examined the relative impact of the six domains based on the job level of the HR professionals. Figure 2.19 shows another consistent pattern in the six domains regardless of the job level of the HR professional. The data are a bit of a surprise, as we would have expected HR professionals at different stages to have differing skill requirements. Perhaps we are capturing in this study the "code" or core competencies for high-performing HR professionals regardless of where they sit in a company.[12] The 44% of variance we are explaining may be this universal code; the unexplained 55% of individual performance may come from a variety of other differentiators not related to these competencies.

Figure 2.19. **Relative Impact of Six Major Competency Domains on Individual Performance by Job Level**

	Individual Contributors	Managers of Individual Contributors	Directors of Managers
Credible Activist	24%	24%	23%
Culture & Change Steward	20%	21%	20%
Talent Manager/Organization Designer	18%	20%	20%
Strategy Architect	17%	15%	18%
Operational Executor	10%	10%	9%
Business Ally	11%	10%	11%
Multiple Regression R²	.423	.428	.455

Figure 2.20. **Relative Impact of Six Major Competency Domains on Individual Performance by HR Channel**

	Functional HR	Centers of Expertise	Embedded HR	Service Centers	Corporate HR
Credible Activist	21%	24%	25%	25%	24%
Culture & Change Steward	19%	20%	20%	21%	20%
Talent Manager/Organization Designer	19%	19%	20%	15%	20%
Strategy Architect	16%	17%	17%	14%	17%
Operational Executor	12%	10%	8%	15%	9%
Business Ally	13%	11%	9%	10%	11%
Multiple Regression R²	.420	.495	.404	.370	.482

Another question that is often raised is the extent to which HR competencies might vary by where the HR professional works in HR, as shown in Figure 2.20. Again, the same pattern holds. Regardless of where you work, you should have the same basic pattern of competencies. The Credible Activist domain is important across the board. For Functional HR, the pattern we have seen earlier seems to hold, with Business Ally being slightly more important. Service Centers value Operational Execution more highly than they do either knowledge of the business or strategy, and on par with Talent Management/Organization Design. Corporate HR folks don't require as much competence in Operational Executor as in other areas of the business.

Figure 2.21 shows that the same pattern seems to hold by gender. Both male and female practitioners require Credible Activist as the primary HR skill set, followed by Culture & Change Steward, Talent Manager/Organization Designer, and Strategy Architect.

Figure 2.21. **Relative Impact of the Six Major Competency Domains on Individual Performance by Gender**

Domain	Male	Female
Credible Activist	22%	25%
Culture & Change Steward	20%	20%
Talent Manager/Organization Designer	19%	19%
Strategy Architect	17%	16%
Operational Executor	10%	9%
Business Ally	12%	10%

Figure 2.22 shows the same basic patterns of how HR competencies affect the individual performance of HR professionals. In smaller businesses, HR professionals tend to be seen as more effective if/when they have more ability as Operational Executors and Business Allies. This may suggest that in smaller firms, HR professionals have a greater expectation to get the day-to-day work of HR done. Larger businesses tend to place higher value on HR professionals if they are strong Strategy Architects, which may indicate increased expectations to work with senior leaders, helping to shape the strategy and to think through execution.

Figure 2.22. **Relative Impact of Six Major Competency Domains on Individual Performance by Size of Business**

	0 to 99	100 to 499	500 to 999	1,000 to 4,999	5,000 to 9,999	10,000 to 24,999	25,000+
Credible Activist	22%	21%	20%	25%	23%	29%	24%
Culture & Change Steward	20%	20%	20%	20%	20%	20%	20%
Talent Manager/ Organization Designer	19%	19%	19%	19%	19%	19%	20%
Strategy Architect	13%	16%	16%	17%	18%	16%	17%
Operational Executor	15%	12%	13%	9%	8%	7%	9%
Business Ally	11%	13%	11%	9%	11%	9%	10%

To sum up, in this section, we have examined how HR competencies correlate with the individual performance of the HR professional. The pattern is the same regardless of how the data are analyzed. For HR professionals to be seen as high-performing, they need to demonstrate Credible Activism. They need to build relationships of trust and have a point of view about how to help the business. They then need to demonstrate competence in Culture & Change Steward, Talent Management/Organization Design, and Strategy Architecture. These three sets of competencies are those that help them align HR work to the business. These are the competencies that enable HR professionals to transform businesses.

Finally, HR professionals need to be good Operational Executors and Business Allies. These are the more transactional competencies for HR professionals. They are the "Figure stakes" or tickets of admission—but if the transactional work is not done well, HR professionals are unlikely to be invited to participate in the strategic or transformational work.

Which of the HR Competencies are Most Important for Predicting Business Performance?

Correlations to Business Performance
The above sections discuss the descriptive state of HR competencies and the relative impact of HR competencies on an HR professional's individual performance. This section examines the extent to which HR competencies impact business performance. Figure 2.23 indicates that the competencies of HR professionals definitely have impact on business performance. Others have found that about half of business performance is explained by things within the control of management and half outside the control of management.[13] We find that when HR professionals have competence, they affect about 20% of business results.[14] Interestingly, the correlation between HR professionals' competencies and business performance is weaker in the eyes of non-HR associates than among HR associates.

All six sets of skills matter in predicting business performance, but Credible Activist, Culture & Change Steward, Talent Manager/Organization Designer, and Strategy Architect have the highest impact (about 75% of total). Also notice the value that non-HR associates place on HR folks knowing the business. Perhaps the issue is clear now that HR folks need to invest much more in business mastery.

Figure 2.23. **Relative Impact of Six Major Competency Domains on Business Performance**

	All Respondents	HR Associates	Non-HR Associates
Credible Activist	22%	22%	19%
Culture & Change Steward	20%	18%	19%
Talent Manager/ Organization Designer	19%	15%	17%
Strategy Architect	12%	17%	18%
Operational Executor	13%	12%	13%
Business Ally	13%	15%	14%
Multiple Regression R^2	.208	.207	.207

Figure 2.24 reports how the competencies of HR professionals in different channels of distribution affect business performance. If you are working in any channel of HR, you need much the same competencies to affect business performance. *For example*, Embedded HR people do Operational Executor the most, quickly followed by Culture and Change Steward and Credible Activist. Different HR channels require different competencies to affect business performance. Functional HR and Service Centers require a high level of competency in Credible Activist. Strategy Architect is most important in Centers of Expertise and Corporate HR. Centers of Expertise require competence in all areas, the highest being Talent Manager/Organization Designer.

Figure 2.24. **Relative Impact of Six Major Competency Domains on Business Performance by HR Channel**

	Functional HR	Centers of Expertise	Embedded HR	Service Centers	Corporate HR
Credible Activist	25%	11%	23%	52%	16%
Culture & Change Steward	23%	16%	24%	17%	8%
Talent Manager/ Organization Designer	20%	22%	10%	4%	31%
Strategy Architect	9%	17%	8%	6%	13%
Operational Executor	10%	15%	27%	0%	16%
Business Ally	12%	19%	8%	20%	17%

Figure 2.25 shows the relative impact of the six competency domains on business performance by gender. Females have more impact on the business when they demonstrate Credible Activism, Culture & Change Steward, and Operational Executor more than males. Males have more impact on the business when they are stronger at Talent Manager/Organization Designer, Strategy Architect, and Business Ally. Women who work in HR seem to have more impact when they build relationships of trust and help shape culture. Men impact the business more when they have depth in managing talent and organization and are business allies. This may be due to differing expectations between men and women who work in HR.

Figure 2.25. Relative Impact of Six Major Competency Domains on Business Performance by Gender

Domain	Male	Female
Credible Activist	19%	25%
Culture & Change Steward	16%	21%
Talent Manager/Organization Designer	22%	15%
Strategy Architect	16%	11%
Operational Executor	9%	17%
Business Ally	18%	11%

Figure 2.26 reports the impact of HR competencies on business performance based on the size of the business. Some of these results are confusing. Very small (0 to 99 employees) and very large (more than 25,000 employees) businesses are more likely to have business success if HR professionals are more competent in the Operational Executor and Business Ally competencies. Smaller companies have to execute by having HR professionals who make things happen. This may come from the HR professional doing administrative work and making sure that the administrative processes operate smoothly.

Larger firms, which are prone to more bureaucracy, face the same challenge of getting administrative work done more efficiently. However, instead of relying on the individual HR professional to do this administrative work, these larger firms are investing in shared services, E-HR, and outsourcing. Larger firms are more likely to experiment with new ways of doing HR work because of the economies of scale.

These results also indicate that mid-size businesses (500 to 5,000 employees) are more successful when HR professionals have greater competence as Culture & Change Stewards. Perhaps, in the changing competitive world we described in Chapter 1, these mid-size firms require more work to shape cultures and make change happen to continue to grow. Clearly, the sample sizes are small here, and more study will be required to figure out how HR professionals help businesses of different sizes become successful.

Figure 2.26. **Relative Impact of Six Major Competency Domains on Business Performance by Size of Business**

	0 to 99	100 to 499	500 to 999	1,000 to 4,999	5,000 to 9,999	10,000 to 24,999	25,000+
Number of Businesses	38	85	65	99	35	28	35
Credible Activist	11%	22%	23%	11%	12%	20%	12%
Culture & Change Steward	20%	16%	26%	29%	10%	19%	13%
Talent Manager/ Organization Designer	18%	19%	15%	20%	10%	19%	15%
Strategic Architect	13%	17%	16%	20%	25%	14%	16%
Operational Executor	23%	10%	9%	8%	5%	15%	22%
Business Ally	15%	16%	10%	12%	38%	13%	21%

Conclusion

What HR professionals know and do clearly affects the performance of the business. The pattern is much the same as the skill set that affects individual performance. When HR professionals are Credible Activists (explored more in Chapter 3) they are not only seen as better individual contributors, but they also help businesses perform better. Following the Credible Activist skill set, HR professionals who are more competent as Culture & Change Stewards (explored in Chapter 4), Talent Managers/Organization Designers (Chapter 5), and Strategy Architects (Chapter 6) will help themselves and their businesses. Then, the HR professionals who are Operational Executors (Chapter 7) and Business Allies (Chapter 8) support personal and business development.

The descriptive statistics and predictive statistics about HR competencies and individual and business performance tell a story about baseline competencies required for HR professionals.

The model introduced earlier in this chapter (see Figure 2.8) is consistent with the overall findings in this study. It shows that HR professionals deliver enormous value and respond to the requirements and conditions laid out in Chapter 1 by mastering specific competencies.

In the next six chapters, we will review the details of each of the six competency domains and review what HR professionals should know, do, and deliver to have greater impact on the business. For each of the six domains, we will follow the same sequence of analysis and commentary. First, we will provide an overview of the domain and the factors that define it. Second, we will present the descriptive statistics for the domain. Third, we will examine the correlations between the domain's factors and individual performance. Fourth, we will look at the correlations with business performance. Finally, we will present some implications for HR professionals, including hands-on suggestions for building competence in each domain and factor.

We began this chapter referring to the HRCS as a progress check along the HR journey. We hope that the message is clear: The HR profession is evolving toward a more business-based, value-added role than it has ever played before. We hope that in each of the chapters that follow, you will find insights and ideas that help you not only survive but thrive during this exciting transition.

CHAPTER 3

Credible Activist

Jason Frank was recently appointed vice president of HR for a bank. He was actively courted by his new company and offered a large signing bonus to leave his former employer where he headed compensation. After two months in his new position, he met with the bank president to discuss his plans to reorganize HR. After listening carefully, the president said, "I like your aggressiveness. But you are new to the company and industry, so let's not make any changes until you have had more time to learn about us and build stronger relationships. We'll talk again in a few months."

Paivi Hansen leads training for the research and development (R&D) division of a global consumer products company, and is respected both in HR and by business partners. She has 20 years with the company, all in training. Recently, the head of corporate training retired and, despite Paivi's experience, someone else was offered the job. She has considered looking at other employment opportunities. The head of HR told her, "Paivi, we don't want you to leave but the top training job needs someone willing to take more initiative. That's not you."

These vignettes help us understand the first competency domain we call Credible Activist. In a farewell essay published in *The Economist*, departing British Prime Minister Tony Blair wrote that one of his goals was for Great Britain to be "a player, not a spectator" on the world stage.[1] A similar point might be made about HR departments and professionals: The high-performers are players, not spectators.[2] They don't need an invitation to take a "seat at the table" because they are already at the table, influencing and impacting business decisions.

This chapter will report and analyze the research results for the Credible Activist domain of HR competence by focusing on the following three areas:
- Defining the Credible Activist domain and its factors.
- Pointing out insights and further questions from the statistical data.
- Offering illustrations and examples of Credible Activism in practice, along with ideas for personal development in this competency domain.

Defining the Domain

Credible Activists are respected and proactive. Credible individuals who are not activists may be respected, but have little impact. Activists who are not credible may have good ideas, but no one listens to them. The matrix below represents these two dimensions in graphic form.

	Less Credible	More Credible
More Activist	Risk of being seen as impetuous, arrogant, or uninformed	Opportunity to have impact
Less Activist	Risk of being seen as a marginal or poor performer	Risk of being seen as irrelevant, not having anything to say, resting on past laurels, or not knowing the business

As the matrix suggests, individuals who are activists but have no credibility are likely to be viewed as impetuous or arrogant. This is Jason's dilemma in the first vignette above. The bank president worries that Jason lacks the company experience, knowledge, and established relationships to realistically assess organizational needs. Hence, the president advises Jason to come back when he is more knowledgeable, has established relationships and can support his recommendations for change. By contrast, individuals like Paivi have credibility but aren't activists. They may be seen as risk averse or resting on past accomplishments. Paivi probably has the skill to lead training, but hasn't earned her manager's confidence. While business leaders may respect Paivi for her technical competence, she most likely will continue to be bypassed if she doesn't figure out how to be seen as a leader and contributor to the business, rather than a responsive and reactive good technician or soldier.

Finally, individuals who are neither credible nor activists are seen as spectators rather than players by their organizations or colleagues. They are at risk
of being replaced by more credible or activist HR professionals.

The idea of personal credibility is not new to the HRCS. For the past 15
years, statistical analysis has demonstrated the importance of being a credible HR professional as shown in the evolution of the HR competency model
in Chapter 2. In this round of the study, however, survey items related to
activism factored statistically with those related to credibility. Evidently, it
is no longer enough for HR practitioners to be trusted and well-liked; they
must also stick their necks out once in a while, take risks, and push their
non-HR colleagues to consider important business issues related to people.
For these reasons, the Credible Activist domain figures prominently in the
graphical depiction of the new HR competency model.

Credible Activist = Strong Individual and Business Performance

As discussed in the previous chapter, Credible Activists proved to have the
most powerful impact in the domain for both individual performance and
business performance. It is, therefore, placed at the nexus of the people and
business vectors. Our research shows four factors associated with the Credible Activist domain:

- Delivering results with integrity.
- Sharing information.
- Building relationships of trust.
- Doing HR with an attitude.

Factor: Delivering Results with Integrity

Equally important to delivering results is that those results are achieved in
the right way. Integrity means several things. It reflects an internal consistency in the HR professional's actions. It means operating in a principled way
and taking action that is consistent with company values, which reflect how
the company wishes to be seen and experienced by customers, investors,
employees, and other stakeholders. The manner in which HR professionals
approach a task speaks volumes about their insight into the organization
and its culture, their commitment to the company, and their professionalism.

HR practitioners should be particularly attentive to the collateral results that
need to be achieved, and the expectations for how work is accomplished. It

is important to go beyond the outcome requirements and understand how the result needs to be delivered.

As with most of the elements of Credible Activism, delivering results with integrity is more about *who a person is* than *what a person does*. An undeviating internal moral compass and an unimpeachable character are traits that build credibility in ways that specific talents or skills cannot. In a post-Enron world, government regulation and ethics training can encourage correct behavior but are not a substitute for a commitment to doing what's right.

Delivering the right results in the right way means something different for HR professionals at different points or stages in their career. For a new HR professional, delivering the right results in the right way focuses on performance basics. Is work completed on time, within budget, and error free? New HR professionals (either new in their career or new to an organization) are consistently being tested; HR leaders and business partners need to determine whether the individual has the aptitude or potential to handle more demanding assignments in the future. High-performers understand the importance of getting the basics right, and recognize that they need to demonstrate that they are worth the company's time, financial, and emotional investment for their career and development.[3]

To deliver results with integrity, HR professionals must:
- Focus on meeting pre-negotiated or pre-stated commitments.
- Strive to be error free.
- Ask important questions that help to frame complex ideas in useful ways.
- Achieve results without violating moral principles or compromising on ethics and values.
- Take responsibility for actions and their consequences.

Factor: Sharing Information

Credible Activists are good communicators. The influence an HR professional has on the business is magnified when good communication skills supplement trust and risk taking. As expressed by Deb Gustavson, manager of employee experience at Takeda Pharmaceutical North America, "How employees experience the company is very directly related to how HR presents company actions and decisions to employees, and keeps people informed about important decisions." HR professionals gain and keep credibility when they are able to articulately and persuasively communicate ideas to others.

The example of Phil Megas (a fictional name) may be helpful. Phil is head of talent management for a large technology company. He has a strong technical background in his area of expertise and is up-to-date on best practices. But he is an introvert and has difficulty building relationships with senior executives. He would prefer to remain in his office, reviewing the data and identifying needs and trends. Phil doesn't understand that his advisory and consulting skills, not just his ability to draw insight from data, make or break his reputation. Right now, his reputation is showing serious stress fractures. Unless he can become an active communicator and establish effective working relationships with his company's executive team, it will be difficult for him to be an effective consultant and advisor.

Factor: Building Relationships of Trust

Phil is a smart professional and an expert in his field. But he hasn't built relationships of trust with his business partners. Relationship building is a crucial skill in HR. It is critical in all professions, but particularly so in HR because so much of what HR does at senior levels is based on trust in their advice and perspective. Without trust, HR can only play a transactional role.

Because HR professionals work with the human side of business, they need to have strong interpersonal skills. They must be able to diagnose and help solve interpersonal problems. Credible Activists create an atmosphere of trust that results in positive working relationships with key internal and external constituents. In the research survey, this skill set was summarized in the phrase "good chemistry," which happens when:

- Core values are shared.
- Common interests are discovered that extend beyond work boundaries.
- The HR professional is empathetic in addressing concerns that may not be directly work-related.
- The HR professional can decompress tense interpersonal issues.

Relationships of trust also depend on knowledge and effort. Credible Activists do their homework. They know what is most important to their business colleagues and keep in touch with internal groups. They understand the goals of key executives, their priorities, and the issues that concern them or keep them up at night. In other words, trust is based on both interpersonal and business understanding. The latter stems from knowing what issues and initiatives are likely to have the greatest impact on achieving business objectives. See Chapter 8 for an extended discussion of the importance of business knowledge.

Factor: Doing HR with an Attitude

In the past five years, HR has earned a seat at the table. The issue is no longer being in the room where decisions are being made, but what to do once there. Too often, HR has been the note taker, scribe, or facilitator in strategy discussions, or the team building resource for senior management. In Chapter 6, we describe the role HR is expected to play as a participant—rather than interested observer or helper—in creating business and company strategy. Being seen as a true Strategy Architect starts with having a strong, informed opinion and speaking up—even when it may be contrary to what the rest of the leadership team is saying.

This candor and fortitude are a large part of what Doing HR with an Attitude is all about. Whether in confronting a manager's inappropriate behavior or providing a recommendation that a leader does not want to hear, Credible Activists aren't afraid of conflict. For example, the retail branch network of a large regional bank was considering shifting its staff of full-time tellers to a mix of full- and part-time tellers. The goal was two-fold: to provide additional staff during the lunch hour when the branches were busiest, and reduce staff levels in the mid-morning and mid-afternoon hours when the branch was slowest. This seemed to make good financial sense.

Fortunately, a forward-thinking HR professional pointed out a significant downside: This staffing model would undermine the customer service framework the bank had put in place, and would create a morale problem for many tellers by forcing some of them to reduce their hours. The HR professional calculated that the potential cost savings would be less than the revenue risk the branches faced if service was compromised. The plan was abandoned. If this particular HR professional played the traditional, non-confronting role, she would have implemented a system she didn't believe in, and the bank would have been at significant risk of lost market share.

Doing HR with an Attitude is the opposite of what one company's HR professionals used to say about their role: "Find out what the business wants and then propose it aggressively." The critical components of this factor include:

- Taking appropriate risks, both personally and for the organization.
- Providing candid observations. HR professionals have a unique and needed point of view.
- Influencing others.
- Not waiting for problems to find you. Anticipating problems increases your credibility and puts you in the role to help the business devise innovative solutions.

Credible Activist by the Numbers

As mentioned above, being a Credible Activist is a crucial competency for HR, since it had the strongest correlations to both individual proficiency and business performance. Fortunately, it is also the domain where HR professionals scored most positively on average (see Figure 3.1). This section will take a look at the following three different sets of numbers for factors within the Credible Activist domain.

- **Descriptive Statistics:** How well did HR professionals score in each of the factors, across a variety of demographic dimensions?
- **Correlations to Individual Performance:** What is the relative importance of each factor to perceived individual performance?
- **Correlations to Business Performance:** What is the relative importance of each factor to business performance (as measured by our business performance index)?

This chapter and the following five chapters lead with the data. This means we will be displaying numerous data figures, and commenting on the preliminary insights afforded, as well as questions raised by each set of numbers. We invite readers to delve into the data, subjecting the numbers to their own analysis and interpretation.

Descriptive Statistics

Descriptive statistics explain the extent to which the HR profession is perceived to be competent in each of the factors within the Credible Activist domain. As shown in Figure 3.1, regardless of respondent type (whether HR participant self scores, HR co-workers, or non-HR colleagues), Delivering Results with Integrity is the factor which scored the highest, and Doing HR with an Attitude scored the lowest. The pattern across respondent types is consistent, with HR associates providing the most generous ratings, followed by participants' self scores. Non-HR associates were the most critical, though the differences are not extreme.

Overall, these are remarkably positive scores and even Doing HR with an Attitude (the lowest of the four factors) receives fairly high marks. It is worth noting that being a Credible Activist is the most personal of the competency domains, which may have something to do with the high scores. In our work with business leaders, we often hear them say, "I love my HR person, but I hate my HR department." For individual HR practitioners, this is good news. For HR departments, the message is a wake-up call. Chapter 9 explores these departmental implications.

Figure 3.1. **Overall Mean Scores by Respondent Type**

	HR Participants	HR Associates	Non-HR Associates
Delivering Results with Integrity	4.27	4.32	4.21
Sharing Information	4.19	4.27	4.21
Building Relationships of Trust	4.00	4.10	4.06
Doing HR with an Attitude	3.97	4.03	3.95

According to Figure 3.2, the overall shape of the findings is consistent across regions, but not the intensity. In all regions except Europe, the highest-scoring component of Credible Activism is Delivering Results with Integrity. This is followed by Sharing Information (which is the top factor in Europe), Building Relationships of Trust and, finally, Doing HR with an Attitude. But while the shape is the same, there are interesting differences. In the United States, Doing HR with an Attitude is a stronger cultural value and more often included in the professional expectations and assessment of HR people than in other regions.

The watch-outs are clear: North American HR professionals (particularly those from U.S.-headquartered companies) who are transferred to other regions need to be sensitive to cultural expectations. For example, the scores for Latin America would lead us to think that too much "attitude" would be a problem there, particularly before there is a track record of results. The flip side of this is also true. Individuals from other regions who are transferred to HR in the United States may find themselves viewed as not having sufficient attitude. They may need to demonstrate more willingness to confront others and take risks.

Figure 3.2. **Overall Mean Scores by Region**

	U.S.	Latin America	Europe	China	Australia	India
Delivering Results with Integrity	4.47	4.23	4.19	4.00	4.33	4.32
Sharing Information	4.43	4.23	4.30	3.97	4.32	4.24
Building Relationships of Trust	4.19	4.13	3.96	3.94	4.04	4.09
Doing HR with an Attitude	4.20	3.88	3.94	3.84	3.99	4.01

The results by industry are not surprising as shown in Figure 3.3. Scores vary widely across industries on all factors. As with the regional data, the big message here is to not assume that all industries have the same expectations of their HR professionals. For instance, industries that are the least dependent on knowledge workers (such as agriculture, mining, and construction) scored lowest on all four factors; manufacturing is an outlier in this respect. Pharmaceuticals and chemicals, banking and real estate, and services are among the industries that generate the highest scores.

One of the more unexpected findings is the strong scores for HR people in public administration. The perception that HR plays a limited and largely transactional role in governmental organizations is inconsistent with how their own colleagues responded. Public administration respondents rated all factors relatively high, including Doing HR with an Attitude.

Figure 3.3. **Overall Mean Scores by Industry (associate raters only)**

	Agriculture	Mining	Construction	Food	Manufacturing	Pharmaceuticals/ Chemicals	Utilities	Wholesale/Retail Trade	Banking & Real Estate	Services	Public Administration
Delivering Results with Integrity	4.03	4.12	4.03	4.18	4.30	4.34	4.38	4.37	4.41	4.41	4.35
Sharing Information	3.99	4.07	4.02	4.17	4.27	4.31	4.41	4.29	4.33	4.40	4.34
Building Relationships of Trust	3.95	4.01	3.87	3.99	4.04	4.15	4.19	4.15	4.20	4.21	4.11
Doing HR with an Attitude	3.82	3.92	3.78	3.94	3.97	4.10	4.11	4.02	4.02	4.13	4.00

Scores in the Credible Activist factors vary somewhat by HR channel, but not as much as we might have guessed, as shown in Figure 3.4. Delivering Results with Integrity and Sharing Information are the highest-rated factors, while Doing HR with an Attitude is lowest (though still high on a comparative basis). There is a clear message in the data regarding Embedded HR: Either this type of role encourages the development of Credible Activism, or Credible Activists are more often selected for Embedded HR positions. The expectations on them are greatest in all of the categories of the Credible Activist. To strengthen your competence as a Credible Activist, you are better off in a front-line role than in E-HR or a Service Center.

Figure 3.4. **Overall Mean Scores by HR Channel (associate raters only)**

	Functional HR	Centers of Expertise	Embedded HR	Service Center	E-HR	Corporate HR
Delivering Results with Integrity	4.17	4.25	4.37	4.18	4.07	4.27
Sharing Information	4.11	4.23	4.36	4.11	4.03	4.27
Building Relationships of Trust	4.06	4.08	4.14	3.93	4.11	4.05
Doing HR with an Attitude	3.91	3.99	4.08	3.82	4.01	3.98

The size of the business in which the HR professional works appears to have some connection to proficiency scores in the Credible Activist factors, as shown in Figure 3.5. In general, competence in these factors grows as the company increases in size. There is a slight decline in scores between the largest two categories, except in Doing HR with an Attitude. Our hypothesis is that HR plays a more visible "activist" role in larger companies, where there is a large, formal HR function and a broad spectrum of HR roles. In addition, the information flow in large organizations is more complex and requires greater savvy and more refined communication skills.

Figure 3.5. **Overall Mean Scores by Business Size (associate raters only)**

	0 to 99	100 to 499	500 to 999	1,000 to 4,999	5,000 to 9,999	10,000 to 24,999	25,000+
Delivering Results with Integrity	4.05	4.17	4.23	4.27	4.27	4.44	4.34
Sharing Information	4.06	4.16	4.22	4.25	4.22	4.38	4.31
Building Relationships of Trust	3.99	4.05	4.05	4.10	4.06	4.17	4.11
Doing HR with an Attitude	3.81	3.85	3.94	3.98	4.03	4.09	4.12

Correlations to Individual Performance

Before we turn our focus to the impact of these four factors on an individual's perceived performance, a brief return to the methodology is warranted. In Chapter 2, we noted that being a Credible Activist accounts for more than its share of an individual's performance. If each of the six competency domains had equal impact on individual performance, they would each account for approximately 17% of the variance in individual performance (100% divided by six). Yet the Credible Activist domain accounts for nearly a quarter (24%) of the variance in individual impact.

Following the same logic, we ran a regression for each of the factors within Credible Activist against individual performance. Essentially, we were trying to answer the question, "How much of the 24% of performance accounted for by Credible Activist can be explained by each of its factors?" We conducted the same analysis for each domain's factors, as shown in subsequent chapters.

According to the global aggregate data, Delivering Results with Integrity shows the strongest correlation to individual performance, accounting for 31% of the variance within the domain. Doing HR with an Attitude is next at 26% of the variance, followed by Sharing Information (24%) and Building Relationships of Trust (19%). The order of impact for these competencies is instructive. The ability to get the job done ethically and as promised is paramount. The "attitude" factor ranks second in its impact, and includes having a point of view, taking appropriate risks, and advocating a strong position. Yet as shown in Figure 3.1, overall competence in Doing HR with an Attitude is the lowest of the four factors in this domain (3.95 on a five-point scale, in the eyes of non-HR respondents). This has clear implications for development planning, which will be examined at the end of this chapter.

Gender is one of the first demographics in our analysis of each domain to see if different factors have greater or lesser impact for men vs. women. As shown in Figure 3.6, differences are minimal. For both men and women, the factors follow the same "order of impact" as in the overall data set (see above). Doing HR with an Attitude has slightly greater impact on performance for women than for men, and its R^2 values are a bit higher for women, indicating a stronger correlation. This could suggest that women stand to gain a bit more than men by developing their HR with an attitude capabilities.

Figure 3.6. **Individual Performance by Gender (associate raters only)**

	Male		Female	
	R^2	%	R^2	%
Delivering Results with Integrity	0.37	32%	0.39	31%
Sharing Information	0.28	24%	0.31	24%
Building Relationships of Trust	0.23	19%	0.24	19%
Doing HR with an Attitude	0.30	25%	0.33	26%

When looking at the performance correlations by region in Figure 3.7, Delivering Results with Integrity accounts for almost one third of the variance in individual performance in Latin America and Australia. Doing HR with an Attitude is the second-most important factor in every region, with a particularly strong showing in North America, China, and India (which has scant data at the time of this writing.) Significantly, Building Relationships of Trust scores higher in Latin America and India than in other regions. This may reflect that business conducted in these cultures is based on relationships.

Figure 3.7. **Individual Performance by Region (associate raters only)**

	North America		Latin America		Europe		China		Australia		India	
	R^2	%	R^2	%	R^2	%	R^2	%	R^2	%	R^2	%
Delivering Results with Integrity	0.36	29%	0.40	32%	0.33	30%	0.34	31%	0.40	32%	0.24	29%
Sharing Information	0.30	24%	0.28	23%	0.25	23%	0.26	24%	0.29	23%	0.16	19%
Building Relationships of Trust	0.24	19%	0.27	21%	0.21	20%	0.19	18%	0.25	20%	0.18	21%
Doing HR with an Attitude	0.34	27%	0.30	24%	0.29	26%	0.30	27%	0.33	26%	0.27	31%

Delivering Results with Integrity is the most critical performance factor for all HR channels, with the exception of Service Centers, where Doing HR with an Attitude scores three percentage points higher as shown in Figure 3.8. This is intriguing. Could it be that in Service Centers, it is even *more* important to have a business point of view and not just function as a glorified helpdesk? On the other hand, Building Relationships of Trust has less impact in Service Centers and E-HR. This makes sense, given the limited face-to-face relationship-building opportunities afforded by these roles. Less clear is why relationship building would have such relatively low impact for those in Functional HR roles. Finally, it should be noted that for those in Centers of Expertise, sharing information is the second-most influential factor, indicating the central importance of effective communication skills in leveraging their expertise across the organization.

The impact of size is relatively slight for individual performance within this domain, as shown in Figure 3.9. Size doesn't appear to differentiate respondent views of the importance of these factors, and across all business sizes, the order of importance remains the same as in the overall findings. The numbers for Building Relationships of Trust, however, tell an interesting story. As the size of the business grows, so does the relative impact of relationship building—a logical conclusion given the increased complexity of relationship building and the larger number of important relationships as business size increases.

Figure 3.8. **Individual Performance by HR Channel (associate raters only)**

	Functional HR		Centers of Expertise		Embedded HR		Service Center		E-HR		Corporate HR	
	R²	%	R²	%	R²	%	R²	%	R²	%	R²	%
Delivering Results with Integrity	0.36	33%	0.44	30%	0.35	32%	0.30	30%	0.31	34%	0.42	31%
Sharing Information	0.26	24%	0.37	26%	0.25	22%	0.23	23%	0.22	24%	0.33	24%
Building Relationships of Trust	0.20	18%	0.29	20%	0.22	20%	0.14	14%	0.16	18%	0.27	20%
Doing HR with an Attitude	0.28	25%	0.35	24%	0.29	26%	0.32	33%	0.23	25%	0.34	25%

Figure 3.9. **Individual Performance by Business Size (associate raters only)**

	0 to 99		100 to 499		500 to 999		1,000 to 4,999		5,000 to 9,999		10,000 to 24,999		25,000+	
	R²	%	R²	%	R²	%	R²	%	R²	%	R²	%	R²	%
Delivering Results with Integrity	0.34	31%	0.38	31%	0.37	30%	0.38	32%	0.38	31%	0.43	30%	0.367	30%
Sharing Information	0.27	25%	0.32	25%	0.3	24%	0.28	24%	0.28	23%	0.33	23%	0.278	23%
Building Relationships of Trust	0.17	16%	0.22	18%	0.23	18%	0.21	18%	0.25	20%	0.29	21%	0.271	22%
Doing HR with an Attitude	0.29	27%	0.33	26%	0.34	28%	0.3	26%	0.31	26%	0.36	26%	0.292	24%

Correlations to Business Performance

In contrast to the individual performance correlations above, the business performance correlations below are quite a bit weaker. This is noted in the R^2 values. For individual performance, the R^2 values for Credible Activist factors range from 0.16 to 0.44, with many in the 0.30 to 0.40 range. In contrast, the R^2 values for business correlations rarely exceed 0.30, with few lower than 0.05. The same trend is seen in the R^2 values for the other competency domains. This indicates that our survey provides a more robust way of correlating the competency domains and factors with perceived *individual* competence than with perceived *business* performance. This creates a significant opportunity for follow-up research to link the competency domains to hard business measures. Now that we've stated this caveat, we will present the correlations to business performance and glean what insights we can from the numbers.

The contribution of the Credible Activist factors to business performance presents an interesting contrast to the findings for individual performance. Delivering Results with Integrity continues to be the highest-impact factor for business performance, after which the views of HR and non-HR raters diverge, as shown in Figure 3.10. For HR respondents, Building Relationships of Trust is a strong second, while for non-HR raters the relationships factor is in last place by a significant margin. Sharing Information is less a factor for HR raters than it is for non-HR, suggesting that business leaders increasingly want HR to be a listening post or an "early warning system" for strategic issues. Supporting this last conclusion, non-HR raters also place higher importance on Doing HR with an Attitude than do HR raters. The message is clear: Business colleagues appreciate HR people who have strong, informed opinions and actively communicate them.

Figure 3.10. **Business Performance by HR or Non-HR (associate raters only)**

	HR		Non-HR	
N	329		361	
	R²	%	R²	%
Delivering Results with Integrity	0.15	29%	0.07	31%
Sharing Information	0.12	23%	0.07	31%
Building Relationships of Trust	0.15	28%	0.03	15%
Doing HR with an Attitude	0.11	20%	0.05	23%

The differences when looking at gender in Figure 3.11 are consistent with the individual performance findings in Figure 3.6. Doing HR with an Attitude counts more for women than for men when it comes to business performance. Again, this hints at the benefit to be gained when women in HR maintain a somewhat hard-edged approach to their HR work.

Figure 3.11. **Business Performance by Gender (associate raters only)**

	Male		Female	
N	295		311	
	R^2	%	R^2	%
Delivering Results with Integrity	0.13	32%	0.17	31%
Sharing Information	0.10	25%	0.14	25%
Building Relationships of Trust	0.08	21%	0.11	20%
Doing HR with an Attitude	0.08	21%	0.13	24%

The results for business size are inconsistent in Figure 3.12 due to the small numbers of businesses in some of the size ranges. In general, Delivering Results with Integrity continues to be seen as the most important of the factors, particularly in smaller businesses. Doing HR with an Attitude is described as having high impact at most size levels, but is relatively trivial in businesses between 5,000 and 9,999 employees. Overall, this is an area where additional data are needed.

Figure 3.12. **Business Performance by Business Size (associate raters only)**

	0 to 99		100 to 499		500 to 999		1,000 to 4,999		5,000 to 9,999		10,000 to 24,999		25,000+	
N	38		85		65		99		35		28		35	
	R^2	%	R^2	%	R^2	%	R^2	%	R^2	%	R^2	%	R^2	%
Delivering Results with Integrity	0.10	42%	0.32	30%	0.11	25%	0.06	32%	0.06	31%	0.40	23%	0.24	28%
Sharing Information	0.05	20%	0.24	23%	0.12	27%	0.04	25%	0.07	36%	0.33	19%	0.22	26%
Building Relationships of Trust	0.04	18%	0.23	21%	0.09	19%	0.05	30%	0.04	23%	0.51	30%	0.15	17%
Doing HR with an Attitude	0.04	20%	0.28	26%	0.14	30%	0.02	13%	0.02	10%	0.46	27%	0.24	28%

For the HR channel in Figure 3.13, the results are confusing and somewhat at odds with the correlations to individual performance in Figure 3.8. Delivering Results with Integrity is viewed as highly important for all HR roles other than the Service Center, where Building Relationships of Trust is perceived to be most crucial for business performance. This is a mirror image of the correlations for individual performance, where relationship building had the least impact and Doing HR with an Attitude had the most. We could hypothesize that Service Center employees need to build relationships of trust in order for the business to gain the advantages and cost economies of the investment.

Figure 3.13. **Business Performance by Channel (associate raters only)**

	Functional HR		Centers of Expertise		Embedded HR		Service Center		Corporate HR	
N	190		165		187		70		126	
	R^2	%	R^2	%	R^2	%	R^2	%	R^2	%
Delivering Results with Integrity	0.12	29%	0.06	32%	0.06	24%	0.04	19%	0.12	37%
Sharing Information	0.06	15%	0.04	23%	0.07	27%	0.05	25%	0.08	24%
Building Relationships of Trust	0.15	36%	0.04	22%	0.05	22%	0.08	36%	0.06	19%
Doing HR with an Attitude	0.08	20%	0.04	24%	0.07	28%	0.04	20%	0.06	19%

Conclusion

What Characterizes Credible Activists?

They get the right things done the right way. This is the first and foremost aspect of Credible Activism. Credible Activists reliably perform and meet commitments. Individuals who do not get the job done, or don't get it done the right way, will not be viewed as Credible Activists.

They seek and accept accountability for outcomes. Credible Activists have a real and firm sense of personal and organizational accountability. Peter Raskind, a senior banking industry executive who is now president of National City Corporation, a large U.S. bank, describes accountability as "owning the outcome." Credible Activists seek accountability, do not duck it when it is given, and believe that accountability is both in response to task assignments and in the need to take initiative.

They know the business and have a point of view about how they can help the business prosper. Credible Activists have a clear perspective about how to best support the business, which is firmly rooted in a broad and deep understanding of the strategic needs of the business. It is also rooted in an informed and thoughtful point of view about how HR can best contribute to business performance.

They do "HR with an attitude." HR professionals need confidence in their skills and in the knowledge that they contribute meaningfully and measurably to business results. Andreas Karl, former head of global HR for Dow Chemical, put it this way: "I am first a member of the business leadership team and, second, an HR professional."

They invest in relationships and relationship skills. Credible Activists are conscientious about their relationships with colleagues and business partners, and invest in these relationships. They are described as having good "chemistry" with senior managers and the management teams they support. Chemistry isn't the result of chance; it is earned by responding quickly to needs, delivering thoughtful and helpful guidance and support, being a student of the team—their personalities and way of working—and doing their homework before recommending a course of action.

They communicate frequently and powerfully. Credible Activists understand the importance of communication. They take communication skills seriously, and become practiced and effective in both writing and speaking.

They take appropriate risks. It is difficult to imagine a Credible Activist who does not take reasonable risks when acting on the company's behalf. Highly effective HR professionals are focused equally on the organization's current and future needs, and act as "path finders" for the business's HR-related needs. This means identifying areas where there is need for improvement in cultural or operational terms. Taking initiative means accepting the risk of being candid in the evaluation of strengths and weaknesses, and advocating change rather than preserving the status quo.

Being well-liked and trusted is no longer adequate for HR effectiveness. Credibility must be coupled with the ability to be an activist—to have an opinion, take appropriate risks, and influence others.

Becoming a Credible Activist

As illustrated throughout this chapter, the Credible Activist domain has the greatest influence on overall HR competence. Conveniently, it also has the greatest impact on overall business results. The point is clear: If you can only focus on one domain, this would be the one to choose.

Of the four factors, Delivering Results with Integrity and Doing HR with an Attitude are the two factors which have the greatest impact within the Credible Activist domain. Understanding how to get things done the right way, having the nerve to express opinions, and taking appropriate risks will have a sizeable impact on your perceived performance as an HR professional.

To illustrate which competency factors seem to be the greatest developmental priorities for HR professionals worldwide, we used a simple mathematical formula to "weight" the 21 competency factors. We call this formula the Developmental Priority Index, or DPI. The logic behind the formula is fairly straightforward: As a profession, HR should work hardest to develop competence in areas where (1) the competency factor has a strong correlation to performance, and (2) there is ample room for improvement. To measure "strong correlation to performance," we used each competency factor's relative impact on individual performance. Our measure for "room for improvement" subtracts the mean score for competency factor (excluding self-scores) from five. Using a competency value of "five minus the score" allows us to measure how far the HR profession is from "perfection" in a given competency.

Remember that the survey scale defined "5.0" as the highest possible score on any question. Thus, if an HR professional were demonstrating a competency *to a very great extent*, she would be scored a "five" by her respondents. Subtracting her actual mean score from five gives us a measure of her "proximity to perfection"—and for our purposes here, we are interested mainly in those competency factors where HR professionals do *not* approximate perfection.

The Developmental Priority Index (DPI) thus converts impact and proficiency scores into relative priorities. The formula is as follows:

Developmental Priority Index (DPI) = (Impact %) * (5.0 – Proficiency Score)[4]

Figure 10.2 in Chapter 10 graphically shows the DPI values for all 21 of the competency factors. The highest DPI value was 7.82 for Sustaining Strategic

Agility (see Chapter 6); the lowest was 3.69, for Designing Rewards Systems (see Chapter 5). The average DPI for all 21 factors was 5.64.

For the Credible Activist factors, the DPI values highlight what the data suggest intuitively: Doing HR with an Attitude is the highest priority for development among the four Credible Activist factors (see Figure 3.14). Note that Delivering Results with Integrity has higher impact on performance (7.85%) than Doing HR with an Attitude (6.53%). But HR professionals already are reasonably competent at Delivering Results with Integrity, reflected in their "5.0-Proficiency" score of 0.73. Thus, the combination of high impact on performance *and* relatively lower proficiency make Doing HR with an Attitude the top developmental priority within the Credible Activist domain.

Figure 3.14. **Developmental Priority Index for Credible Activist Factor**

Competency Factor	% Impact	5.0-Proficiency	DPI
Delivering Results with Integrity	7.85%	0.73	5.71*
Sharing Information	6.06%	0.75	4.56
Building Relationships of Trust	4.81%	0.92	4.40
Doing HR with an Attitude	6.53%	1.00	6.55*

* = Value above the average DPI for all 21 factors (5.64)

As you plan for your development, remember the eccentricity principle developed by the late Kathleen MacDonald of Exxon Chemical (and a variation of Ed Hollander's concept of idiosyncratic credit): "You are allowed to be as eccentric as you are perceived to be competent." The message: Build competence first. Credibility precedes activism.

Developmental Actions for the Credible Activist Domain

Factor: Delivering Results with Integrity

- Create HR measures that track both the output of HR and the means of generating the output.
- Apply Six Sigma quality standards and processes to improve the accuracy of all HR activities and practices.
- Ensure that line management clearly understands and accepts HR standards, receive feedback from internal clients about the extent to which standards are achieved, and make appropriate improvements.

- Practice drawing visual images of complex problems that clarify key issues.
- Lead an HR or management team in a discussion on ethical issues. Include a clarification of the company's ethical parameters and a definition of the processes that will be used to ensure compliance.
- Examine your HR practices from the standpoint of unanticipated consequences. Do any of your HR practices, such as measurements, rewards, and promotions, inadvertently encourage employees to perform in ways that might result in violation of the firm's ethical parameters?

Factor: Sharing Information

- Make a presentation to a major conference on an HR activity in your company. Also arrange to present the topic to an internal audience.
- Write an article about a major business issue for publication in an internal or external magazine, newspaper, or journal.
- Have some of your written material critiqued by a writing coach or English instructor from a local college or university.
- Arrange to speak at an in-house training program. Request that the speaker evaluation form include a section for feedback on the verbal communication issues you have greatest interest in improving.
- When listening to effective speakers in any forum, take notes about the content of the message and the speaking techniques they use to get their messages across.

Factor: Building Relationships of Trust

- Elicit feedback from colleagues on your interpersonal skills. Act on the feedback. Don't be defensive. Translate the feedback into simple and focused action.
- Avoid using the word "I" for an entire day.
- Practice nonjudgmental empathizing with family members or close friends.
- Diagnose the root cause behind an interpersonal problem that you have with an associate at work. Determine what needs to be done to establish a more effective relationship and take action.
- Defuse an interpersonal problem between colleagues that is causing a productivity or performance problem.

Factor: Doing HR with an Attitude

- Examine your HR practices from the standpoint of unanticipated consequences. Do any of your HR practices, such as measurements, rewards, or promotions, inadvertently encourage people to perform in ways that might result in violation of the firm's ethical parameters?

- Honestly evaluate your willingness to express opinions and ideas in staff meetings or other forums. If you have a tendency to be quiet or hesitant in these meetings, make a goal to remedy the situation.
- Find something that is within your power to fix and fix it. Don't let your actions or inactions fall subject to co-worker approval.

CHAPTER 4

Culture & Change Steward

In December 1984, the Qingdao Refrigerator factory in China was falling apart—literally and figuratively. Burdened under enormous debt, the private company (not a state-owned enterprise) had not paid its workers for months. Work standards were non-existent. Three top executives had come and gone in less than a year. More than 20 years later, China's best-known global company (now called Haier) is a home-appliance giant with annual sales in excess of $13 billion. The company's turnaround is a rare story of complete cultural transformation. Indeed, Zhang Ruiminthe, a visionary leader who saw potential value in a dilapidated factory that turned out shoddy products, attributes much of the company's success to "a corporate culture that embraces constant progress and the belief that victory comes through change."[1]

Zhang's succinct statement captures the highly paradoxical essence of the Culture & Change Steward domain. Culture is, by definition, a relatively stable and slow-changing aspect of an organization. Change, on the other hand, is change. We take no credit for putting these two contradictory elements together; we never would have thought to do so. Statistical factor analysis revealed that the two must go hand in hand for HR to be effective in today's world. Regardless of other cultural attributes that your organization may possess, it needs a flexible, adaptive, innovative culture with a changing foundation. And HR professionals play the role of steward in this process.

Culture is an underlying pattern that endures over time. Change is making events happen on time and faster. HR professionals need to make change happen (e.g., implement programs, policies, and other activities). But, they also need to see the connection of the independent events into a pattern or culture change. Change without culture becomes random activities. Culture without change becomes staid and outdated.

This chapter reports and analyzes the research results for the Culture & Change Steward domain of HR competence, focusing on the following three areas:
- Defining the Culture & Change Steward domain and its factors.
- Pointing out insights and further questions from the statistical data.
- Offering illustration and examples of effective practices in culture and change.

Defining the Domain

Culture has been an important feature in our HR competency studies since 1997. That year, both Culture and Change emerged as statistically distinct competency domains. In the 2002 study, culture and change were the dominant factors in a larger domain labeled Strategic Contribution; together, these two factors accounted for 66% of HR's impact on business performance within the Strategic Contribution domain. The 2007 study marks the first time that culture and change have factored together into a separate domain of their own.

This suggests that in the current business climate, HR professionals need to recognize, articulate, and help shape an organization's culture to make change happen. Culture is a pattern of activities more than a single event. The latest thinking on culture takes an "outside-in" approach, starting with clarity around external customer expectations.[2] What does the organization want to be known for by its target or best customers? This external expectation is then translated into internal employee and organization patterns of behavior.

Stewards of Culture
As stewards of culture, HR professionals respect those aspects of the past culture that should be respected, at the same time helping to shape a new culture that will facilitate organization success. They coach managers in how their actions reflect and drive culture, they weave the cultural standards into HR practices and processes, and they make culture real to employees.

Additionally, successful HR professionals facilitate change in two ways. First, they help develop the right culture in the organization. Second, they develop disciplines to make change happen throughout the organization. This may include implementation of strategy, projects, or initiatives. In the graphical illustration of the 2007 model, Culture & Change Steward occupies a unique position, halfway between the "people" and the "business" axes of the diagram. This is intended to show the integrative function of an effective company culture, which forms a bridge between the business imperatives and the day-to-day actions of people. HR professionals help turn what is known into what is done.

The Culture & Change Steward domain is made up of four interrelated factors: Crafting Culture, Facilitating Change, Personalizing Culture, and Enacting Culture.

Factor: Crafting Culture

Crafting culture is having a clear concept of the culture that is required by your business and defining that culture in a way that is understood by those both inside and outside your company. High-performing HR professionals clearly understand the culture required to deliver the business strategy, and communicate the desired culture broadly and frame it in ways that engage employees. They also put systems and practices into place that align individual behavior and organizational goals at all levels.

Factor: Facilitating Change

Given the world in which HR now functions, change alone matters little; the right changes need to be coupled with speed to create any competitive advantage, and the culture needs to incorporate this "fast change" as a capability. Change often means turning what we know into what we do. To ensure that the right changes happen quickly, HR professionals must work with the management team and other key individuals to ensure that decisions are made quickly; ensure that the human, financial, and informational resources are aligned with the desired change; monitor the progress of key change initiatives; capture lessons learned; and apply these lessons to improve future change efforts.

Another startling finding from the 2007 HRCS is the integration of culture and change competencies into a single, statistically-similar domain. To play a uniquely value-added role, HR professionals can't be good at one and not the other. Neither is culture without change, nor change without culture in the fast-paced world we now inhabit.

Factor: Personalizing Culture

Culture at the organizational level should translate to individual actions and beliefs. Almost every HR professional has the best intentions when it comes to helping people; that's the human side of "human resources." Individualizing a company culture makes the lives of those you serve better. An HR professional or department that successfully personalizes culture helps employees find purpose and meaning in their work. When a business has successfully personalized culture, employees understand exactly how their work benefits the company and how it benefits themselves. In this type of culture, employees are valued as people, not just as employees, and are recipients of things such as work-life balance, flexible schedules, tuition reimbursement, etc.

When the culture of an organization becomes personal, it moves from a wish list of descriptive sentences regarding what the organization would like to be to a cohesive integration of what it has actually realized.

Factor: Enacting Culture

Enacting culture involves unifying the culture that has been crafted and making sure that it is consistent, coherent, and cohesive across business functions, as well as in the minds of customers and shareholders. Culture turns events into patterns and connects different parts of the business. When linked to external stakeholders such as customers and investors, culture becomes a firm brand. HR professionals who enact culture actively measure the influence that their culture has on the performance of the business and leverage that information to adjust the culture as necessary. They use culture to unify different factions of the business to make the whole more than the sum of its parts. They also ensure that the culture of the business is recognized in the mind of external stakeholders such as customers and investors.

The critical issue here is to ensure that the organization's unifying culture is congruent with the company's identity in the minds of key customers and investors. Any disconnect will measurably (and negatively) impact the company's results.

As illustration, consider the experience of BP (British Petroleum) in 2006. After an expensive campaign in which it proclaimed itself the "green," environmentally-conscious oil giant, its inattention to pipeline mainte-nance and sloppy management practices resulted in a catastrophic oil spill at their North Slope operations in Alaska. Not only was this a PR disaster for the company, its stock valuation also took a significant immediate hit in the form of a much lower price-to-earnings ratio than the rest of Big Oil. The moral of the story: HR needs to make sure that leadership and employee behavior internally mirrors the company's external image.

Culture & Change Steward by the Numbers

Descriptive Statistics

Figure 4.1 shows the overall mean scores for each of these factors by respondent type. These scores suggest that, in general, HR professionals are better at helping define the culture (Crafting Culture) than at actually implementing it (Enacting Culture). Perhaps this reflects the way cultural interventions are often undertaken. In many cases, they are driven by pro-cesses that involve managers and employees in defining corporate vision and values. These vision and value statements are then framed and hung in the lobbies of corporate buildings, featured on the corporate website, and/or made into laminated cards that each employee tacks onto the wall of his or her work space.

This is one approach to Crafting Culture—or, at least, to crafting a state-ment of intended culture. But often the initiative stops there. The hard work of aligning executive and employee behavior with the stated culture, creating measurements and rewards for behavior consistent with the culture, and measuring the impact of the culture on business success—in short, Enacting Culture—takes place less frequently, less uniformly, and less effectively.

Figure 4.1. **Overall Mean Scores by Respondent Type**

	HR Participants	HR Associates	Non-HR Associates
Crafting Culture	3.89	3.92	3.83
Facilitating Change	3.85	3.87	3.76
Personalizing Culture	3.69	3.71	3.63
Enacting Culture	3.47	3.62	3.55

When the Culture & Change Steward factors are compared across regions, an interesting pattern emerges. Scores for each factor are similar in regions with developed economies—the United States, Europe, and Australia. In developing regions, we see a stark contrast between the scores in Latin America and China. Latin American scores approximate those of the developed regions, while the scores from China lag noticeably as shown in Figure 4.2.

One explanation for this difference is that, even though the economies in Latin America are still developing, the HR profession is relatively established and maturing. In contrast, HR is a new profession in China, focused more on getting the operational details right rather than tinkering with something as abstract and amorphous as the corporate culture. (See Chapter 7.) Furthermore, the Western business press has offered a plethora of books on business culture in the past 20 years.[3] While the West has been addressing the culture of business, emerging organizations in China are just beginning to understand its power. This chapter's opening vignette, however, illustrates that some Chinese companies definitely "get it" when it comes to corporate culture.

Figure 4.2. **Overall Mean Scores by Region (associate raters only)**

	U.S.	Latin America	Europe	China	Australia	India
Crafting Culture	4.04	3.93	3.91	3.58	3.92	3.84
Facilitating Change	3.96	3.86	3.85	3.59	3.81	3.77
Personalizing Culture	3.80	3.70	3.62	3.53	3.65	3.72
Enacting Culture	3.68	3.65	3.55	3.45	3.59	3.57

A look at the scores by industry tells a story similar to that of the regional analysis in Figure 4.3. Scores for the Culture & Change Steward factors are significantly lower in agriculture, mining, and construction—all of which are commoditized and capital intense industries with low margins and an emphasis on operational efficiency. A second group of industries have scores somewhat higher than the commodities, but lower than the rest of the industries: food and manufacturing. Pursuing the same logic, these represent industries where efficiency and process control are paramount. Their cultures might change more slowly than others.

The high scores for the utilities industry are both striking and revealing. Few industries have come so quickly from a stable, regulated environment to an intensely competitive one. The resulting turbulence forces successful utilities to think and act differently; i.e., to reinvent themselves and their cultures. Like the Haier example that opens this chapter, successful utilities have navigated enormous change as they have moved from public trusts to privately traded entities. Industry consolidation has resulted in a host of mammoth mergers and takeovers—again surfacing cultural issues as former competitors become integrated under the same corporate umbrella. This is an industry in change, and the culture that has shaped the industry must change. The scores evidently recognize the role HR is playing in this transition.

Figure 4.3. **Overall Mean Scores by Industry (associate raters only)**

	Agriculture	Mining	Construction	Food	Manufacturing	Pharmaceuticals/ Chemicals	Utilities	Wholesale/ Retail Trade	Banking & Real Estate	Services	Public Administrations
Crafting Culture	3.65	3.72	3.53	3.82	3.88	3.98	4.03	3.94	3.98	4.03	3.92
Facilitating Change	3.63	3.70	3.52	3.76	3.83	3.95	3.97	3.83	3.87	3.93	3.86
Personalizing Culture	3.55	3.62	3.44	3.60	3.63	3.69	3.80	3.68	3.73	3.81	3.74
Enacting Culture	3.49	3.54	3.39	3.53	3.52	3.63	3.71	3.64	3.65	3.74	3.61

The implications of the data on HR channels are fascinating as shown in Figure 4.4. First, HR professionals in Service Centers and E-HR have lower scores in this area. Logically, they probably have less to do with shaping culture than do their counterparts in Embedded or Corporate HR. Centers of Expertise are often called upon to help design and implement organization change initiatives; their high scores, therefore, make sense. Functional HR—with its traditional "silos" of activity—scores lower because culture change is an integrative effort. HR integration occurs much more naturally (and scores in these factors are highest) in Embedded HR, because these people are closer to the business and must make change happen.

Figure 4.4. **Overall Mean Scores by HR Channel (associate raters only)**

	Functional HR	Centers of Expertise	Embedded HR	Service Center	E-HR	Corporate HR
Crafting Culture	3.69	3.90	3.98	3.71	3.69	3.91
Facilitating Change	3.69	3.83	3.89	3.66	3.75	3.86
Personalizing Culture	3.59	3.71	3.71	3.58	3.64	3.68
Enacting Culture	3.49	3.66	3.61	3.53	3.57	3.60

Figure 4.5 indicates that HR's competence in cultural matters increases with size of business. This is consistent with numerous theories about the development of organizational cultures.[4] Culture is rarely explicit in smaller companies. It develops naturally as leaders and employees make decisions on internal structure and processes, and adapt to external conditions. The decisions that lead to successful outcomes tend to become repeated and over time adopted as "the way we do things" (often subconsciously). Once the organization achieves a certain size, people begin paying attention to culture specifically. Size complicates work and requires more explicit attention to patterns. In smaller firms, things happen more naturally without having to consciously "craft" or "enact" them.

Figure 4.5. **Overall Mean Scores by Business (associate raters only)**

	0 to 99	100 to 499	500 to 999	1,000 to 4,999	5,000 to 9,999	10,000 to 24,999	25,000+
Crafting Culture	3.70	3.75	3.84	3.87	3.90	3.97	3.97
Facilitating Change	3.70	3.67	3.78	3.79	3.84	3.95	3.93
Personalizing Culture	3.60	3.61	3.64	3.66	3.66	3.74	3.74
Enacting Culture	3.56	3.51	3.56	3.60	3.61	3.62	3.63

Correlations to Individual Performance

Correlations to individual performance provide insight into the relative impact of the four factors. For the HR professional to be seen as competent and high-performing, which counts more—Crafting Culture, Enacting Culture, Personalizing Culture, or Facilitating Change?

Gender is the first point of comparison, and the story is basically "no difference" (see Figure 4.6). The men's individual performance is derived slightly more from Personalizing Culture than is the women's (21% vs. 20%). This is a seemingly small difference, but statistically significant due to the large sample size. The corollary finding is that women get more performance mileage out of their ability to define (i.e., "craft") the culture. Could it be that we value take-charge women and sensitive new-age men? Of course, we pose this question with tongue firmly implanted in cheek, but the slight difference is intriguing.

Figure 4.6. **Individual Performance by Gender (associate raters only)**

	Male		Female	
	R^2	%	R^2	%
Crafting Culture	0.324	29%	0.328	30%
Facilitating Change	0.328	29%	0.312	29%
Personalizing Culture	0.236	21%	0.219	20%
Enacting Culture	0.235	21%	0.224	21%

Regional differences appear minimal, with the possible exception of Europe (see Figure 4.7). Effective European HR professionals are credited less with Personalizing Culture and more with Crafting Culture. This is somewhat surprising, given the history in Europe with its heavy emphasis on the "personal" (employee- or worker-centric) approach to organization culture. The social democratic tradition emphasizes worker rights and individual dignity, which are related to the "personalizing" factor. These findings could reflect a shift toward the business-oriented side of culture (e.g., the direction-setting and strategy-aligned aspects of Crafting Culture). They may also reflect a tendency for European HR professionals to enjoy the theory or conceptual approaches to culture.

Figure 4.7. **Individual Performance by Region (associate raters only)**

	North America		Latin America		Europe		China		Australia		India	
	R^2	%	R^2	%	R^2	%	R^2	%	R^2	%	R^2	%
Crafting Culture	0.318	29%	0.311	29%	0.283	32%	0.300	27%	0.327	29%	0.265	25%
Facilitating Change	0.296	27%	0.317	29%	0.259	29%	0.326	29%	0.336	30%	0.342	32%
Personalizing Culture	0.228	21%	0.221	20%	0.148	17%	0.271	24%	0.249	22%	0.217	21%
Enacting Culture	0.237	22%	0.230	21%	0.198	22%	0.234	21%	0.221	20%	0.233	22%

Differences between the HR channels are subtle, as shown in Figure 4.8. The percentages look remarkably similar, though the R^2 scores show greater differentiation. Corporate HR, E-HR and Centers of Expertise each have noticeably higher R^2 scores than Functional HR, Embedded HR, and Service Centers. This suggests that when E-HR, Corporate HR, and Centers of Expertise do culture management well, it has greater impact on their competence than for people in the other HR channels.

Figure 4.8. **Individual Performance by HR Channel (associate raters only)**

	Functional HR		Centers of Expertise		Embedded HR		Service Center		E-HR		Corporate HR	
	R^2	%	R^2	%	R^2	%	R^2	%	R^2	%	R^2	%
Crafting Culture	0.301	28%	0.36	30%	0.286	30%	0.286	32%	0.482	30%	0.366	29%
Facilitating Change	0.313	29%	0.362	30%	0.279	29%	0.254	29%	0.388	24%	0.345	28%
Personalizing Culture	0.241	23%	0.246	20%	0.188	19%	0.165	19%	0.383	24%	0.27	22%
Enacting Culture	0.216	20%	0.24	20%	0.21	22%	0.18	20%	0.373	23%	0.261	21%

Size doesn't present much in the way of individual performance differences (see Figure 4.9). True, effective HR people in very small companies such as start ups evidently don't have to be quite as good at change as those in larger companies. An anomalous finding requiring additional analysis is the blips for HR in the companies with 1,000 to 4,999 employees, and in the largest companies with 25,000+ employees. For these HR professionals, competency in cultural issues seems to have less impact on individual performance, though our current analysis does not suggest why.

Figure 4.9. **Individual Performance by Business Size (associate raters only)**

	0 to 99		100 to 499		500 to 999		1,000 to 4,999		5,000 to 9,999		10,000 to 24,999		25,000+	
	R^2	%	R^2	%	R^2	%	R^2	%	R^2	%	R^2	%	R^2	%
Crafting Culture	0.329	30%	0.367	29%	0.392	30%	0.287	29%	0.328	28%	0.315	32%	0.28	28%
Facilitating Change	0.276	25%	0.355	28%	0.359	28%	0.296	30%	0.336	29%	0.285	29%	0.3	30%
Personaliz-ing Culture	0.253	23%	0.273	22%	0.275	21%	0.193	20%	0.243	21%	0.2	20%	0.2	20%
Enacting Culture	0.251	23%	0.26	21%	0.269	21%	0.205	21%	0.248	21%	0.19	19%	0.21	21%

Correlations to Business Performance

As noted in Chapter 3, the correlations between HR competency factors and business performance are weaker than the correlations between these factors and individual performance. That said, the correlations to business performance allow us to raise some worthwhile questions.

HR professionals' self-perceptions of the impact of cultural competence on business performance have a different profile from that of non-HR associates as depicted in Figure 4.10. For HR, Facilitating Change is a much stronger predictor of performance than for non-HR respondents, who see Crafting Culture as more important. In the eyes of their business associates, HR people could be more proactive in shaping the culture early on, rather than just focusing on making it real to employees. Non-HR respondents may see the value of culture is sustaining change more than HR professionals.

Figure 4.10. **Business Performance by HR vs. Non-HR (associate raters only)**

HR vs. Non HR	HR		Non-HR	
	329		361	
	R^2	%	R^2	%
Crafting Culture	0.122	27%	0.097	32%
Facilitating Change	0.116	26%	0.069	23%
Personalizing Culture	0.095	21%	0.064	21%
Enacting Culture	0.114	26%	0.075	25%

Figure 4.11. **Business Performance by Gender (associate raters only)**

	Male		Female	
	295		311	
	R^2	%	R^2	%
Crafting Culture	0.134	32%	0.147	[2]26%
Facilitating Change	0.109	26%	0.133	23%
Personalizing Culture	0.093	22%	0.135	23%
Enacting Culture	0.083	20%	0.159	28%

Men seem to have greater impact through Crafting Culture, while women do so through Enacting Culture (see Figure 4.11). This is a reversal of our finding above, where correlations to individual performance showed men (slightly) stronger in Personalizing Culture and women in Crafting Culture. Here, men in HR seem to help businesses succeed more when they are involved in culture up front (Crafting), while women achieve business impact more in translating culture to employee behavior (Personalizing) and building it into systems (Enacting).

In Figure 4.12, the percentages in boldface reflect the factor that accounts for the largest portion of business performance, within each of the size categories. The differences are noticeable, though the pattern is inconsistent. For example, HR in small companies (fewer than 500 employees) has greatest impact through Facilitating Change. In these small companies, Personalizing Culture has less impact, perhaps because it is already personalized. In very large companies, HR professionals who are more able to Enact Culture make a bigger difference, implying that HR works more on the back end of culture. In between these two extremes, companies having 10,000 to 25,000 employees seem to achieve greater business results when HR pays attention to Crafting Culture. Companies with 500 to 999 employees could focus their HR efforts more on Enacting Culture.

Figure 4.12. **Business Performance by Business Size (associate raters only)**

	0 to 99		100 to 499		500 to 999		1,000 to 4,999		5,000 to 9,999		10,000 to 24,999		25,000+	
	38		85		65		99		35		28		35	
	R^2	%	R^2	%	R^2	%	R^2	%	R^2	%	R^2	%	R^2	%
Crafting Culture	0.135	25%	0.207	25%	0.155	25%	0.134	26%	0.047	26%	0.498	33%	0.250	26%
Facilitating Change	0.187	35%	0.260	31%	0.075	12%	0.145	28%	0.036	20%	0.270	18%	0.224	24%
Personalizing Culture	0.075	14%	0.220	26%	0.172	28%	0.120	23%	0.041	23%	0.319	21%	0.179	19%
Enacting Culture	0.141	26%	0.147	18%	0.214	35%	0.124	24%	0.058	32%	0.444	29%	0.296	31%

Last (and in this case, perhaps least), the comparisons across the HR channel are more confusing than enlightening (see Figure 4.13). Service Center professionals score extremely high in their impact when Personalizing Culture—when they make the culture real in day-to-day transactions with employees. And their 2% score in Enacting Culture would indicate that they simply don't have much ability to do this aspect of culture stewardship, though the score seems exaggeratedly low. In contrast, Embedded HR scores quite high in Enacting Culture. In their partnership with the business, they're the ones implementing and building processes and systems that reinforce the desired culture.

Figure 4.13. **Business Performance by Channel (associate raters only)**

	Functional HR		Centers of Expertise		Embedded HR		Service Center		Corporate HR	
	190		165		187		70		126	
	R^2	%	R^2	%	R^2	%	R^2	%	R^2	%
Crafting Culture	0.128	28%	0.077	25%	0.062	24%	0.042	29%	0.076	28%
Facilitating Change	0.102	22%	0.094	31%	0.063	24%	0.015	10%	0.067	24%
Personalizing Culture	0.107	23%	0.061	20%	0.040	15%	0.087	59%	0.068	25%
Enacting Culture	0.119	26%	0.073	24%	0.096	37%	0.003	2%	0.063	23%

Conclusion

This competency domain is about the fusion of culture and change—and we learn from physics that fusion is a process that releases enormous amounts of energy. When culture and change are considered and implemented as parts of a single competency rather than separate competencies, the result can dramatically impact both an individual HR professional's effectiveness and an organization's competitiveness. Any company embarking on a culture change program should enlist HR professionals in defining and enacting the culture. When HR professionals have the skills to make culture real, they help their companies become competitive.

We have seen many large traditional companies work to change their cultures where HR has had not only a voice, but a visible impact on making it happen. General Motors has been in the midst of a renaissance in globalizing their business, creating more innovative products and services, and upgrading their quality of management. HR professionals at GM have been instrumental in defining these initiatives and making them happen. When executives sense that their culture needs to change, they should be able to turn to HR professionals for insight and advice.

HR is better at Crafting Culture than Enacting Culture. Processes that create vision and values statements are the easy part. The real work begins once such statements are created. More important, the absence of input by ex-

ternal stakeholders is telling. Most HR professionals Craft Culture via an entirely inside-out process. A simple procedure we have devised can provide an
important check and balance in this process. Once the vision and values are
articulated, have them reviewed by key customers and investors. Ask these
stakeholders, "If we are successful in demonstrating these values and achieving this vision, will we create the kind of experience that you expect of us?"
If their answer is "yes," then the model stands. If "no," the next question is
obvious: "What do we need to change in order to reflect your priorities and
needs?"

Culture & Change Steward appears to be a more salient competency for HR
in larger firms. Culture is less explicit in smaller organizations. It is still in
the process of being defined and solidified. This indicates that HR professionals in small organizations have an even greater opportunity to consciously guide the development of an outside-in culture. In large firms, a culture is
already in place and, in many cases, it is quite rigid. Culture has been called
the DNA of the organization, indicating that it can be difficult for competitors to clone—but also difficult for large companies to change.

Culture appears to matter less—and is practiced less by HR—in commod-
ity-driven industries. When the focus is on costs and efficiencies, HR seems
to pay less attention to cultural variables, perhaps because managers in these
industries see culture as a "soft" and less important issue. An exception is
Southwest Airlines. The organization positions itself as a low-cost provider
in a brutally competitive industry, yet its culture is written up in case studies
as the primary source of its unparalleled business performance. Southwest
Airlines is intensely clear on the experience it wants to create for its customers: fun, on time, and cheap. All of its HR processes—recruitment, selection,
development, job design, celebrations, etc.—reinforce playfulness, speed, and
cost-efficiency.[5]

Becoming a Culture & Change Steward

As illustrated throughout this chapter, the Culture & Change Steward
domain has tremendous impact on one's overall HR competence. Each of its
four factors scores above the average on the Developmental Priority Index,
as shown in Figure 4.14. It is the only competency domain to achieve this
distinction. (For a quick explanation of how to calculate the DPI, refer to
endnote #4 in Chapter 3.)

Figure 4.14. **Developmental Priority Index for Culture & Change Steward Factors**

Competency Factor	% Impact	5.0-Proficiency	DPI
Crafting Culture	6.70%	1.12	7.51*
Facilitating Change	6.59%	1.18	7.76*
Personalizing Culture	4.68%	1.33	6.21*
Enacting Culture	4.70%	1.41	6.61*

*= Value above the average DPI for all 21 factors (5.64)

Of the four Culture & Change Steward factors, Facilitating Change received the highest DPI value—7.76 (a value that is second-highest among all 21 factors in our study). Clearly, this competency domain is one where developmental efforts can reap great benefits to HR professionals.

Developmental Actions for the Culture & Change Steward
Factor: Crafting Culture

- Design a change process that will lead to an important shift in your organization's culture and will better align with the expectations of external customers.
- Evaluate your work processes and HR practices from the point of view of the signals they send about the experience you're trying to create for key customers.
- Gather information from internal and/or external sources regarding the future of your business. Does your current culture support future success? If not, what needs to change? How will you change it?

Factor: Facilitating Change

- Work with an HR team to ensure that HR processes are in place to support current change initiatives. Do you have the right people, with the right information, doing the right things, with the right measurements and the right incentives?
- Redesign your most effective change tools from a speed perspective.
- Develop and implement meeting guidelines that help make decisions happen more quickly and with better follow-through and consistently measurable results—in ways that drive the expected customer experience.
- Work with a key line executive to ensure that management team members consistently send the same messages about the desired direction of change through their words, time allocation and behaviors.

Factor: Personalizing Culture

- In one-on-one interaction with co-workers, help them see the purpose and meaning in their work.
- Whenever possible, connect current initiatives with the organization's history, founding, or major accomplishments.
- Ask the question: "What do our customers expect of us? How do we reflect this expectation in our HR practices?"
- Reinforce culturally consistent behavior by "catching people doing something right."
- Coach managers to be more sensitive to the symbolic messages they are constantly sending. Help them eliminate messages that are off-target or hypocritical with the organization's desired culture.

Factor: Enacting Culture

- Conduct a cultural audit alone or with an HR or management team. Identify the cultural characteristics that your business must have to meet the needs of stakeholders and advance your business strategy. Identify the gaps between what is and what should be.
- Identify how your managers and employees need to behave in the future if they are to achieve their goals and outperform your business competitors.
- Find and celebrate people who exemplify your organization's desired culture.
- Audit key management practices (budgeting, performance management, communication, meetings, etc.) for alignment with the culture. Are certain practices unintentionally sending symbolic messages at odds with the expected customer experience?
- Collect stories of behavior that models the desired culture. Share these stories in conversations, presentations, and newsletters.
- Help managers understand the significance of what they pay attention to. Employees can tell what's really important by watching how their managers spend their time and energy.

CHAPTER 5

Talent Manager/ Organization Designer

In the late 1980s, Taco Bell was drifting. Revenues were in a rut, growth was sluggish, and other fast-food purveyors were competing aggressively. To address the challenge, company president John Martin adopted a risky but compelling strategy: reduce the cost of its food, while maintaining quality to the point that other companies simply couldn't keep up. Doing so meant reviewing every aspect of Taco Bell's operations, with particular scrutiny devoted to the company's talent and organization.

Taco Bell's HR organization took the lead on the talent/organization analysis. The HR team soon realized that the front-line store manager was the pivotal role in driving cost savings and innovation. This prompted a fundamental redesign of the store manager position. Historically, store managers were low-paid, low-skilled, high-turnover employees. Now, Taco Bell was almost expecting them to be junior general managers at the local level, running a tight ship and finding ways to grow revenues. This was a huge change.

HR worked closely with management to identify the competencies required of store managers and assess the current workforce against this new model. Almost a third of the incumbents were replaced with new recruits who previously would have been overqualified for the position. Many of the new store managers had university degrees; some even had MBAs. They were asked to find creative new channels to sell or distribute Taco Bell's products. In exchange, they could make significantly more money (both base and bonus) than was previously possible at the store-manager level.

To operationalize the idea of greater accountability and autonomy at the store level, HR helped re-engineer reporting relationships, removing three levels of middle management in the process. A new role called "market manager" was established, with a span of control of up to 30 store managers. Organizational refinements followed, as the company learned from its excesses and, with HR's help, adapted its structure accordingly. Streamlined operations, such as centralizing or outsourcing all "cooking," allowed the stores to merely "warm and assemble" the ingredients, further driving down costs.

This radical restructuring produced dramatic results. Taco Bell quickly established itself as the low-cost leader for consistently good fast food—an advantage it has sustained for nearly 20 years. In addition, by removing three layers of bureaucracy and providing incentives for innovation, Taco Bell unleashed a storm of creativity at the store level. Store managers tried some novel concepts—such as airport kiosks, beach and park food carts, school cafeteria partnerships, and outlets in supermarkets and gas stations—which have since been adopted or adapted by nearly all fast-food companies.

Taco Bell's HR leadership played a crucial role in this remarkable success story—a role that in many ways epitomizes the Talent Manager/Organization Designer domain of HR competence. The two components of this domain—talent management and organization design—are strange bedfellows. Talent management focuses on how individuals enter and move up, across, or out of the company; organization design deals with the structure, governance, and processes that shape how the organization utilizes. In many companies, these two aspects of HR are structurally separate and handled by different groups of people. We didn't put them together merely for the perverse pleasure of creating a long and unwieldy title.[1] Rather, our statistical analysis factored these tasks together, reinforcing the need for integration or at least cooperation between the way people are recruited, developed, evaluated, paid, and promoted, and the way organizations are designed in terms of jobs, teams, workflow, reporting relationships, and cross-functional coordination.

In short, the numbers told us that HR is not just about talent or just about organization, but about the two of them together. This same insight emerges from the Taco Bell case. HR had to integrate talent management with organization design to achieve the desired business results. Imagine if Taco

Bell had implemented the talent strategy without the reorganization: High-octane store managers would be smothered by three layers of oversight for every new idea they wanted to implement. Alternatively, what if Taco Bell had reorganized without changing its talent strategy? The flat structure and 30-to-1 spans of control would translate into chaos at the store level, where many of the managers with little training and experience would have felt lost—or worse, empowered. Empowerment without capability is a dangerous prospect.

This chapter will report and analyze research results in three areas for the Talent Manager/Organization Designer domain of HR competence. It will define the Talent Manager/Organization Designer domain, focusing on the relationship between the two components for HR effectiveness; point out insights and additional questions from the statistical data; and provide practical examples of the talent management and organization design integration, along with ideas for personal development.

Defining the Domain

Ask 20 random people on the street, "What do human resources professionals do?" and at least 17 will respond about some aspect of talent management. Attracting, developing, and retaining talent is the most familiar and recognizable function of HR work. And indeed, the best HR professionals work closely and effectively with business leaders to identify competency needs, align resources with responsibilities, and convert talent into contribution. If anything, the importance of this work has expanded in recent years. The war for talent[2] wages on a global scale. Corporate executives often identify finding and keeping top talent as their No. 1 priority. The non-profit world struggles equally with a talent gap.[3] "Human capital" has become a buzzword and a business imperative. As is often the case, however, this represents a bit of an overreaction by business leaders and HR professionals. The value of the human asset appreciates or depreciates in direct proportion to the intelligence and effectiveness of the organization's design.

In a nutshell, organization design is about ensuring that the structure reinforces the desired organization capabilities. This should start, as mentioned in Chapter 4, with a strong idea of firm brand or identity. What does the organization want to be known for by its best customers? Once this brand is identified, organization design focuses on mapping the flow of raw materials, people, and work to deliver the capabilities that will perpetuate the brand. In the Taco Bell example, critical capabilities were speed, efficiency and innovation. All of HR's actions—from reducing levels of bureaucracy to hiring more capable store managers—were designed to build these three organization capabilities.

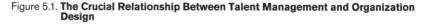

Figure 5.1. The Crucial Relationship Between Talent Management and Organization Design

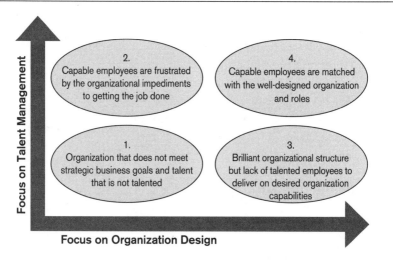

The data from this round of the HRCS make a provocative statement about the role of HR professionals and departments: The combination of talent management and organization design represents a whole greater than the sum of the two parts. Talented individuals who work in badly designed roles (or in ill-fitting organization structures) are frustrated and their contribution is constrained. Sports history is replete with examples of underachieving "all-star," teams whose expensive players couldn't work well together, had differing goals, or both. Equally hapless are the well-managed teams populated with so-so athletes.

Figure 5.1 depicts these "mismatch" situations, along with the ideal, desired situations. Paying too much attention to either axis will result in under-performance. Savvy HR professionals strike a balance between getting and developing the right talent, and making sure that the organization's structure is conducive to delivering the desired organization capabilities.

Organization Design Ensures Efficient Business Units/Functions
The war for talent needs to be waged on two fronts. Externally, it requires securing the right people with the right skills in the right numbers to execute the business strategy. Internally, it revolves around ensuring that work roles, teams, and business or functional units are designed for effectiveness and efficiency, and are connected to one another through appropriate processes.

Our research indicates five separate statistical factors associated with this domain—the most of any of the domains in the competency model. We will examine each of these factors in greater detail.

Factor: Ensuring Today's and Tomorrow's Talent

HR professionals are responsible for finding, mining, and aligning the talent needed by a business, now and in the future. The basic talent equation has three components:

Talent = Competence x Commitment x Contribution

HR helps define what competence looks like, through competency modeling and performance management tools. Commitment is bolstered by maintaining a balance between what employees give to the organization and what they get in return—and often, the most significant "gets" are non-monetary, such as respect, autonomy, opportunities for growth, etc. Finally, contribution is enabled when an employee's competence and commitment are constantly aligned with the business's needs.

Procter & Gamble (P&G) is known for its ability to attract and grow talent. In addition to simply recruiting talented individuals today, P&G's HR works hard to recruit the right talent for the future. Thinking ahead 10 to 15 years is not easy, but it forces business leaders and recruiters to define "success factors" that anticipate changes in technology and global markets. This helps P&G remain remarkably agile for a large, multinational corporation. In addition, P&G's HR focuses its recruitment efforts on recent graduates, maintaining solid affiliations with strong universities and fostering relationships with key professors. With a "grow talent from within" strategy, it strives to ensure that talented employees have significant (and visible) roles, skilled managers and mentors, and a voice in their own developmental trajectory and "next assignments."

Factor: Developing Talent

Developing talent involves actively setting performance standards, providing means for development, producing mechanisms for measurement, and giving appropriate and timely feedback. The design and implementation of these activities fall under the purview of HR. Developing talent leads to robust leadership pipelines, increased organization capabilities, higher retention rates, and more productive employees. HR plays a critical role in developing talent by:

- Providing individuals with opportunities to engage in high value-added and challenging work assignments.
- Offering training programs that focus on basic skills (basic literacy and computer skills, for example), technical skills (activity-based costing, inventory management), leadership skills (strategy, organizing, coaching), and cultural skills (the organization capabilities of speed, collaboration, creativity, inclusion, etc.).
- Linking training to an individual's career development plan.
- Providing mechanisms for follow-up to reinforce personal change and growth.
- Ensuring a clear succession path to maintain expertise in critical roles.
- Coaching managers in how they provide on-job development support to their people.

General Electric (GE) is known for developing world-class talent. It didn't build this reputation by accident. For example, GE's HR engages all functions and business units in "growth dialogues," which are discussions revolving around how to grow talent organically within their respective areas. Business leaders discuss ways to improve and develop current talent to meet the future needs of the company. Furthermore, performance evaluations are a key part of talent development and are *everyone's* responsibility. HR trains employees to take responsibility and to see performance evaluation not as something HR does to them, but as an organization improvement mechanism. Additionally, GE has established the John F. Welch Leadership Center in New York, a corporate-run business school devoted entirely to developing leadership talent. GE puts its money where its mouth is—the leadership development program costs more than $1 billion annually.

Many companies have attempted to replicate GE's success in talent and leadership development. GE's whole-organization commitment is what sets it apart. The organization has succeeded in branding itself as *the* talent development company—and this brand produces bottom-line results. Investors have tremendous confidence that GE will continue to be guided by the best leaders in the world.

Factor: Shaping Organization

While the previous factor (Developing Talent) focuses on improving individuals within an organization, Shaping Organization focuses on the organization as a whole. Within this factor, two sub-components emerged: organizational development (OD) and organization structure. Organizational development generally refers to change interventions at the organizational level. Organization structure refers to the structure an organization needs to accomplish its strategic goals.

In a world of fast change, shaping an organization is anything but a one-time process. It requires line management and HR professionals to continuously analyze the processes and flow of information, work, and people to decide what is working and what is not working and adjust accordingly.

Headquartered in Stavanger, Norway, Statoil has grown from a relatively minor national oil company into one of the largest global energy companies with a market capitalization approaching $70 billion. In 2007, the company announced a $30 billion merger with Norsk Hydro, as well as a second smaller acquisition in Canada. The Hydro merger significantly expands the combined opportunities of the new company, but also their talent challenge. For Jens Jenssen and his HR team, the challenges are two-fold. First, they must make sure the company retains Statoil's and Hydro's most capable employees. To do this, however, they need to establish an organization structure that puts the right people in the right roles, rationalizes the combined organization, and boosts Statoil's ability to be world class in oil exploration and production.

Jenssen and his team have had to answer the following questions as they help shape the new Statoil:
- Are the goals of the organization clear? Do individuals know what is expected of them? Is there a clear line of sight from organization goals to team goals to individual goals?
- Are the roles and role relationships clear? Do teams and individuals have a clear understanding of what others need and expect from them, and what they need and expect from others?

- Are jobs designed to be successful? Do individuals have the resources, tools, and authority they need to get the job done?
- Is growth built in? Is developmental "head room" built into the job? Will it continue to energize and interest individuals over time?

Factor: Fostering Communication

Good communication operates in all directions: up, down, across, and out. Employees rely on executive communication for direction on goals, priorities, and values. Executives rely on upward communication to stay in touch with what employees are thinking and feeling. Effective horizontal communication ensures that teams, functions, and business units are cooperating. Communication is how an organization builds its reputation as an employer of choice and its brand as a developer of leadership talent.[4]

In a world where access to information is growing far faster than the ability to use it wisely, HR professionals must be able to accurately select and clearly communicate the most critical messages for organizational success. Effective HR professionals are able to foster communication by:
- Facilitating and the design of internal communication processes (how information moves into, out of, and through the company).
- Working with managers to send clear and consistent messages.
- Developing a comprehensive internal communication strategy and plan.

An excellent example of fostering communication comes from Sears, where Tony Rucci (the senior HR executive at the time) and the HR team engaged dozens of managers and hundreds of employees in constructing Sears' Employee-Customer Profit Chain. They identified the key employee attitude metrics that measured the extent to which Sears was a "compelling place to work." Using advanced statistical procedures, the HR team found that a 5% improvement in employee attitude metrics resulted in a 1.3% increase in positive customer impressions. This, in turn, resulted in a 0.5% increase in revenue growth per store, which added up to hundreds of millions of dollars. The basic logic was simple: Creating a compelling place to work would result in a compelling place to shop; creating a compelling place to shop would result in a compelling place to invest. This message was constantly communicated throughout the company and beyond, including a case study that was published in the *Harvard Business Review.*

Factor: Designing Rewards Systems

Strategic rewards and compensation have an effect on both the organization as a whole and on the talent that can be attracted and developed within that organization. Our data analysis, however, showed an intriguing discrepancy in how this factor is perceived. HR respondents tended to associate compensation and rewards as parts of the Operational Executor domain—day-to-day, transactional elements of their HR work. In contrast, the non-HR respondents saw compensation and rewards as inseparable from the strategic part of managing talent and designing organizations.

Two aspects must be considered in designing strategic rewards systems: measurement and rewards. Below are considerations for each of these two aspects:

Measurement	Rewards
· Measure the full value-added components of individual jobs.	· Base compensation is required but too often is not linked to performance and hence does not alter behavior.
· Differentiate between high- and low-performing teams and individuals.	· Rewards need to be valued by the receiver, not the giver.
· Be simple but complete. Measurement should measure results and behaviors. Measuring results captures past performance. Behaviors can be predictors of future performance.	· Remember the importance of visibility. For many people, rewards need to be visible to the receiver as well as to those whose opinions are valued by the receiver.
· Be credible by capturing multiple viewpoints and using several sources.	· Link to motivation. Non-monetary rewards, such as the opportunity to do high-value, cutting-edge work, often have more power than money.
· Utilize key benchmarks such as other individuals performing the same tasks, or preset goals.	· Avoid "one-way street" rewards. Rewards need to be taken away if performance is not sustained.

At biotech giant Amgen, rewards systems are utilized to get the right talent into the company, and then encourage the right culture and behaviors. Its 401(k) plan provides a simple example of this philosophy. Not only does Amgen match 100% of an employee's contribution up to 5%, it also contributes an additional 5% regardless of the employee's contribution. Amgen sees this as a message to employees that it cares about them and wants them to stick around for the long term. In addition, Amgen recently restructured its compensation system to give managers greater latitude to reward people or groups who make extraordinary contributions to the business. Supervisors are given the ability to identify and reward employees up to a certain percent of their salary. The rewards can be either in cash or stock grants (not just stock options). This program clarifies the employee value proposition: Working hard gets immediately rewarded.

Talent Manager/Organization Designer by the Numbers

This section will look at three different sets of numbers for factors within the Talent Manager/Organization Designer domain:

- Descriptive statistics: How well did HR professionals score in each of the factors, across a variety of demographic dimensions?
- Correlations to individual performance: What is the relative impact of each factor on perceived individual performance?
- Correlations to business performance: What is the relative impact of each factor on business performance, as measured by our business performance index?

Descriptive Statistics

Descriptive statistics explain the extent to which the HR profession is perceived to be competent in each of the factors within the Talent Manager/Organization Design domain—essentially, a big-picture view of the profession's strengths and weaknesses. The overall mean for this domain placed it as the one that HR does third best, after Credible Activist and Culture & Change Steward.

The first comparison is overall scores by respondent type. Figure 5.2 shows scores provided by the HR participants themselves, their HR associates and their non-HR associates. Overall perception of competency among the factors associated with this domain generally maintains the same pattern regardless of the respondent group being considered, with one exception: HR participants or associates feel that they are better at Developing Talent than Shaping Organization, whereas non-HR associates feel that HR is better at Shaping Organization. This is a curious observation. Could it be that HR's traditional comfort zone is in talent development rather than organization structure? If so, it is useful to realize that non-HR colleagues appreciate HR's expertise in organization design and ascribe greater competence than HR people feel they deserve. Remember, a working definition of expertise is to know just enough to be helpful. Even though they are not highly confident of their own organization design skills, HR professionals probably know "just enough more" than their line manager colleagues—and, thus, are valued by them.

The same phenomenon can be seen in the area of Designing Rewards Systems. HR participants scored themselves quite low compared to their non-HR associates (a spread of almost 0.3). This is particularly interesting in light of the factor analysis alluded to briefly above. When using data from HR participants and respondents, Designing Rewards Systems factored with the tactical domain of Operational Executor. Using non-HR associate data, Designing Rewards Systems factored strongly with the development of talent. In the collective mind of the global HR profession, the message seems to be this: "Compensation and rewards is low-value-added work, and we're not very good at it." This is a bit of a wake-up call to the profession: Non-HR colleagues value the work HR professionals do in compensation and rewards, and appreciate their expertise. Rewards systems are notoriously difficult to get right. In the words of the old one-liner, "Money may not buy happiness, but it buys the kind of misery we enjoy." When trying to figure out the details of a rewards system, we're always dealing to some extent in "preferable levels of misery." Don't let that deter you. Your line-manager colleagues need your help.

The data also make clear that, while HR professionals must balance the roles of Talent Manager and Organization Designer to make sure that both work together and receive the proper emphasis, scores for the factors Ensuring Today's and Tomorrow's Talent and Shaping Organization indicate that HR professionals are much more apt (and probably more comfortable) with the talent manager component of this competency than they are with the organization designer component. In the immediate future, HR professionals should focus on the development of the organization. Otherwise, they run the risk of turning human resources into nothing more than the management of human capital.

Figure 5.2. **Overall Mean Scores by Respondent Type**

	HR Participants	HR Associates	Non-HR Associates
Ensuring Today's and Tomorrow's Talent	3.92	3.94	3.88
Developing Talent	3.70	3.78	3.69
Shaping Organization	3.68	3.77	3.74
Fostering Communication	3.87	3.88	3.82
Designing Rewards Systems	3.20	3.34	3.49

When looking at factor scores by region, you will see the same sorts of trends we have seen in other domains—namely, higher scores for the United States and Europe, and lower scores for China as shown in Figure 5.3. Interestingly, China's scores for all factors fall within 0.1 of each other, indicating that China's HR professionals and their associates see themselves as performing equally in all of these factors. China's scores are among the lowest for all factors with the exception of Designing Rewards Systems, which garnered one of the highest scores of all regions. The reason for this could be that in China (and perhaps in India and Latin America as well), strategic HR is a relatively new concept. The focus of HR has been on the basics, such as getting people their paychecks.

Figure 5.3. **Overall Mean Scores by Region**

	U.S.	Latin America	Europe	China	Australia	India
Ensuring Today's and Tomorrow's Talent	4.10	3.89	4.02	3.62	3.88	3.93
Developing Talent	3.84	3.76	3.82	3.51	3.79	3.76
Shaping Organization	3.81	3.77	3.78	3.69	3.69	3.89
Fostering Communication	3.96	3.97	3.82	3.63	3.86	3.82
Designing Rewards Systems	3.32	3.50	3.28	3.52	3.26	3.73

When looking at industries, our data show clear distinctions (see Figure 5.4). Pharmaceuticals and chemicals, utilities, and services score among the highest in Ensuring Today's and Tomorrow's Talent. In contrast, agriculture, mining, and construction are the lowest-scoring sectors. This likely reflects differences in the percentages of "knowledge work" across these industries. Pharma and chemicals are knowledge-intensive industries, while agriculture, mining, and construction rely on less-skilled labor that is more easily replaced. Banking, trade, and manufacturing fall in between these two extremes.

A similar trend can be seen within Developing Talent, Shaping Organization, and Fostering Communication. Designing Rewards Systems again scores lower than the other factors within this competency.

Figure 5.4. **Mean Scores by Industry (associate rater scores only)**

	Agriculture	Mining	Construction	Food	Manufacturing	Pharmaceuticals/ Chemicals	Utilities	Wholesale/Retail Trade	Banking & Real Estate	Services	Public Administrations
Ensuring Today's and Tomorrow's Talent	3.74	3.75	3.61	3.84	3.93	4.08	4.03	3.96	3.96	4.02	3.95
Developing Talent	3.66	3.63	3.43	3.66	3.75	3.84	3.87	3.71	3.80	3.85	3.81
Shaping Organization	3.69	3.76	3.61	3.70	3.78	3.86	3.84	3.72	3.68	3.79	3.73
Fostering Communication	3.70	3.72	3.65	3.76	3.88	3.93	4.01	3.79	3.93	3.99	3.92
Designing Rewards Systems	3.49	3.48	3.44	3.28	3.37	3.46	3.38	3.38	3.27	3.43	3.37

The scores by HR channel also are revealing, according to Figure 5.5. Embedded and Corporate HR professionals provide the highest scores for all factors other than Designing Rewards Systems, where they score lowest. This may indicate that HR professionals in these two channels have more opportunity to influence talent management and organization design due to the nature of their jobs than their counterparts in more functional and specific roles. The low scores for these two channels in Designing Rewards Systems, especially at the corporate level, are a little puzzling. A number of the survey questions in this factor are quite specific to traditional compensation and benefits work. It could be that, unless participants were currently working in compensation and benefits, they scored themselves (and were scored by others) quite low.

Figure 5.5. **Mean Scores by HR Channel (associate rater scores only)**

	Functional HR	Centers of Expertise	Embedded HR	Service Center	E-HR	Corporate HR
Ensuring Today's and Tomorrow's Talent	3.71	3.88	4.06	3.71	3.72	3.93
Developing Talent	3.59	3.77	3.82	3.54	3.64	3.81
Shaping Organization	3.64	3.80	3.82	3.62	3.73	3.77
Fostering Communication	3.73	3.86	3.95	3.72	3.76	3.85
Designing Rewards Systems	3.43	3.46	3.34	3.52	3.43	3.38

Finally, size of business data indicate that the larger the organization, the greater the perceived HR expertise in talent management, organization structure, and communication (see Figure 5.6). Business size appears to have no appreciable relationship to competence in Designing Rewards Systems. As noted in previous chapters, HR professionals in smaller companies tend to be jacks of all trades, including compensation. In larger organizations, the HR function tends to be subdivided into specialties, leading HR people to feel that unless they work specifically in compensation and benefits, they really don't have much expertise in it.

Figure 5.6. **Mean Scores by Business Size (associate raters only)**

	0 to 99	100 to 499	500 to 999	1,000 to 4,999	5,000 to 9,999	10,000 to 24,999	25,000+
Ensuring Today's and Tomorrow's Talent	3.73	3.73	3.86	3.87	3.97	4.02	4.04
Developing Talent	3.63	3.60	3.70	3.70	3.80	3.85	3.84
Shaping Organization	3.70	3.62	3.71	3.71	3.80	3.79	3.91
Fostering Communication	3.73	3.74	3.87	3.85	3.84	3.97	3.90
Designing Rewards Systems	3.52	3.40	3.43	3.39	3.43	3.24	3.41

Correlations to Individual Performance

As we begin to focus on the impact of these five factors on an HR professional's perceived performance, it is worth remembering that Talent Manager/Organization Designer accounts for approximately 19% of the variance in individual performance (see Figure 2.16). If each of the six competency domains had equal impact on individual performance, they would each account for approximately 17% of the variance in individual performance (100% divided by six). So the Talent Manager/Organization Designer domain is slightly above average in its impact on an HR professional's perceived overall competence.

As we have done with other factors in other domains, we ran a regression for each factor within the Talent Manager/Organization Designer domain against individual performance. Essentially, we were trying to answer the question: How much of the 19% of performance accounted for by the Talent Manager/Organization Designer domain can be explained by each of its factors?

Figure 5.7 presents the data on perceived individual performance by gender. Women appear to gain greater performance leverage than men from Ensuring Today's and Tomorrow's Talent and Fostering Communication, while men seem to gain more mileage than women in Designing Rewards Systems and Shaping Organization. The differences are slight, but interesting. Male HR practitioners evidently gravitate a bit more to the organizational and analytical factors within this domain, women to the staffing- and verbal-related factors. The two genders are dead even when it comes to the impact of Developing Talent.

Regressions by region are shown in Figure 5.8. Across nearly all regions, the pattern is similar, with Ensuring Today's and Tomorrow's Talent having the greatest impact on the perception of an individual HR professional's competence. The second-place factor varies, however, between Developing Talent (in the United States and India) and Shaping Organization (in Latin America,

Figure 5.7. **Individual Performance Regression by Gender (associate raters only)**

	Male		Female	
	R^2	%	R^2	%
Ensuring Today's and Tomorrow's Talent	0.323	26%	0.328	29%
Developing Talent	0.250	20%	0.227	20%
Shaping Organization	0.271	22%	0.226	20%
Fostering Communication	0.267	21%	0.258	23%
Designing Rewards Systems	0.136	11%	0.096	8%

Figure 5.8. **Individual Performance by Region**

	U.S.		Latin America		Europe		China		Australia		India	
	R^2	%	R^2	%	R^2	%	R^2	%	R^2	%	R^2	%
Ensuring Today's and Tomorrow's Talent	0.310	27%	0.311	24%	0.263	29%	0.322	24%	0.305	25%	0.304	23%
Developing Talent	0.257	23%	0.264	21%	0.197	22%	0.26	19%	0.267	22%	0.33	24%
Shaping Organization	0.215	19%	0.287	22%	0.202	23%	0.301	22%	0.279	22%	0.256	19%
Fostering Communication	0.228	20%	0.248	19%	0.156	17%	0.256	19%	0.265	21%	0.261	19%
Designing Rewards Systems	0.123	11%	0.17	13%	0.075	8%	0.205	15%	0.125	10%	0.196	15%

Europe, and China). Fostering Communication is in third place in the United States, and in fourth place (or tied for third) in all other regions. Designing Rewards Systems has the least impact, but HR professionals in developing regions received higher impact scores just as they received the highest mean scores in this factor.

Analyzing the data by HR channel continues to show that Ensuring Today's and Tomorrow's Talent has the greatest impact on individual performance, regardless of channel (see Figure 5.9). Functional HR and E-HR see greater relative impact from Fostering Communication, while HR professionals in the majority of the other channels see stronger correlations to Shaping Organization. Designing Rewards Systems brings up the rear for all channels—even Centers of Expertise, which would presumably contain a greater concentration of compensation and benefits specialists.

Figure 5.9. **Individual Performance by Channel**

	Functional HR		Centers of Expertise		Embedded HR		Service Center		E-HR		Corporate HR	
	R^2	%	R^2	%	R^2	%	R^2	%	R^2	%	R^2	%
Ensuring Today's and Tomorrow's Talent	0.319	26%	0.36	27%	0.289	28%	0.204	25%	0.473	25%	0.352	27%
Developing Talent	0.258	21%	0.283	22%	0.235	23%	0.179	22%	0.469	25%	0.286	22%
Shaping Organization	0.232	19%	0.266	20%	0.215	21%	0.177	22%	0.346	18%	0.282	21%
Fostering Communication	0.267	22%	0.264	20%	0.206	20%	0.132	17%	0.423	22%	0.247	19%
Designing Rewards Systems	0.136	11%	0.14	11%	0.081	8%	0.108	13%	0.196	10%	0.153	12%

Size has an interesting impact on the perception of HR competence (see Figure 5.10). In general, as size increases, the perceived importance of talent management and development grows, and the importance of Designing Rewards Systems reduces in perceived impact. This may be because as an organization grows, compensation and rewards systems become quite institutionalized, leaving little room for the individual HR professional to change them.

At about 10,000 employees, communication seems to become slightly more important than organization design. Again, this could be attributed to increased bureaucratization and structural rigidity in larger companies, and greater need for communication between organization units and across structural boundaries.

Figure 5.10. **Individual Performance by Business Size**

	0 to 99		100 to 499		500 to 999		1,000 to 4,999		5,000 to 9,999		10,000 to 24,999		25,000+	
	R^2	%	R^2	%	R^2	%	R^2	%	R^2	%	R^2	%	R^2	%
Ensuring Today's and Tomorrow's Talent	0.302	26%	0.391	28%	0.345	25%	0.285	28%	0.318	26%	0.336	32%	0.316	27%
Developing Talent	0.264	23%	0.299	22%	0.303	22%	0.204	20%	0.28	23%	0.233	22%	0.281	24%
Shaping Organization	0.244	21%	0.278	20%	0.266	19%	0.217	21%	0.277	22%	0.192	18%	0.242	21%
Fostering Communication	0.217	19%	0.269	19%	0.295	21%	0.208	20%	0.242	20%	0.219	21%	0.234	20%
Designing Rewards Systems	0.14	12%	0.15	11%	0.177	13%	0.11	11%	0.122	10%	0.087	8%	0.085	7%

Correlations to Business Performance

In contrast to the individual performance correlations, business performance correlations are overall quite a bit weaker. This is noted in the R^2 values. For individual performance, R^2 values range from 0.085 to 0.473, with most in the 0.2 to 0.3 range. In contrast, R^2 values for business correlations rarely exceed 0.15, with more than a few lower than 0.01. In other words, our survey provides a much more robust way of correlating the competency domains and factors with perceived individual competence than with perceived business performance. This creates a significant opportunity for follow-up research to link the competency domains to hard business measures. With that caveat, we will present the correlations to business performance and glean insights we from the numbers.

Looking at HR vs. non-HR raters provides an interesting perspective on how relative contribution is viewed (see Figure 5.11). For non-HR associates, Ensuring Today's and Tomorrow's Talent makes the largest contribution to business results, with over a third of the total attributed to the five factors. Developing Talent is a distant second. Although Shaping Organization is clearly seen as playing a role, the size of its perceived impact on business performance is viewed as much greater by HR associates (22% vs. 15%) than for non-HR associates.

Figure 5.11. **Business Performance by Respondent Type**

	HR		Non-HR	
	R^2	%	R^2	%
Ensuring Today's and Tomorrow's Talent	0.099	26%	0.094	34%
Developing Talent	0.084	22%	0.061	22%
Shaping Organization	0.085	22%	0.042	15%
Fostering Communication	0.077	20%	0.053	19%
Designing Rewards Systems	0.042	11%	0.029	10%

Cutting the data by gender and then running regressions against business performance provides us with an interesting contrast to findings for individual competence (see Figure 5.12). The top-loaded factor for women's impact on business results is Fostering Communication (which was second to Ensuring Today's and Tomorrow's Talent in the correlations to individual performance). The increase in the Ensuring Today's and Tomorrow's Talent factor for men is even more surprising. It jumps to 31% of business impact from 25% for individual impact.

Figure 5.12. **Business Performance by Gender (associate raters only)**

	Male		Female	
	R^2	%	R^2	%
Ensuring Today's and Tomorrow's Talent	0.148	31%	0.101	25%
Developing Talent	0.110	23%	0.085	21%
Shaping Organization	0.092	19%	0.075	18%
Fostering Communication	0.073	15%	0.121	30%
Designing Rewards Systems	0.062	13%	0.026	6%

Figure 5.13 shows the data for impact of competency factors on the business vs. business size. The data are full of unexplained anomalies. This is

due in part to the low R^2 values for many of the size ranges. At the 100 to 499, 10,000 to 24,999, and 25,000+ size ranges, the R^2 values allow us to draw some inferences. At the sub-500 employee level, bringing in talent and Facilitating Communication appear to have the greatest impact on business results. This also applies at the 10,000 to 24,999 employee levels, with Fostering Communication showing slightly stronger impact on business results. At the 25,000+ level, Shaping Organization comes to the fore, followed by Designing Rewards Systems. Clearly, more research is needed here. If the data can be trusted, HR professionals in the largest organizations need to pay more attention to strategic compensation and rewards systems. This is the factor with the lowest mean scores in this domain, yet the highest impact on business results in large companies.

Figure 5.13. **Business Performance by Business Size (associate raters only)**

	0 to 99		100 to 499		500 to 999		1,000 to 4,999		5,000 to 9,999		10,000 to 24,999		25,000+	
	R^2	%	R^2	%	R^2	%	R^2	%	R^2	%	R^2	%	R^2	%
Ensuring Today's and Tomorrow's Talent	0.140	30%	0.305	29%	0.105	34%	0.088	22%	0.050	25%	0.422	24%	0.223	16%
Developing Talent	0.179	39%	0.177	17%	0.082	26%	0.047	11%	0.057	29%	0.368	21%	0.211	15%
Shaping Organization	0.063	14%	0.198	19%	0.049	16%	0.109	27%	0.008	4%	0.309	18%	0.384	28%
Fostering Communication	0.044	9%	0.267	26%	0.056	18%	0.105	26%	0.076	38%	0.470	27%	0.238	17%
Designing Rewards Systems	0.036	8%	0.099	9%	0.022	7%	0.059	14%	0.008	4%	0.159	9%	0.339	24%

Finally, the data for business performance by HR channel (or role) provides an interesting insight into how different roles are seen to contribute (see Figure 5.14). For Functional HR and for Centers of Expertise—both of which play a corporate role—Ensuring Today's and Tomorrow's Talent and Shaping Organization are seen as critical areas for business contribution. For Embedded HR, the greater leverage comes from Developing Talent, Fostering Communication, and Designing Rewards Systems. For the Service Center people, ensuring talent and developing it are the areas of greatest importance. Communication, which should be an important part of what the Service Center does, doesn't register at all. Again, however, we point out the low R2 values for all of these regressions.

Figure 5.14. **Business Performance by Channel (associate raters only)**

	Functional HR		Centers of Expertise		Embedded HR		Service Center		Corporate HR	
	R²	%	R²	%	R²	%	R²	%	R²	%
Ensuring Today's and Tomorrow's Talent	0.110	27%	0.132	31%	0.022	13%	0.035	59%	0.152	33%
Developing Talent	0.076	19%	0.060	14%	0.046	27%	0.017	30%	0.075	16%
Shaping Organization	0.106	26%	0.112	27%	0.018	10%	0.003	5%	0.093	20%
Fostering Communication	0.065	16%	0.064	15%	0.045	26%	0.000	0%	0.109	23%
Designing Rewards Systems	0.043	11%	0.051	12%	0.042	24%	0.003	6%	0.038	8%

Conclusion

Competent Talent Managers/Organization Designers pay attention to both talent and organization. Effective HR professionals have learned how to balance the organization's development and design with the need to obtain good talent. All-star teams don't spell success, but all-star teams coupled with the right organizations do.

Competent Talent Managers/Organization Designers use alternate strategies for ensuring today's and tomorrow's talent. Even though the McKinsey book was somewhat overstated, there really is a war for good talent, especially in certain professions (think risk analysis experts) and industries (think health care). This doesn't always mean waging traditional warfare.

HR professionals can access talent in the following ways: build, buy, bounce, borrow, bound, and bind.

Build. Businesses can grow their own talent by hiring inexperienced employees and providing the training, work experiences, and rewards that encourage retention over the course of a career. P&G uses this strategy brilliantly, and has become what we've called "branded talent developers."[5]

Buy. Another strategy is to buy experienced talent from the outside. This strategy makes sense when the organization hasn't the infrastructure or the time to grow from within, or when key skills are missing.

Bounce. A third strategy is to manage out poor performers. For example, Exxon Mobil annually manages out the bottom 5% to 10% of performers through a forced distribution of performance. The organization continuously upgrades the quality of its employee population. Adopting such a system can be disastrous, however, without the proper mechanisms to ensure fairness. The company must have a carefully crafted a performance-oriented culture that won't feel violated.

Borrow. This refers to "renting" rather than owning resources. Alternatives range from utilizing contractors or consultants that supplement internal resources, to lending specialized resources from one part of the company to another, to fully contracting out a particular activity or function.

Bound. Making sure that the right people get identified early for additional responsibilities, and then putting them into positions where they can prove themselves, is the essence of the "bound" strategy. Ideally, succession planning systems help achieve this goal.

Bind. Bind means ensuring that top performers are retained, principally by offering the kinds of growth opportunities and experiences that they cannot find elsewhere.

HR professionals design organizations to deliver firm brand. Organization design should begin with the desired firm brand and organization capabilities needed to deliver the firm brand. Once the organization capabilities are determined, they align systems and processes to ensure the correct flow of information, people, performance and work to deliver these capabilities.

Becoming a Talent Manager/Organization Designer

Building your competence in the Talent Manager/Organization Designer domain is a powerful way to have greater impact as an HR professional. Of the five factors within the domain, Ensuring Today's and Tomorrow's Talent has much greater impact on the perception of personal competence and, in most cases, on business results as well. The Development Priority Index scores for these five factors show that Ensuring Today's and Tomorrow's Talent has a greater priority for the HR profession overall (see Figure 5.15). Developing Talent is a close second. Designing Rewards Systems is an area that does not score very high (in fact, it had the lowest DPI score in Round 5 of the study), but remains an important foundational area of HR competence.

Figure 5.15. **Development Priority Index Values for Talent Manager/Organization Designer Domain**

Competency Factor	% Impact	(5.0 Proficiency)	DPI
Ensuring Today's and Tomorrow's Talent	6.69%	1.09	7.28*
Developing Talent	5.37%	1.25	6.74*
Shaping Organization	5.02%	1.24	6.22*
Fostering Communication	4.92%	1.15	5.64
Designing Rewards Systems	2.31%	1.60	3.69

* = Value above the average DPI for all 21 factors (5.64)

Developmental Actions for the Talent Manager/Organization Designer

The following lists of specific developmental experiences may help you build capability in each of the factors within the Talent Manager/Organization Designer domain:

Factor: Ensuring Today's and Tomorrow's Talent

- Practice translating general cultural attributes into specific behaviors. (If someone were flexible, cost conscious, team-focused, creative, or disciplined, what specific and observable behaviors would she/he exhibit?)
- Be involved in college recruitment with a team of experienced recruiters.
- Work in a volunteer position within an association that requires you to evaluate members for promotions.
- Review the talent pipeline of your organization and organize focus groups to help identify what works well and what needs to work more effectively.
- Work with a line manager to identify the technical and cultural competencies that he/she may need in the future. Identify competencies where there is a shortage or surplus, and decide what needs to be done to correct the situation.

- Evaluate your chances for promotion against both technical and cultural criteria.
- Participate in the talent review of a unit or team. If the company doesn't conduct regular talent reviews, start one. General Electric, Exxon and PepsiCo all offer "best practice" approaches for doing so.

Factor: Developing Talent

- Create inventories of key developmental jobs and experiences. Identify what the incumbents learn from these experiences, and how such learning prepares them for greater contribution and leadership.
- Work with managers to create simple, realistic lists of potential successors to key jobs and roles.
- Pay attention to the development of core technical people, not just future executives.
- Identify "just-in-time" learning catalysts that can give people the skills and perspectives they need just prior to taking on new responsibilities. (Example: arrange mentoring by an experienced supervisor for people who've just been promoted to their first supervisory job.)
- Identify both the business deliverables and developmental objectives for each job assignment, and coach managers to hold their people accountable for both.
- Keep a list of developmental resources (training consultants, coaches, executive programs, etc.) that have provided measurable impact in the past.

Factor: Shaping Organization

- Engage your work team in identifying and reducing low-value work.
- Be involved in an organization restructuring task force.
- Write a critique of a recent organization restructuring. What problems were solved? What problems were created? How might the created problems be resolved?
- Work with a department to create a more effective work process design.
- Identify alternative organizational integration processes that will make the organizational whole worth more than the sum of its parts.
- Identify how different units (or companies) review the effectiveness of their organization structure, compare and identify best practices that can be generalized in the company or implemented.

Factor: Fostering Communication

- Compare communications efforts within your industry. What do competitors do better than your company? Identify one improvement that you can adapt from each of your best competitors and share it with colleagues and business partners.
- Develop an internal communication plan that effectively disseminates customer or shareholder information.
- Conduct a communication audit of your organization. Evaluate how well information travels up, down, and across the company. Share your findings with your supervisor.
- Evaluate current methods for disseminating information throughout the company, find the weaknesses and propose/implement a solution.
- Streamline/simplify a communication process that has too many steps or too much red tape.
- Make a presentation to a conference on an HR activity or issue in your organization. Arrange to repeat the presentation for an internal audience.
- Expand your network to include people from different parts of the organization (or outside the organization) who don't usually communicate. This puts you in a "knowledge broker" position, transferring critical information between groups.
- Write an article about a major business issue for publication in an internal or external magazine, newspaper, or journal.
- Coach a manager on the design and delivery of a key presentation. Teach basic techniques; critique and offer feedback.
- Volunteer to take the lead on designing the communication strategy for an upcoming organizational change (such as the implementation of a new policy, system or process).

Factor: Designing Rewards Systems

- Work with a management team to identify behaviors that are critical to your company's performance. Formulate these behaviors into an evaluation process.
- Identify key opportunities to perform high-value, challenging work and build them into your rewards system.
- Identify what percentage of employees create 90% of the wealth. Interview them concerning what they desire by way of financial and non-financial rewards. Design customized rewards for those individuals.

- Determine what percentage of your rewards system is at risk and what percentage is entitled. Determine what might be done to tie your rewards system more closely to performance.
- With a management team, determine what percentage of your rewards system should be contingent on results and what percentage should be contingent on behaviors.
- If you are on the board of a volunteer organization, or your church or synagogue, consider initiating a talent and organization review process. They are rarely found in non-profit organizations, and the need is just as great.
- Ask to be involved in improvement efforts that will provide you with a better focus on corporate rewards, and how they align with (or not) the competencies that are most important to the company's performance.

CHAPTER 6

Strategy Architect

D ue to changing market conditions, a large business is in the process
of considering the acquisition of its largest competitor. Knowing
that the acquisition of so large a company will require major adjustments
in product line, branding, manufacturing, and financial organization, the
CEO is putting together a two-day leadership team offsite to discuss the
acquisition and its myriad implications. Department heads from finance,
marketing, operations, and purchasing are invited, but the CEO isn't
sure about inviting HR. "This is a strategy discussion," he tells his CFO.
"We'll definitely want to involve HR down the road once the strategy is
defined—especially to help us figure out how we're going to deal with all
the extra headcount. But I'm wondering what they'll add to this discussion." In the end, he follows his CFO's advice and invites the vice president of HR—but, to be sure, it is mostly out of political correctness. It
would look strange (and send a damaging message) to have all of the
other functional heads in the room without HR.

This example is a bit extreme and somewhat dated, but it highlights a
persistent question: How can HR play a truly strategic role? In past years,
when the topic was mergers, globalization, innovation, customer service,
or financial performance, HR tended to join the conversation on the back
end. Its role was tactical, not strategic. Whether this was caused by, or
was the cause of, an inferiority complex, the result was the same: HR
professionals had to work doubly hard to achieve a "seat at the table," a
metaphor that symbolizes a deserved and permanent role in such business
and strategy discussions.

In recent years, line managers have begun to blur the distinction between strategy formulation and execution. Without the ability to make strategy happen, its formulation is little more than an intellectual exercise. Consequently, managers are seeking HR's input earlier. And not only are HR professionals invited to the table, they are expected to be more than note takers once seated.

At its core, the Strategy Architect domain is about how to prepare, what to say, and how to say it when participating in business discussions. To contribute, the HR professional must be able to take a strategic perspective not only of his or her HR work, but of the business overall. Much of this perspective grows out of a deep understanding of the external customer—an "outside-in" approach similar to what we advocated in Chapter 4 regarding organizational culture and change.

This chapter will present the research results for the Strategy Architect domain of HR competence. We will focus on the following three areas:
- Defining the Strategy Architect domain and its factors.
- Pointing out insights and further questions from the statistical data.
- Offering illustration and examples of effective practices of Strategy Architects.

Defining the Domain

This particular domain of HR competence was not easy to label. We knew from the factor analysis that the domain consisted of such behaviors as helping establish business strategy, having a vision of the future, providing alternative insights on business issues, understanding external customers, and working with business leaders to articulate purpose and meaning for the organization. Clearly, this was a strategy-anchored set of skills. We considered the term "strategy partner" to describe HR's role, but the word is overused and carries too much baggage (i.e., some people think that "partner" connotes "not really a part of the team"). "Strategic player" was another choice but again, the connotations were too passive. We settled on "architect" as closest to the meaning we wanted to convey. Architects have unique information that enables them to build blueprints that guide decision making.[1]

This domain, however, requires additional definition. When they first hear the term Strategy Architect, many people think of a CEO, general manager, or high-priced consultant—a brilliant mastermind who dreams up the organization's strategy. Such is not a typical role for even the most senior HR executives. Senior line leaders define and are accountable for the business strategy, but there is a more subtle aspect of the Strategy Architect's role that we wish to emphasize. Professional architects are schooled in the underlying principles of form and function, style and structure. They didn't invent these principles, but they know them well and can intuitively apply them to their work. Architects are not quite engineers and not quite artists, but can converse intelligently with both groups—and, more importantly, with the client to uncover needs, wishes, and an overall vision for the space they are helping to create.

In a remarkably similar way, HR professionals must thoroughly master the strategic architecture of the businesses in which they work. They need an in-depth appreciation of the company's business portfolio and what makes each business distinctive in customers' eyes. HR leaders most likely did not "invent" the strategy, but unless they ground all of their HR work in its fundamental principles, the systems and processes they create will be unstable, unaesthetic, and, ultimately, unsatisfying to the customer.

Perhaps an illustration will be helpful. Over the past 40 years, there has been a seismic shift in the way a company's market value is determined. In the 60s, a publicly traded company's overall worth in the stock market was dependent primarily on one factor: its ability to produce quarterly earnings. Today, financial earnings account for about half of a company's stock-market value. The other half is based on what accountants and economists call "intangibles," a category that includes such "soft" assets as the R&D organization's *past*, its track record. Intangibles increase an investor's confidence in the company's ability to produce *future* earnings.

The process for building intangible value is, ironically, quite tangible. The required steps are specific and concrete—an architecture of sorts—as depicted in Figure 6.1. Step 1 is for the business to keep its promises to investors, customers, and the community. Doing so engenders trust; without this trust, the following steps don't matter. Step 2 is to articulate a compelling strategy—a simple statement of how the business intends to grow. Such statements yield clarity and unity. Step 3 involves making sure the company has the requisite technical competence to deliver on its strategy. The result: execution. The final step is to create the organization capabilities that make business unique and are almost impossible for competitors to imitate, resulting in distinctiveness.[2]

Figure 6.1. **The Architecture for Intangibles**

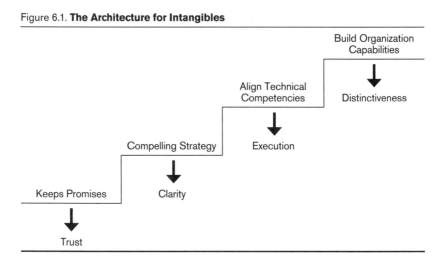

As shown in Figure 6.1, HR may influence intangibles in four ways. First, an HR professional coaches leaders to make and keep promises. This sometimes means moderating expectations and always means delivering on results. Second, a fully competent HR professional understands and contributes to defining and articulating the strategy by helping make sure that the strategy is clearly defined and focused on the future. Third, HR practices such as staffing, training, and performance management are critical to aligning technical competencies. And fourth, as discussed in Chapter 5, HR—more than any other function—owns processes related to creating and maintaining organization capabilities. These four steps—the "Architecture for Intangibles"—are among the handful of strategic fundamentals in which HR practitioners need to be fluent.

Strategy Architect Domain
Statistical analysis uncovered two distinct factors within the Strategy Architect domain: Sustaining Strategic Agility, and Engaging Customers. We'll discuss each of these factors in turn.

Factor: Sustaining Strategic Agility

HR professionals must understand the business strategy and align HR practices with it. This includes being able to identify the problems central to the business strategy, recognize marketplace trends and their impact on the business, and translate the strategic direction into annual business and HR initiatives.

By understanding the strategy and the potential obstacles to its success, HR professionals are able to maintain the organization's agility. High-performing HR professionals:

- Ensure the availability of resources (money, information, and people) that facilitate needed change.
- Have a vision of the future for the business.
- Are proactive in contributing to business decisions.

In a behemoth like IBM, with over 350,000 employees, Sustaining Strategic Agility would seem almost impossible to achieve. In addition, IBM boasts the lowest turnover in the IT industry. This lack of "fresh blood" would also seem to impede agility. Yet IBM's business and HR leaders are convinced that Sustaining Strategic Agility and employee turnover are inversely correlated: As turnover decreases, agility increases. Why? Because when people know their jobs well and have confidence in their future with the company, they can adapt to new situations more quickly. Additional examples of how IBM's HR leadership team helps the company stay nimble include:

- **Anticipating future needs.** In an industry that changes rapidly, staying ahead of the curve is essential to maintaining nimbleness. HR leaders look two to three years into the future to forecast the skills and people they will need to have—and where they will need them—in order to maintain IBM's competitive advantage.
- **Leading the transformation.** While many companies may have HR professionals that facilitate strategic planning meetings, IBM's HR leadership plays a much more active role in defining and executing strategy.

Be careful not to confuse novelty with strategy. Many HR professionals get distracted by each new management fad; they seem to feel that new approaches will keep them at the cutting edge, no matter what that edge is cutting. Chasing each new idea is a sure way to sacrifice the strategic unity and sustained direction necessary to have impact. Sticking to the business's strategic direction and staying close to its external customers are the perfect antidotes.

Factor: Engaging Customers

It is fascinating that unbiased statistical analysis would group Engaging Customers with Sustaining Strategic Agility. Understanding the impact of internal systems and processes on the external customer is an indispensable part of being a Strategy Architect. Engaging Customers involves the following behaviors:

- Facilitating the dissemination of customer information throughout the organization.
- Contributing to the building of the company's brand with customers, shareholders, and employees.
- Facilitating the integration of different business functions.
- Reducing or eliminating work that ultimately adds little or no value to the external customer.

These behaviors suggest that HR plays an important role in amplifying important signals—such as customer feedback and information—and transmitting these signals throughout the company. The end result is that people know how their work links directly to the strategy and the customer.

Lafarge, a large construction materials company, has operations in several countries and 71,000 employees worldwide. Lafarge's HR professionals dedicate time each month for interaction directly with customers. This policy has several benefits. First, HR professionals gain first-hand knowledge of the wants and needs of the external customers. Second, the customer visits put a "name and a face" on an otherwise abstract group of stakeholders, which in turn motivates HR professionals to create HR practices that build the company's brand for those external customers. Finally, understanding the outside customers gives HR professionals insights that they can then disseminate to the organization and share in leadership meetings. The resulting credibility enables them to meaningfully contribute to strategy discussions when they arise. Instead of being seen as an internally focused cost center, Lafarge HR is poised to directly affect the company's bottom line.

Strategy Architect by the Numbers

The first set of data figures in this chapter will discuss the relative performance of HR professionals in the two factors of the Strategy Architect domain, as seen by different groups of respondents. Understanding how the profession is doing in these areas, coupled with their relative importance (to be discussed further on in the chapter), can help HR professionals focus attention where it best serves the business.

Not surprisingly, HR associates view their colleagues as better at Sustaining Strategic Agility than do non-HR respondents, as shown in Figure 6.2. Chalk it up to functional solidarity; on the whole, HR sees itself as a group of strategic thinkers. Individuals' self-perceptions were less generous, however, scoring below even the perceptions of non-HR associates. Individual HR professionals evidently feel less than fully confident in their strategic skill set.

More interesting is the difference between the two factors. HR professionals, regardless of which group is rating them, are seen as being much better at Sustaining Strategic Agility than they are at Engaging Customers. This represents a significant opportunity for development. As a profession, HR has not yet broadened its perspective outside the organization's boundaries.

Figure 6.2. **Overall Mean Scores by Respondent Type (associate raters only)**

	HR Participants	HR Associates	Non-HR Associates
Sustaining Strategic Agility	3.54	3.72	3.62
Engaging Customers	3.33	3.47	3.44

Almost regardless of region, as shown in Figure 6.3, Sustaining Strategic Agility seems to be more of a strength compared to Engaging Customers. The exception is in China, where Sustaining Strategic Agility is rated slightly higher (a difference of 0.08). While Chinese HR professionals scored in the middle of the pack on Engaging Customers, they scored lower than any region on Sustaining Strategic Agility. As we have mentioned in previous chapters, China tends to be an anomaly in this data set, most likely due to the relative newness of the HR field within the region. In addition, a large percentage of the participating Chinese firms were state-owned enterprises (SOEs), for which many strategic decisions are made by government planners.

Figure 6.3 also shows noticeably lower scores for Europe and Australia in Engaging Customers. Perhaps the HR profession remains somewhat more functionally-oriented in these areas.

Figure 6.3. **Overall Mean Scores by Region (associate raters only)**

	U.S.	Latin America	Europe	China	Australia	India
Sustaining Strategic Agility	3.79	3.62	3.73	3.55	3.64	3.70
Engaging Customers	3.48	3.49	3.40	3.47	3.37	3.55

HR shows the strongest performance on both factors in companies in the services industry, according to Figure 6.4. This is especially logical for the Engaging Customers factor, given the preeminence and proximity of the customer in most service-based firms. Following this logic, however, it is somewhat surprising that HR in the retail industry surfaced relatively low scores on engaging the customer. Utilities show strong scores overall, followed by pharma/chemicals. And as seen in our analysis of other domains, public administration is demonstrating greater strength here than would be suggested by the stereotype of the slow-moving, customer-ignoring government bureaucracy.

Figure 6.4. **Overall Mean Scores by Industry (associate raters only)**

	Agriculture	Mining	Construction	Food	Manufacturing	Pharmaceuticals/ Chemicals	Utilities	Wholesale/Retail Trade	Banking & Real Estate	Services	Public Administrations
Sustaining Strategic Agility	3.57	3.64	3.44	3.64	3.65	3.77	3.76	3.66	3.62	3.78	3.69
Engaging Customers	3.47	3.50	3.32	3.37	3.39	3.46	3.50	3.39	3.44	3.55	3.47

Figure 6.5 contains some numbers that are confusing. Across channels, E-HR shows up with the highest scores for both Sustaining Strategic Agility and for Engaging Customers. We are struggling to rationalize this, since e-anything often conjures pictures of computer-filled back rooms littered with empty Red Bull cans and populated by geeks in sneakers who work odd hours. Perhaps the stereotype is misleading. In recent years, the creation of E-HR centers has often been seen as a clear strategic choice, involving HR in the financial cost-benefit calculations. To a greater degree than their tradi-

tional HR counterparts, leaders in E-HR could feel directly connected to the business's profitability.

As for the Engaging Customers scores, we believe the confusion here may have resulted from a misinterpretation of the survey questions. "Customer" usually means "internal customer" (i.e., the company's managers and employees), and E-HR tends to be extremely focused on meeting these people's needs. They know that they're one step away from being outsourced. In a similar way, Centers of Expertise score above the norm on Engaging Customers, again reflecting their role as a "central service" whose existence is justified by the service levels it provides to its (internal) customers.

On the other hand, the scores for Corporate HR and Embedded HR make a lot of sense. Both channels score quite high in Sustaining Strategic Agility. In other words, those defining the corporation's HR practices and policies, and those helping line managers implement and adapt these policies, are in the best positions to understand the business strategy and influence decisions about the future.

Figure 6.5. **Overall Mean Scores by HR Channel (associate raters only)**

	Functional HR	Centers of Expertise	Embedded HR	Service Center	E-HR	Corporate HR
Sustaining Strategic Agility	3.55	3.71	3.72	3.56	3.75	3.70
Engaging Customers	3.44	3.51	3.44	3.44	3.58	3.43

Looking at performance scores by business size in Figure 6.6 provides a couple of interesting insights. First, the highest score for Engaging Customers belongs to HR people in the smallest organizations. In companies with fewer than 100 employees, HR is by necessity less compartmentalized, less isolated, and more involved in the overall business. In fact, small-company HR people often wear multiple hats.

In contrast, Sustaining Strategic Agility is best executed by HR professionals in large organizations. Large companies have more disciplined processes for creating and communicating strategy, and need more people involved in making strategy process happen.

Figure 6.6. **Overall Mean Scores by Business Size (associate raters only)**

	0 to 99	100 to 499	500 to 999	1,000 to 4,999	5,000 to 9,999	10,000 to 24,999	25,000+
Sustaining Strategic Agility	3.62	3.48	3.61	3.62	3.74	3.80	3.81
Engaging Customers	3.55	3.37	3.43	3.44	3.47	3.46	3.51

Correlations to Individual Performance

For HR professionals to be seen as competent and high-performing Strategy Architects, which of its two factors matters more? To answer this question, we have parsed the data into several subsets. Overall, the Strategy Architect domain explains about 17% of the average HR professional's individual performance (see Figure 2.17). The scores below show the proportion of that 17% accounted for by each of the factors. In most cases, Sustaining Strategic Agility was seen to have almost twice the impact of Engaging Customers. Our interest, therefore, is in the subtle differences shown by the various cuts of the data.

When the correlations to individual performance are cut by gender, a slight difference is seen in Figure 6.7. Women tend to gain proportionally more impact from Sustaining Strategic Agility than do men (see the percentages below), but the R^2 values are somewhat higher on both factors for men than women, indicating a stronger link for men than women between these factors and individual performance.

Figure 6.7. **Individual Performance by Gender (associate raters only)**

	Male		Female	
	R^2	%	R^2	%
Sustaining Strategic Agility	0.308	61%	0.276	63%
Engaging Customers	0.195	39%	0.161	37%

The regional data in Figure 6.8 provides further insight into the relative importance of these two factors. For emerging economies (Latin America, India, and China), the relative impact of the two factors is far less polarized than for already established economies (U.S. and Canada, Europe, and Australia). This may indicate that HR professionals in these emerging economies should place special emphasis on understanding their external customers, which will naturally lead to playing a more strategic role in their respective companies.

Figure 6.8. **Individual Performance by Region (associate raters only)**

	U.S. and Canada		Latin America		Europe		China		Australia		India	
	R^2	%	R^2	%	R^2	%	R^2	%	R^2	%	R^2	%
Sustaining Strategic Agility	0.279	66%	0.289	58%	0.247	65%	0.307	53%	0.296	62%	0.341	54%
Engaging Customers	0.145	34%	0.213	42%	0.131	35%	0.270	47%	0.180	38%	0.285	46%

Differences across the various HR delivery channels raise some intriguing questions (see Figure 6.9). For example, Functional HR, Service Centers, and E-HR show the narrowest gap between the two factors, which means that Engaging Customers scores somewhat higher in terms of impact. Corporate HR, Centers of Expertise, and Embedded HR tend to achieve a larger proportion of impact from Sustaining Strategic Agility. The R^2 values are strongest for E-HR, indicating that the correlation between these factors and individual performance is strongest in that channel of HR delivery.

Figure 6.9. **Individual Performance by HR Channel (associate raters only)**

	Functional HR		Centers of Expertise		Embedded HR		Service Center		E-HR		Corporate HR	
	R^2	%	R^2	%	R^2	%	R^2	%	R^2	%	R^2	%
Sustaining Strategic Agility	0.273	58%	0.322	61%	0.258	66%	0.189	60%	0.440	57%	0.310	61%
Engaging Customers	0.200	42%	0.202	39%	0.135	34%	0.128	40%	0.330	43%	0.200	39%

It is difficult to interpret the data on business size in Figure 6.10. No consistent pattern emerges, other than confirmation that Sustaining Strategic Agility accounts for a larger percentage of individual performance than Engaging Customers, at all business sizes. The R^2 values are relatively similar across business size as well.

Figure 6.10. **Individual Performance by Business Size (associate raters only)**

L	0 to 99		100 to 499		500 to 999		1,000 to 4,999		5,000 to 9,999		10,000 to 24,999		25,000+	
	R^2	%	R^2	%	R^2	%	R^2	%	R^2	%	R^2	%	R^2	%
Sustaining Strategic Agility	0.209	64%	0.296	56%	0.33	63%	0.269	61%	0.311	59%	0.254	62%	0.29	67%
Engaging Customers	0.119	36%	0.23	44%	0.196	37%	0.17	39%	0.214	41%	0.154	38%	0.14	33%

Correlations to Business Performance

In addition to measuring each of these factors against the individual performance of HR professionals, we also measured them against the overall performance of the business in which the HR professional operates. We are interested here not only in what boosts the perception of HR competence, but in what HR professionals should be doing to demonstrate greater impact on business performance. The following figures show the relative impact of these two factors with respect to the overall business performance.

The first analysis displays differences of opinion between HR and non-HR raters in Figure 6.11. Sustaining Strategic Agility has twice as much impact as Engaging Customers in the eyes of non-HR associates. The spread between the two factors is less pronounced when looking at the HR associate responses.

Figure 6.11. **Business Performance by HR vs. Non-HR (associate raters only)**

	HR		Non-HR	
N	329		361	
	R^2	%	R^2	%
Sustaining Strategic Agility	0.116	56%	0.068	67%
Engaging Customers	0.089	44%	0.033	33%

In Figure 6.12, we see somewhat the opposite of what we learned when we looked at gender with respect to individual performance. Comparing men to women, it is more important for business results that men focus on Sustaining Strategic Agility, and that women work on Engaging Customers. The difference between the two factors (Sustaining Strategic Agility percentage minus Engaging Customers percentage) is much larger for men than it is for women—quadruple, in fact (24% vs. 6%). Perhaps this reflects a difference in stereotyped expectations, where men are "expected" to be strategists and women are "expected" to be relationship builders, working more closely and naturally with external customers.

Figure 6.12. **Business Performance by Gender (associate raters only)**

	Male		Female	
N	295		311	
Male vs. Female	R²	%	R²	%
Sustaining Strategic Agility	0.101	62%	0.121	53%
Engaging Customers	0.062	38%	0.107	47%

Business size is one of the few places within this analysis where Engaging Customers shows up with higher business impact than Sustaining Strategic Agility, as shown in Figure 6.13. In both very small companies and very large firms, focusing HR professionals on the task of Engaging Customers appears to have a proportionally greater impact on overall business performance. In small firms, this could be a reflection of the omnipresence of customer relationships. Along with everyone else in a small company, HR is never very far removed from the company's end users, and losing even a few customers can make or break a small company. On the other hand, very large firms see the impact more from Engaging Customers largely because of the amount of press coverage they receive. Microsoft, Nike, Walmart, GE, etc., are constantly in the news—and the reports aren't always flattering. To the extent that their HR professionals can help them understand, engage, and connect with their customers, these companies stand to gain market share, build good will, and strengthen their "intangibles."

Figure 6.13. **Business Performance by Business Size (associate raters only)**

	0 to 99		100 to 499		500 to 999		1,000 to 4,999		5,000 to 9,999		10,000 to 24,999		25,000+	
N	38		85		65		99		35		28		35	
	R^2	%	R^2	%	R^2	%	R^2	%	R^2	%	R^2	%	R^2	%
Sustaining Strategic Agility	0.086	39%	0.259	69%	0.107	72%	0.104	63%	0.100	10%	0.309	51%	0.282	40%
Engaging Customers	0.134	61%	0.115	31%	0.042	28%	0.062	37%	0.151	15%	0.296	49%	0.420	60%

When we look at the correlations to business performance by HR channel in Figure 6.14, we get the distinct impression that, once again, survey respondents were interpreting the word "customer" to mean those within the company whom they serve. This would explain why Service Centers and Embedded HR buck the overall trend, showing a higher correlation between business performance and Engaging Customers than Sustaining Strategic Agility. Embedded HR people are surrounded by their internal "customers," and Service Centers take care of internal customer needs constantly. Note, however, that the R^2 values are very low for nearly all the HR channels, showing that the correlation is quite weak regardless of HR channel.

Figure 6.14. **Business Performance by Channel (associate raters only)**

	Functional HR		Centers of Expertise		Embedded HR		Service Center		Corporate HR	
N	190		165		187		70		126	
	R^2	%	R^2	%	R^2	%	R^2	%	R^2	%
Sustaining Strategic Agility	0.100	59%	0.094	60%	0.056	49%	0.003	24%	0.112	60%
Engaging Customers	0.068	41%	0.064	40%	0.057	51%	0.011	76%	0.076	40%

Implications

In recent years, the HR profession has seen a growing emphasis on becoming strategic contributors. Our data support this emphasis, and indicate that there remains significant room for improvement in this competency domain.

The following observations summarize the key implications of our research in the Strategy Architect domain.

Don't confuse "architect" with "owner." You're not in charge of the business strategy. Your job as an HR professional is to understand the principles of business strategy to the point that you can apply them to your daily work, much the same way an architect understands and applies the principles of design and engineering in her daily work. Architects are not owners. When building a house with an architect, the owner makes the final decision, but the architect offers choices and alternatives the owner may not have considered.

Facilitate the strategy creation process. HR does often take responsibility for the process of creating the strategy. When they surface, seize such opportunities. As you prepare to facilitate a strategy discussion, ask yourself: Are the right people in the room? Have you involved the leaders who will need to buy into the strategy so it can be executed effectively? Are the right people speaking up? Is the timing right? What meetings should be held? Who should attend? What is the agenda for those meetings? Strategy creation is less an event than an ongoing series of conversations, which HR can help orchestrate.

Help clarify and articulate the strategy. You can make an enormous contribution by "taking the strategy to the masses" through clarification and communication. Studies have found that only one-third of workers feel empowered to reach their most important goals and only about 40% of workers clearly understand their most important goals.[3] Clarification is key. We've sat through many meetings in which consultants and executives present hundreds of slides documenting their market analysis and proposing a number of strategic options. Our reaction often is to raise our hand and ask, "So what's the strategy?" Unless that question can be answered in 15 words or less, using language that everyone in the company understands, the company lacks a clear strategy.

One company put on one page their vision, mission, strategies, goals, objectives, values, and priorities. In small type, this one page showed about 35 issues in which the company took interest. They had sent this one page and an accompanying video to 55,000 employees worldwide. Our view is that they created more concept clutter than strategic clarity. None of the employees, let alone the executives, could remember the 35 items on the page.

A good example of strategic clarity is Mill Steel, a family-owned steel processing business in western Michigan. Theirs is a little-engine-that-could story, in which they faced stiff competition and a unionized workforce. For the past five years, due to its progressive strategy and approach to growth, Mill Steel has been named one of the 10 Elite Winners of "West Michigan's 101 Best and Brightest Companies to Work For" by the Michigan Business and Professional Association.

Mill Steel's leadership team is crystal clear about its strategy: Get the customer what they want when they want it. This mantra is communicated throughout the organization, and reinforced through HR practices. For example, Mill Steel has partnered with Grand Valley State University to ensure access to a diverse group of incoming workers and jointly engage in research and development efforts. In addition, its performance-based bonus system has created a culture of ownership—no small feat in a family-owned company. The organization includes staff in discussions dealing with business planning for the future, in addition to monthly lunches that allow all staff to discuss opportunities and challenges with the leadership team.

Management and HR's attention to aligning the people practices with the overall business strategy has allowed Mill Steel to build an environment that inspires ownership at all levels of the company; as a result, in a rapidly changing environment, Mill Steel has found a way to provide a level of service far greater than their competitors can.

Bring the outside view in. As noted in this chapter, HR professionals too often see their customers and clients as line managers and employees within the organization. In order for HR professionals and departments to be effective, the definition of *customer* must be focused externally: the outside customer or end user, the investor, and the community where the business operates. True, HR is about people—but external customers, investors, and community leaders are people too! Get to know their motives, drives, and needs. Doing so will have a profound impact on the way you approach your HR-specific work. To become a Strategy Architect and have greater impact on bottom-line performance, your customer needs to be the same one that everyone else on the leadership team is talking about.

HR can involve customers through their presence (the physical inclusion of customers in traditional HR practices) or their essence (having their ideas or input in the room even if they are not physically there). The marketing department can provide a lot of information on current and target customers. Digest this information. Assess how well your internal processes (hiring, training, rewarding, etc.) relate to that outside customer. For example, ask key customers to look at your performance appraisal form and let you know if the behaviors and outcomes evaluated on the form are consistent with their expectations. Or invite key customers (or investors) into company-hosted training events so that employees can experience first-hand customer expectations—and follow up with these customers, asking, "Will the training you saw us providing our employees make them better able to meet your needs?"

Ensure execution of the strategy by aligning HR practices. In their book, *The Strategy-focused Organization: How Balanced Scorecard Companies Thrive in the new Business Environment,*[4] Kaplan and Norton cite a study of 275 portfolio managers who reported that the ability to execute strategy was more important than the quality of the strategy itself. And after a business strategy is defined, tweaked, or in some cases completely revamped, HR usually assumes the huge task of acting as a sort of project manager for the implementation. Although the execution of the strategy on the front lines should clearly be owned by line management, coordination of the overall effort falls to HR—especially when it comes to minimizing roadblocks and maximizing the flow of information and work across boundaries.

In their article "The Silent Killers of Strategy Implementation and Learning," Beer and Eisenstat outline six roadblocks that they call "strategy killers."[5] Two of these strategy killers are related to implementation, where HR plays a major role: poor coordination across functions, businesses, or borders; and inadequate down-the-line leadership skills. Understanding these killers can position HR professionals to help the company avoid large mistakes during the massive chaos that is strategy implementation.

Align leadership behavior to strategy. HR professionals can coach leaders to make sure that leadership actions are congruent with strategic intent. HR professionals may track a leader's calendar to ensure that their personal time matches their organization's goals. A global strategy should translate to leaders spending time in global markets. An innovation strategy should be reflected in leaders spending time in R&D and with new products and lighthouse customers. A cost strategy should show up with leaders focusing on process improvements and efficiency efforts.

Becoming a Strategy Architect

Building your competence in the Strategy Architect domain is one of the best ways to demonstrate leadership as an HR professional. If you are in a role that does not currently offer a lot of opportunity to influence business strategy, then perhaps this domain would not be one of your immediate developmental priorities. For those in HR leadership positions, or those interacting closely and frequently with line managers, the Strategy Architect domain is crucial.

Of the two factors within the domain, Sustaining Strategic Agility has much greater impact on the perception of personal competence, and (in most cases) on business results as well. The Development Priority Index scores for these two factors show that Sustaining Strategic Agility has a greater priority for the HR profession overall, as shown in Figure 6.15. In fact, Sustaining Strategic Agility had the highest DPI score of any of the 21 factors. One of the reasons for this high score is that HR professionals generally lack in the strategic skills defined in this chapter.

Figure 6.15. **Development Priority Index Values for Strategy Architect Domain**

Competency Factor	Impact %	5.0-Proficiency	DPI
Sustaining Strategic Agility	5.91%	1.32	7.82*
Engaging Customers	3.62%	1.54	5.59

*= Value above the average DPI for all 21 factors (5.64)

Interestingly, this may be a case where one factor supports and enables the other. Getting to know your business's external customers and their needs is one of the best ways to broaden your strategic perspective and credibility.

Developmental Actions for the Strategy Architect

The following lists of specific developmental experiences may help you build capability in each of the factors within the Strategy Architect domain:

Factor: Sustaining Strategic Agility
- Serve on a cross-functional team whose task is to identify customer buying habits and recommend steps to improve market share.
- Conduct an industry analysis that includes a detailed plan for increasing the performance of your company relative to the competition.
- Work on a future scenario-building team whose task it is to develop a vision for the future of your company and the industry within which you compete.
- Prior to facilitating a decision-making process, develop your own recommendations for each issue that is likely to be raised.
- Develop an HR strategy. Devote the first three pages to a detailed examination of the state of your company relative to its competitors. Specify the steps that need to be taken to ensure company success. Base your recommendations on data, not on guesswork.
- Work with a not-for-profit on their strategy. Help them figure out how to position themselves in their market.

Factor: Engaging Customers
- Visit customers directly to elicit feedback about company performance.
- Work with the marketing department to involve employees more extensively in market research efforts. Ensure that information gathered through such an effort is used to solve customer problems and to improve customer-satisfaction indicators.
- Work with facilities management to ensure that the physical arrangement of office space or plant layout facilities optimizes internal communications and reinforces key values and strategies of the company.
- Conduct management team discussions on how to reduce low-value work and replace it with high-value work.
- Act as a customer to use your company's products or services.
- Talk to friends and associates who use your company's products or services and sense what they are experiencing.
- Look at your HR practices and see the extent to which they reflect customer expectations.

CHAPTER 7

Operational Executor

Exactly what sorts of problems and issues take most of an HR professional's time?

In an attempt to answer this question, the HR department of an internationally-known company asked its HR staff to post the types of questions and requests they field most often. Here is the resulting list, straight from their intranet site:

- How do I access my stock options?
- When are performance ratings due?
- How do I submit a request for paid time off?
- I can't access the Employee Service website.
- What is my salary mid-point?
- I have a medical claim question that the benefit center can't answer.
- How do I change my address?
- I need an employment verification letter to travel.
- What are the extra taxes taken out of my check?
- What is the tuition reimbursement policy? Whom do I give my documents to?
- How do I change the directory or phone book?
- How can I find my completed training records (learning history)?
- What is the end-of-year vacation cut-off date?
- How do I use or find the recognition tool?
- How do I find out information about a short-term transfer?
- How do I find information about my visa?
- Who is my HR contact?

- How do I get my 10-year service pen fixed?
- My passport is damaged and I need to travel. What do I do?
- Was I nominated for stock during the annual review? I saw my increase on my paycheck but my manager never communicated it to me.
- How do I change my tax withholdings?
- How much will I pay in taxes if I relocate to your location?
- How can I update my profile?
- Where can I get more ink for my service-award pen?
- Can I get an extra ID card?
- My email address is incorrect. IT told me that it was an HR issue.
- I'm not in the IT Master system yet. IT/Security told me it was an HR issue.
- How do I get a badge for a contractor? IT said it was an HR issue.
- How do I get network access for a contractor?
- I have an international employee coming next week to work. Does he need a work visa?
- I need a new visa stamp. Will the company pay for a personal trip for my family and me to get my new stamp?
- When will I receive my severance checks?
- I'm not seeing my retirement savings match and need to roll it over.
- My paid-time-off balance is incorrect.
- Can we bring creamer back to the break rooms?

We're not making up this stuff. Anyone who has worked for long in HR will recognize these as actual queries. "And the most maddening part of it," lamented a senior HR manager, "is that the answers to nearly all of these general policy questions are readily available on-line."

It's almost too ironic that the previous chapter was about being a Strategy Architect. "Sounds great," agree many of the HR professionals we've talked to. "I'd love to be a strategist. But I'm too busy dealing with all manner of menial and outlandish requests." Indeed, HR seems to occupy the low ground in many companies; all issues that no one else wants to deal with find their way to HR. It's hard to be a strategic, value-added player when you're finding ink refills for people's 10-year service pens.

This is the core issue for the Operational Executor domain: how to deliver on basic HR services without getting trapped in "help desk" mode. One of HR's roles is to take care of the operational details of working with people.

The key is to do so intelligently and efficiently—and to find ways to fix the administrative systems that seem to be broken in so many companies.

This chapter will report on the research results for the Operational Executor domain. Along the way, we will answer four questions:
- What is the history and evolution of this kind of work in organizations?
- What characterizes excellent "Operational Execution" in HR?
- How does this competency domain vary across geographies, gender, size of company, and other factors?
- What can we learn from leading companies about how to organize for operational excellence without allowing such work to dominate the HR agenda?

The Historical Perspective

Not too many years ago, operational and policy issues were the primary work performed by "personnel" departments. Personnel handled the paperwork related to people—hiring, firing, paying, promoting. Operational Execution was the name of the game; identifying it as a competency for high-performers would have bordered on redundant—like pointing out that high-performing fish can actually swim. The personnel department began by focusing on the terms and conditions of work and managing the administrative systems to help people get work done.

As our economy continued to shift away from manufacturing and toward knowledge work, the importance of more strategic contributions from HR grew apace. HR found itself being pulled into areas of complexity and depth: leadership development, team-based organizations, workforce planning, organization capability diagnosis, and executive compensation. The next step in the evolution was to create "shared services" organizations, where basic services were offered at low cost with a high degree of standardization. Company-wide policies appeared more efficient for many HR matters. HR took on the role of defining and "policing" such policies.

With continuing advancements in information technology and communications infrastructure, such "shared services" achieved the next step in their evolution: outsourcing. Companies realized that much of the fundamental administrative work didn't have to be done on-site or even by company employees. A company in Los Angeles could easily have its benefits administration handled from Lincolnshire, Illinois—or from Bangalore. The unrealistically high promises of low-cost, high-efficiency HR outsourcing haven't come completely true quite yet, however. Many employees who have come to expect personal attention from their HR representative continue to rely on such. Managers aren't sure they trust the information on the internet, or the answer from the person on the other end of the phone (and the other end of the world). Perhaps most significantly, HR professionals themselves, who have traditionally defined their value in terms of serving people's pressing needs, have trouble letting go of that role. We've heard countless HR people confide that one of the most difficult things for them to do is to overcome the legacy image of being the policy police.

Clearly, there are significant structural implications in the realm of Operational Executor. How does a company organize its HR function to provide the daily support, while not driving out the opportunity for strategic contribution? We will examine this question near the end of this chapter. For now, let's turn our attention to the definition of this competency domain and its factors.

Defining the Domain

As presented in Chapter 2, the definition of the Operational Executor domain is not complicated. It revolves around the HR professional's ability to execute the operational aspects of managing people and organization. Such activities as drafting, adapting, and implementing policies are central to this domain. In addition, employees need to be paid, relocated, hired, trained, etc. HR professionals are obligated to ensure that these fundamental needs are efficiently met. This operational work is akin to Herzberg's famous "hygiene factors"[1] Get it right and no one notices. Get it wrong and everyone is up in arms. Flawless application of consistent policies earns trust and opens the door to more strategic contributions.

Our factor analysis of the Operational Executor domain yielded two statistically distinct factors: Implementing Workplace Policies and Advancing HR Technology.

Factor: Implementing Workplace Policies

This factor centers around the day-to-day activities and systems that must happen to ensure that a company runs smoothly. These more tactical items often get taken for granted, but that doesn't lessen their importance. Flawlessly implementing workplace policies includes the understanding and execution of the following:

- Managing labor policies and procedures.
- Understanding labor legislation in the industry in which your business operates, including the legal rights of the people at work.
- Managing the arrangement of physical space and workplace environment.
- Designing flexible work schedules that fulfill the needs of the business while accommodating the needs of individual employees.

Factor: Advancing HR Technology

This factor consists of the application of electronic technology to HR administrative services. Advancements in this area have gotten to the point where it is almost commonplace for employees to be able to handle scheduling, payroll, travel reimbursements, benefits enrollment and changes, even quitting, through a company HR portal. In the past five years, we have seen these systems increase in scale, scope, efficiency, and effectiveness. The value of HR technology lies in its ability to offer transactional HR services at the click of a mouse, freeing up time and energy for more transformational activities.

As with most competencies, too much emphasis on operational efficiencies becomes counterproductive. When Operational Executor becomes the competency domain that is optimized, HR departments run the risk of applying policies inflexibly. As illustration, consider the case of a large global company that had developed a remarkable set of HR policies covering recruitment, recognition, relocation, and other matters. These policies made perfect sense in the cultural context of the company's North American headquarters. As its business shifted overseas, however, HR became known as the "policy police," insisting (for example) that the operations in China offer the standard mantle clock as a service award—even though clocks are a symbol of death and decay for the local Chinese workers. So a caveat is in order: Watch out for the attitude that "anything worth doing is worth overdoing." A little bit of standardization goes a long way when it comes to HR policies; HR professionals are wise to stay attuned to the principles behind the policies, not the policies themselves.

Operational Executor by the Numbers

Descriptive Statistics

As was noted in Chapter 2, Operational Executor is not one of the domains where HR professionals are rated highly by their non-HR respondents. The overall mean score for the domain is 3.63, slightly higher than Strategy

Architect (3.58) and Business Ally (3.48), but well below Culture & Change Steward (3.75), Talent Manager/Organization Designer (3.76), and Credible Activist (4.14). The good news, however, is that the score for Operational Executor is up from the 2002 study (when it was 3.35). We take this as a sign that progress is being made, though HR has room for improvement in delivering basic HR services. We have to continue to highlight that these administrative basics are prerequisites to longer-term success. Unless the basics are done and done well, the rest does not matter. Quite obviously, if employees are not paid on time or benefits processed in a timely way, they don't care much about strategy and long-term success. Indeed, we are disappointed that these administrative scores are not higher in this round of data.

Figure 7.1 shows the overall mean scores for each of the factors in the Operational Executor domain. As with four of the six domains, HR professionals score themselves less positively than their non-HR colleagues when it comes to Operational Execution. In other words, they are not self-deceived about the need for improvement. Scores do not show meaningful differences between the two factors, however.

Figure 7.1. **Overall Mean Scores by Respondent Type**

	HR Participants	HR Associates	Non-HR Associates
Implementing Workplace Policies	3.47	3.58	3.63
Advancing HR Technology	3.49	3.66	3.58

Regional differences are minimal, though HR in Latin America seems to be doing a better job in these two factors than their colleagues in the rest of the world, as shown in Figure 7.2. Europeans score at the bottom in these factors. A possible explanation has to do with the importance and complexity of labor relations in Europe—and labor-related items represent two of the seven specific questions in the Implementing Workplace Policies factor. It is interesting that China scores higher in the workplace policy factor than most of the rest of the world. This may again point to the current state of HR in China, where a focus is on administrative efficiency.

Figure 7.2. **Overall Mean Scores by Region (associate rater only)**

	U.S.	Latin America	Europe	China	Australia	India
Implementing Workplace Policies	3.59	3.71	3.48	3.63	3.52	3.66
Advancing HR Technology	3.73	3.70	3.52	3.53	3.58	3.73

Industry comparisons offer a number of questions for consideration in Figure 7.3. Services, banking & real estate, and utilities are leading the charge in HR Technology, it seems. This could well be a reflection of the crucial role played by information technology in general in these industries, in contrast to more "heavy" industries such as agriculture, mining, and manufacturing. The scores show less of a spread for the Implementing Workplace Policies factor.

Figure 7.3. **Overall Mean Scores by Industry (associate rater only)**

	Agriculture	Mining	Construction	Food	Manufacturing	Pharmaceuticals/ Chemicals	Utilities	Wholesale/Retail Trade	Banking & Real Estate	Services	Public Administrations
Implementing Workplace Policies	3.57	3.63	3.57	3.48	3.60	3.62	3.66	3.57	3.59	3.66	3.58
Advancing HR Technology	3.47	3.60	3.49	3.49	3.63	3.69	3.72	3.61	3.72	3.76	3.65

Predictably, E-HR and Service Centers are the channels that score highest in these two factors in Figure 7.4. Over time, as the outsourcing trend continues, we expect the difference to grow even larger, as Service Centers and E-HR become synonymous with a large portion of the operational issues in HR.

Figure 7.4. **Overall Mean Scores by HR Channel (associate rater only)**

	Functional HR	Centers of Expertise	Embedded HR	Service Center	E-HR	Corporate HR
Implementing Workplace Policies	3.60	3.63	3.59	3.68	3.73	3.57
Advancing HR Technology	3.61	3.66	3.61	3.73	3.75	3.66

Smaller businesses appear to make less use of HR technology, probably reflecting the expense of such systems, according to Figure 7.5. The
threshold appears to be at the 500 to 999 employee level. Businesses this
size and larger scored much more positively than smaller companies. The
same did not hold true, however, for Implementing Workplace Policies.
Businesses at the smaller end generally got more positive marks on this
dimension. This could be related to two issues. First, smaller businesses
tend to have fewer policies to implement, thus making it easier to do so
consistently. Second, HR plays a more "jack of all trades" role in smaller
businesses, getting involved in a wide variety of administrative activities,
including the design and allocation of office space. (Two of the seven
questions in the Implementing Workplace Policies factor relate to involvement in allocating and designing the physical work environment.) Larger
companies no doubt have separate facilities departments that handle
many of these issues—and this is a lost opportunity in some ways for HR.
The physical work environment is being recognized more and more as a
large contributor to productivity, team dynamics, employee satisfaction,
and other important measures. As Winston Churchill famously said, "We
shape our buildings; thereafter they shape us."

Figure 7.5. **Overall Mean Scores by Business Size (associate rater only)**

	0 to 99	100 to 499	500 to 999	1,000 to 4,999	5,000 to 9,999	10,000 to 24,999	25,000+
Implementing Workplace Policies	3.64	3.54	3.67	3.60	3.58	3.56	3.61
Advancing HR Technology	3.56	3.52	3.70	3.62	3.66	3.65	3.64

Correlations to Individual Performance

Correlations to individual performance basically answer one question:
When it comes to the perception of HR professionalism, which counts
more—the policy side of HR work, or the technology side?

Gender appears to be an insignificant variable when regressed against
individual performance in the Operational Executor domain. Scores for
both men and women are essentially identical in Figure 7.6. Some differences are observable, however, in the regressions against individual performance by region in Figure 7.7. HR professionals in Latin America get

much more performance mileage out of Implementing Workplace Policies than Advancing HR Technology. The pattern is similar in China and Australia, though less extreme. In Europe and North America, the two factors account for nearly equal proportions of an individual's performance.

Figure 7.6. **Individual Performance by Gender (associate rater only)**

	Male		Female	
	R^2	%	R^2	%
Implementing Workplace Policies	0.176	52%	0.155	51%
Advancing HR Technology	0.163	48%	0.151	49%

Figure 7.7. **Individual Performance by Region (associate raters only)**

	U.S.		Latin America		Europe		China		Australia		India	
	R^2	%	R^2	%	R^2	%	R^2	%	R^2	%	R^2	%
Implementing Workplace Policies	0.147	52%	0.239	58%	0.073	51%	0.296	54%	0.176	55%	0.226	53%
Advancing HR Technology	0.137	48%	0.175	42%	0.069	49%	0.255	46%	0.141	45%	0.2	47%

The differences are a bit more dramatic for individual performance by HR channel in Figure 7.8. Professionals in E-HR rely on HR technology by definition. In other HR channels, the effect of the two factors on performance is either equal or in favor of Implementing Workplace Policies. HR professionals in Service Centers, with their emphasis on consistent solutions to employee problems, had the strongest correlation between the policy aspects of HR and their individual performance—a finding that is not unexpected.

Figure 7.8. **Individual Performance by HR Channel (associate rater only)**

	Functional HR		Centers of Expertise		Embedded HR		Service Center		E-HR		Corporate HR	
	R^2	%	R^2	%	R^2	%	R^2	%	R^2	%	R^2	%
Implementing Workplace Policies	0.203	49%	0.191	50%	0.121	52%	0.206	55%	0.382	47%	0.172	52%
Advancing HR Technology	0.211	51%	0.188	50%	0.110	48%	0.167	45%	0.431	53%	0.158	48%

Size tells a story not unlike the effect of business size on the descriptive statistics. In smaller organizations, individual performance derives much more from policy and procedures than from technology, as shown in Figure 7.9. In larger organizations (1,000 employees and above), the two areas—policy and technology—tend to become one in the same, reflected in the near-equal scores in the figure below.

Figure 7.9. **Individual Performance by Business Size (associate rater only)**

	0 to 99		100 to 499		500 to 999		1,000 to 4,999		5,000 to 9,999		10,000 to 24,999		25,000+	
	R^2	%	R^2	%	R^2	%	R^2	%	R^2	%	R^2	%	R^2	%
Implementing Workplace Policies	0.246	58%	0.226	52%	0.265	54%	0.147	52%	0.139	50%	0.120	48%	0.138	51%
Advancing HR Technology	0.175	42%	0.211	48%	0.23	46%	0.137	48%	0.136	50%	0.129	52%	0.133	49%

Correlations to Business Performance

If you had to guess which area—policy vs. technology—accounted for more of an organization's business performance, you'd likely guess policy. In the eyes of both HR professionals and their non-HR associates, this seems to be the case, as show in Figure 7.10. However, when looking at business performance by gender, the numbers suggest a difference in Figure 7.11. Men seem to have somewhat stronger Luddite tendencies—their impact on the business is disproportionately (3:2) from the policy area rather than from technology.

Figure 7.10. **Business Performance by HR vs. Non-HR (associate raters only)**

	HR		Non-HR	
	329		361	
	R²	%	R²	%
Implementing Workplace Policies	0.085	53%	0.053	53%
Advancing HR Technology	0.076	47%	0.047	47%

Figure 7.11. **Business Performance by Gender (associate raters only)**

	Male		Female	
N	295		311	
	R²	%	R²	%
Implementing Workplace Policies	0.062	59%	0.113	50%
Advancing HR Technology	0.043	41%	0.115	50%

Business size is a variable that offers no consistent pattern in the correlations between Operational Executor factors and business performance in Figure 7.12. Technology wins out at three size increments, is tied with policy at one (10,000 to 24,999 employees), is somewhat lower at the two extremes, and is absolutely inconsequential for businesses between 5,000 and 9,999 employees. If we were to interpret the data literally, we would advise companies of this size not to invest a penny in HR technology—it simply has no correlation with business performance. Clearly, there is some noise in the data that we haven't been able to eliminate. Stay tuned for further research on this issue.

Figure 7.12. **Business Performance by Business Size (associate raters only)**

	0 to 99		100 to 499		500 to 999		1,000 to 4,999		5,000 to 9,999		10,000 to 24,999		25,000+	
	38		85		65		99		35		28		35	
	R²	%	R²	%	R²	%	R²	%	R²	%	R²	%	R²	%
Implementing Workplace Policies	0.176	55%	0.147	47%	0.048	35%	0.044	44%	0.024	99%	0.326	50%	0.430	66%
Advancing HR Technology	0.146	45%	0.167	53%	0.090	65%	0.055	56%	0.000	1%	0.322	50%	0.222	34%

It is somewhat of a surprise to see that Service Centers' impact on business results comes exclusively from the Advancing HR Technology factor, as shown in Figure 7.13. We reported the finding above that HR professionals in Service Centers derive more of their *individual* performance from the policy factor than from technology. This question clearly demands greater exploration. In both Corporate and Embedded HR, as well as in Centers of Expertise, business impact correlates quite a bit more with Implementing Workplace Policies than with Advancing HR Technology. Perhaps in these channels, business associates care far more about the administrative HR aspects themselves than the medium by which they are handled.

Figure 7.13. **Business Performance by Channel (associate raters only)**

	Functional HR		Centers of Expertise		Embedded HR		Service Center		Corporate HR	
N	190		165		187		70		126	
	R^2	%	R^2	%	R^2	%	R^2	%	R^2	%
Implementing Workplace Policies	0.076	46%	0.086	56%	0.082	56%	0.000	0%	0.084	62%
Advancing HR Technology	0.087	54%	0.069	44%	0.064	44%	0.012	100%	0.052	38%

Implications

As we begin to summarize the key empirical findings, it is worth mentioning again a data point that may have passed unnoticed in Chapter 2: Non-HR respondents place greater value on the Operational Executor domain (11% of an individual's performance) than do the HR participants themselves (7%). Perhaps this is an unintended consequence of the shared services and outsourcing movements. HR professionals seem to have attempted to distance themselves from the operational aspects of their work, telling themselves that this stuff is not sexy, not cool, and not strategic. But policy, procedure, and technology are definitely important. They are like housework—no one notices unless you don't do it. When we visit family or friends, we often see dirt or mess in their house that they have become accustomed to. And vice versa when they visit our house.

Secondly, individual HR professionals can easily feel victimized by the splintered and haphazard collection of policies that they are supposed to implement. In most cases, they did not have a hand in creating the policies. In fact, many policies are legacy ideas passed down from an earlier, simpler, more standardized, less global point in the company's history. HR professionals often are the first to realize that the policies no longer meet the needs of the business, yet they must implement them nonetheless. This is a difficult position in which to be placed.

Lest we go too far down the victimization path, however, we will share a couple of success stories from individuals who've figured out how to play the Operational Executor role effectively, and from companies where the structure and systems work efficiently and generate less frustration.

Individual Implications

Cheryl Kwok (disguised name) is an operational HR provider for a large manufacturing organization. At a site with more than 1,000 employees, hers is the challenge to provide all of the day-to-day, administrative, nuts-and-bolts HR support that is needed. She doesn't get involved in the strategic discussions with plant management. Nor does she dream up new talent management systems. Those areas fall under the stewardship of the plant's HR director. Cheryl's value is in managing the operational stuff competently, cheerfully, and quickly.

"I don't see myself staying in this role forever," Cheryl confides. "I mean, there are days when it really wears you down. But other days are extremely rewarding. The employees know I'm on their side. They see me solving their problems with them. And in the process, I'm getting a solid grounding in all kinds of HR issues—everything from discrimination lawsuits to maternity benefits. It will make a big difference to my career in the future, to have spent significant time on the firing line. I'll be able to talk the language that employees understand."

Cheryl's description highlights two important implications of the Operational Executor domain for individual HR professionals:

Look for the immediate rewards. Cheryl's description of the rewarding aspects of her work reminds us of a colleague who once said that he loved to change the baby's diaper. When we asked why, he said, "It's a concrete task with a clear start and a clear end, and when I'm finished I know I've made the world a better place for at least one person." Making the company a better place for one person at a time is not a bad description of much of the work that falls under the Operational Executor heading. ʹ

See it as a developmental step on your HR journey. No one would want to "change diapers" for his or her entire career. Cheryl has been able to embrace the Operational Executor domain as a crucial ticket to punch in her career progression. With a strong foundation in the fundamental people issues, she needs to continue to develop her business acumen (see Chapter 8). This will prepare her to be an HR leader who knows the business from the ground up.

Organizational Implications

When Embedded HR "business partners" find themselves overwhelmed by operational HR work, it's not just because they don't know how to say no. There is a structural issue involved as well. Service Centers do some operational tasks, but not the ones requiring personal attention. Centers of Expertise are hampered by their lack of local business knowledge, so Embedded HR professionals get pulled into this operational work even when encouraged to be strategic.

A missing role in the structure of HR services is the capacity to deliver and implement the corporate-driven initiatives while maintaining focus on the business and its customers. We see a variety of responses to this structural challenge:

- Create a specific operational role. As in the case of Cheryl Kwok, some companies are establishing the role of "junior business partners" assigned to HR generalists or business partners. These individuals turn the strategic ideas into operational practice within the business.
- Set up a pool of HR operational consultants. These are individuals assigned to a business to help turn the strategy into action. They focus on implementing specific projects within the business.
- Send implementation experts from corporate. We know of a company that uses a case advisor who comes from the Service Center to follow through on employee requests.

A large regional bank has pioneered the development of operational HR. Its solution has been to create an operational HR consulting pool. A team of high-performing, mid-level HR professionals is managed as a unit, reporting to the head of HR. They help implement solutions to important HR projects.

For example, one team helped develop and implement a strategy to reduce attrition in the call centers run by retail banking. Historically, Service Center and Embedded HR professionals would work together to scope the need, but would lack the resources to actually implement. The operational HR pool solves this problem, and has been responsible for a number of important deliverables.[2]

These structural solutions point to a future evolution of the Operational Executor role: to be the experts in implementing state-of-the-art strategies tailored to the business's needs. These HR professionals will be required to not only mind the implementation of policies and HR technology, but to meld what the business requires for success (driven by the Embedded HR professionals) with innovative and state-of-the-art HR practices (driven by the Centers of Expertise) into an operational plan that can be executed in a timely way.

Some of the challenges for organizations that are thinking of creating an operational HR capability are as follows:

Select the right individuals. Operational HR roles require people who are execution- and implementation-oriented. Over time, HR organizations may find that operational HR is a mix of long-timers (people who like to do this work) and rotational resources.

Develop the skills needed to be successful. Project and implementation management skills are crucial for operational HR professionals, but also team skills. Some diagnostic skills are also important. Operational HR resources should not be seen as simply "pairs of hands" to implement but, rather, involved early in developing solutions.

Manage priorities and workloads. Choosing what projects are appropriate for operational HR is an important process task. It could be tempting for HR to use its operational HR resources on work that other HR professionals simply do not want to do. This would trivialize the operational HR work and operational HR resources.

Measure contribution. Operational HR is project- and implementation-oriented, so its performance should be measured accordingly.

While it is easy to discount competencies in Operational Execution as either passé or outsourced to someone else, it is critical that the administrative processes within an organization be done flawlessly. A decade ago, many in HR advocated a "from-to" logic where HR should move from day-to-day to long term, from administrative to strategic, and from transaction to transformation. While appealing to the short term, this shift is fundamentally flawed. The logic we advocate is "and/also." The day-to-day, administrative, and transaction work must be done, and done well, to enable HR professionals to remain credible. The Operational Executor competencies in workforce policies and in technology make this happen.

Becoming an Operational Executor

As illustrated throughout this chapter, the Operational Executor domain has some impact on one's overall HR competence, but is not one of the "heavy hitters" in this regard. Each of its factors scores below average on the Developmental Priority Index, as shown in Figure 7.14. (For a quick reminder of how we calculate the DPI, refer to endnote #4 in Chapter 3.)

Figure 7.14. **Developmental Priority Index for Operational Executor Factors**

Competency Factor	Impact %	5.0-proficiency	DPI
Implementing Workplace Policies	3.35%	1.40	4.70
Advancing HR Technology	3.22%	1.37	4.41

* = Value above the average DPI for all 21 factors (5.64)

Developmental Actions for the Operational Executor
Some specific on-the-job experiences for boosting your competence as an Operational Executor are listed below:

Factor: Implementing Workplace Policies
- Visit with local companies that have established effective working relationships with their unions and make a presentation to management about what you learn.
- Conduct an informal survey of employees to discover how the company could help them better meet their non-work demands.
- Create an on-line bulletin board or blog where people can share ideas for achieving more satisfying work schedules.

- Apply Six Sigma quality standards and processes to improve the accuracy of all HR activities and practices.
- Compare your company's position on key legal issues to those of your competitors.
- Interview two on-staff attorneys to identify the major legal threats that potentially face your company. What are the major issues? What is the likely outcome?

Factor: Advancing HR Technology

- Work on a team to design an on-line competency evaluation process.
- Draw a graphic representation of the flow of major HR information in your HR department and identify the points at which HR technology might be more effectively utilized.
- Identify how to leverage 360-degree feedback more effectively through on-line follow-up.
- Determine which critical competencies within HR can be best taught through on-line technology, which are best taught on the job, and which are best taught in a classroom setting.
- Determine how your employee recruitment process might be redesigned to use less paper, replacing it with electronic tools.
- Experiment on employee portals from other companies.

CHAPTER 8

Business Ally

For more than five years, Acme Co. had a corner on the market for portable MP3 players. The competition was so far behind that Acme got fat and lazy. Then, a shift occurred in the competitive landscape. ABC Co., one of Acme's smaller competitors, released a greatly improved MP3 player that quickly became the "it" product. Despite its size and what used to be a massive market share, Acme found itself in the unfamiliar position of playing catch-up to ABC's new toy.

John Smith, Acme's vice president of HR, had been emphasizing HR process improvements throughout the five years of Acme's market dominance: How could HR's business benefits be defined and delivered more efficiently? How could Acme streamline hiring practices? What new people-management software was available? As useful as some of these improvements were, the HR department had been largely internally focused, referring to Acme employees as the "customers" of HR.

Acme's board of directors determined that the CEO had been asleep at the switch and replaced him with a new chief executive from the outside. In John's first meeting with the new CEO, he expected some praise for the HR improvements he'd implemented over the years. Instead, the CEO made it clear to John that he expected something else. John had statistical "proof" that HR was operating efficiently, but the CEO wasn't interested. "Unless HR can prove its efforts are having direct impact on the customer—the real external customer—the department is not creating value," he said. "HR should be so much more than an efficiently operated cost center. It should be having direct, measurable impact on the business. If not, most of the other stuff can be outsourced."

This got John's attention. As he thought of ways to connect HR more closely to the business, he realized he didn't really have a grasp of the business itself. He always had thought he understood his role, and that business knowledge was a "nice to have" rather than a "must have." After all, knowing how Acme made money didn't help deliver benefits any faster; nor did it help to mainstream the hiring process. With a growing sense of unease, he pondered the CEO's injunction and wondered how he could make HR something other than an efficient provider of internal services.

John Smith is not alone in his identity crisis. In working with HR professionals at all levels, we often find that their first instinct is to focus inside on their companies' HR practices. To force them outside their comfort zone, we often require that they interview one of their business executives prior to attending one of our HR leadership workshops. In this interview, the HR person is supposed to learn about the challenges the business is facing, what is keeping the executive awake at night, and so on. As they report on their interviews during the first morning of the workshop, the HR professionals spend around 80% of their time sharing the executives' impressions of HR practices. When we confront them and ask, "Why aren't you sharing with us the actual business challenges you uncovered," the response is telling. "This is what our business executive wanted to talk about," they say. "We didn't want to be rude and take over the conversation. Besides, it was great to hear our executive talking about what we do!"

In other words, business executives often don't even talk to HR people about the business. They have been conditioned over the years to steer the conversation toward HR practices whenever they engage with an HR professional. This is changing, of course, particularly for HR people who work in business-facing roles (Embedded HR, senior HR execs, etc.). But for many people in our profession, being considered a true Business Ally remains an important and somewhat elusive goal.

This chapter will report and analyze the research results for the Business Ally domain of HR competence. We will focus on the following three areas:
- Defining the Business Ally domain and its factors.
- Pointing out insights and further questions from the statistical data.

- Offering illustration and examples of effective practices in becoming true Business Allies.

Defining the Domain

As John Smith found out, HR professionals are increasingly expected to contribute *directly* to the success of the business. Businesses succeed by profitably responding to changing external conditions. HR professionals help drive the success of the business by knowing the "social context" or broader setting in which the business operates.

In addition, HR professionals must understand the value chain of the business—how it makes money, how it converts less-valuable inputs into more-valuable outputs, and how resources within the company are arranged to deliver on customer expectations. Further, HR professionals (like their counterparts in other functions) should understand the value proposition of the business: who its customers are, and why these customers buy the company's products and services.

Being a Business Ally is much more than simply understanding the business. It's using that in-depth understanding to anticipate issues and offer solutions that will drive business success. By understanding the business and the social context in which the business operates, HR becomes better positioned to influence business decisions. Over the years, the term "HR business partner" has gained popularity. We have found recently, however, that some organizations no longer favor the term. "Please don't call us 'partners,'" said a group of mid-level HR managers at a well-known international telecommunications company. "Being a 'partner' implies we're separate from the business. We consider ourselves—and more importantly, our fellow managers consider us—full-fledged members of the management team. We just happen to focus on people issues rather than finance, research, sales, or operations."

This shift to "business people" rather than "business partners" anticipates a natural evolution of the profession. Over the 20 years we have conducted this survey, the role of Business Ally has shifted dramatically. Originally, understanding the business was very important for an HR professional to be perceived as competent. This held true until 2002, when for the first time "understanding the business" became one of the weakest statistical predictors of an HR professional's overall competence. It isn't that understanding the business has become less important; it is perhaps more important than ever. However, it is now considered "table stakes" rather than a differentiator. Being a Business Ally is expected, something you must have to even begin to play. Not understanding your business, your industry, and how it fits into the global market will hinder you from being able to contribute to more strategic areas at the intersection of people and business. And being a Business Ally means not only understanding the business, but acting on that understanding (with a bit of "attitude"—see Chapter 3 on being a Credible Activist).

Business Ally Domain Factors
Factor: Interpreting Social Context
The world continues to flatten, markets continue to open, and expectations of consumers and shareholders continue to rise. In addition, we've seen an increase in the importance of "good will," or a firm's reputation and credibility in the local and global communities. Understanding the context of the global economy, geopolitical realities, technological changes, and demographic shifts helps HR professionals create practices and processes that positively influence stakeholders, both within and (especially) outside a company.

HR professionals that can effectively Interpret Social Context are skilled at:
- Identifying the globalization of business and its implications.
- Grasping the external political environment.
- Being able to clarify social issues that may impact their industry.
- Recognizing the demographic trends that influence their business.
- Understanding government regulation and how HR practices are affected by this regulation.

Factor: Serving the Value Chain
To add value to business decisions, to have greater credibility, and to more effectively deliver HR practices, HR professionals need knowledge of all activities that comprise the value chain. The value chain consists of several elements that link market demand with internal supply, starting with knowledge of external customers, suppliers, and competitors. The dynamics and requirements of the competitive environment are then translated into internal financial and production requirements. Finally, products and services are distributed to the marketplace through various channels.

Not all activities in the value chain are of equal value. In discount retailing, purchasing and store layout are generally more critical to success than individual sales efforts. In pharmaceuticals, R&D tends to be more important than manufacturing. Since the importance of activities in the value chain can change as business conditions evolve, HR must understand the value chain and remain current on the activities that are most critical to the company. As discussed in Chapter 6, understanding the value chain is a prerequisite to being a true Strategy Architect.

In our work with HR professionals, we often ask, "So who is your customer?" Almost without thinking (as if it's a silly question), they nearly always respond, "The employees of the company." In one sense, this is to their credit; HR people are and should be concerned about the people they serve internally. At the same time, this single-minded focus on employees is too narrow, too limiting. The "customers" of any group in a company are those who take money out of their wallets or purses and give it to the company— real customers who buy the company's products and/or services. When HR professionals develop the reflex to focus on real customers, they will design and deliver programs and services that better align with the business.

Serving the Value Chain requires skills and understanding in the following areas:
- Competitor analysis.
- Knowing the requirements of external customers.
- Understanding supplier relationships.

Factor: Articulating the Value Proposition

One of the most difficult challenges for many HR professionals is to formulate a clear definition of their company's value proposition. A value proposition is a clear, concise series of factual statements that describes the appeal of your company's products or services. A strong value proposition would suggest that customers would be crazy to do business with one of your competitors. Naturally, such a value proposition would deliver results such as increased revenue, increased market share, and improved customer retention levels.

HR professionals who are able to Articulate the Value Proposition know how their companies create wealth. For example:

- Companies can create wealth by developing a portfolio of businesses that maximize returns while mitigating risks. To do this effectively, they need to determine which businesses they will buy, keep, and divest. They must also determine which tasks will be conducted internally and which should be outsourced.
- Companies can create wealth by determining which businesses they will emphasize, which markets they will pursue, and which marketing efforts will be used in selected markets.
- Companies create wealth by identifying the basic processes through which products and services will be provided and the quality standards that are acceptable.

HR professionals who can Articulate the Value Proposition for their company play a more proactive part in strategy discussions and develop systems and procedures to aid in resulting decisions.

Factor: Leveraging Business Technology

Technology has changed the way that business is conducted. Understanding that technology and being able to leverage it as HR professionals create the systems through which the flow of people, work, and information can greatly add to the business's overall success. HR professionals who Leverage Business Technology are aware of, and are able to, leverage:

- New emerging technologies.
- E-commerce.
- Production and manufacturing processes.
- Design of work processes.
- Computer information systems.

Business Ally by the Numbers

According to non-HR respondents, overall scores for Business Ally were the lowest among the six competency domains, both in terms of proficiency (in the eyes of all respondent groups) and impact on individual performance (in the eyes of the non-HR respondent group) (see Figures 2.9 and 2.17). However, as mentioned earlier in this chapter, being a Business Ally provides an important foundation for more strategic work.

At the level of the individual factors within the Business Ally domain, performance and impact vary by respondent group. As in the preceding five chapters, we will present the comparative data for all four factors across the different respondent groups, and point out unusual or suggestive differences in the findings as we go.

By looking at proficiency scores for the four factors, we immediately notice the lower self scores across the board (see Figure 8.1). HR participants judge themselves to be less competent in these four factors than do either their HR counterparts or their non-HR associates. Perhaps non-HR associates *assume* that HR professionals understand the business when this is not true. Keep in mind that these four factors scored the lowest of any factors in any domain within the new competency model. Clearly, this is an area where both self-perception and peer perception indicate that progress could be made.

For decades, many have talked about HR "knowing the business" but it is either not happening or the bar is being raised more quickly than the HR profession can keep up. HR professional accreditation tests need to revisit their emphasis on business acumen. To be sure, we are somewhat frustrated that the profession of HR has not made more progress in business acumen. It is past time for HR professionals to not only know the theory and practice of HR, to be able to form positive relationships, and to work well with others, but to also master the basics of business.

Figure 8.1. **Overall Mean Scores by Respondent (associate raters only)**

	HR Participants	HR Associates	Non-HR Associates
Interpreting Social Context	3.57	3.69	3.71
Serving the Value Chain	3.42	3.56	3.45
Articulating the Value Proposition	3.30	3.48	3.38
Leveraging Business Technology	3.28	3.47	3.36

Interestingly, the pattern across all three respondent groups was the same. Interpreting Social Context was the strongest of the four, while Leveraging Business Technology was the weakest. Non-HR associate raters, while they were generally more severe critics across the four factors, did give HR participants the highest score for Interpreting Social Context.

By looking at the data across regions, we see the same pattern that we have in other regional comparisons. Scores for more established economies, such as the U.S., Europe, and Australia, are higher than scores for emerging economies such as China (see Figure 8.2). The pattern of the scores across the factors is also similar, in that each region's relative strengths and weaknesses match the overall data, with two exceptions. First, Latin America gets a particularly low score (in comparison to its other scores) for Articulating the Value Proposition. Second, China's scores are remarkably similar across the board, with a 0.10 spread between them as opposed to the 0.30 spread in other regions. Additionally, the Chinese scores are lower than the scores in all other regions. This could be due to the relative newness of the HR profession in China. It could also be due to the development of the economy itself. As China opens up from a state-controlled, communist economy to the "one country, two systems" model, learning the ins and outs of capitalism presents a steep learning curve for some HR professionals.

Figure 8.2. **Overall Mean Scores by Region (associate raters only)**

	U.S.	Latin America	Europe	China	Australia	India
Interpreting Social Context	3.76	3.72	3.77	3.54	3.68	3.83
Serving the Value Chain	3.55	3.52	3.54	3.45	3.48	3.79
Articulating the Value Proposition	3.50	3.42	3.44	3.44	3.36	3.53
Leveraging Business Technology	3.41	3.52	3.32	3.45	3.36	3.62

Cutting the data by industry offers some noteworthy comparisons (see Figure 8.3). For example, pharmaceuticals/chemicals scores the highest by far in Interpreting Social Context. This is not surprising, given the pharmaceutical industry's competitive landscape. It is extremely global, R&D-intensive, highly regulated, and dependent not only on understanding the needs of current customers but society in general. Making sure that HR professionals can understand and interpret social context would be a logical focus for companies in the pharmaceutical industry.

The service industries score highest across the four factors, and rank No. 1 compared to other industries in Serving the Value Chain, Articulating the Value Proposition, and Leveraging Business Technology. Services-industry HR people evidently are more in tune with the entire delivery process (given the customer-facing nature of their companies) than their counterparts in many of the other industries represented.

Figure 8.3. **Overall Mean Scores by Industry (associate raters only)**

	Agriculture	Mining	Construction	Food	Manufacturing	Pharmaceuticals/ Chemicals	Utilities	Wholesale/Retail Trade	Banking & Real Estate	Services	Public Administrations
Interpreting Social Context	3.61	3.66	3.50	3.62	3.73	3.85	3.73	3.70	3.60	3.77	3.71
Serving the Value Chain	3.52	3.49	3.45	3.45	3.47	3.53	3.50	3.50	3.53	3.66	3.54
Articulating the Value Proposition	3.47	3.46	3.44	3.38	3.45	3.49	3.40	3.45	3.39	3.50	3.39
Leveraging Business Technology	3.42	3.48	3.43	3.34	3.43	3.43	3.45	3.31	3.38	3.49	3.45

There are some obvious findings in the HR channel comparisons as shown in Figure 8.4. As expected, E-HR is best (by far) at Leveraging Business Technology. Interpreting Social Context is most important for Embedded HR and Corporate HR, where there is more interaction with the business environment and where understanding the business, industry, and community have much more impact. Serving the Value Chain is performed best by those in a Center of Expertise, where the focus is on fulfilling the needs of different areas within the value chain.

Figure 8.4. **Overall Mean Scores by HR Channel**

	Functional HR	Centers of Expertise	Embedded HR	Service Center	E-HR	Corporate HR
Interpreting Social Context	3.59	3.71	3.75	3.56	3.65	3.73
Serving the Value Chain	3.47	3.56	3.53	3.49	3.55	3.50
Articulating the Value Proposition	3.39	3.49	3.43	3.38	3.64	3.48
Leveraging Business Technology	3.45	3.47	3.39	3.43	3.61	3.43

Cutting the data by business size also provides some insights, as shown in Figure 8.5. In general, the larger the company, the better it is at Interpreting Social Context. Large multinationals typically have more complex sets of interrelationships with governments, business partners, customers, and communities around the globe—and larger companies tend to have more impact on society than smaller companies. Regarding Leveraging Business Technology, small companies and large companies seem to understand and leverage business technology better than companies in the middle. Very small companies are often technology-dependent and rely on innovative technology to grow. Very large companies may also require technology to be transformed, and are able to invest in the latest information systems and data base applications.

Figure 8.5. **Overall Mean Scores by Business Size (associate raters only)**

	0 to 99	100 to 499	500 to 999	1,000 to 4,999	5,000 to 9,999	10,000 to 24,999	25,000+
Interpreting Social Context	3.59	3.56	3.66	3.66	3.78	3.72	3.81
Serving the Value Chain	3.59	3.42	3.48	3.48	3.58	3.58	3.54
Articulating the Value Proposition	3.46	3.33	3.41	3.40	3.50	3.46	3.54
Leveraging Business Technology	3.46	3.35	3.47	3.43	3.41	3.40	3.46

Correlations to Individual Performance

To what extent does proficiency in each of Business Ally's four factors affect an individual's perceived competence as an HR professional? Again, we have analyzed the data several ways to highlight similarities and provide insights into how different groups view the impact of each factor on individual performance. The data are important not only for general understanding of the HR profession, but for personal development planning. Understanding how each factor affects the perception of performance gives you further information for prioritizing your development needs.

The first analysis compares the impact of the four factors on individual performance by gender in Figure 8.6. Little difference is seen between men and women on these factors. The Business Ally's factors have a stronger correlation to performance overall for men than for women, as seen in the higher $R2$ values. The order of impact is similar, with minor differences. Interpreting Social Context clearly has the greatest influence on an individual's perceived competence. For women, Leveraging Business Technology has slightly less relative impact than for men.

Figure 8.6. **Individual Performance by Gender (associate rater only)**

	Male		Female	
	R^2	%	R^2	%
Interpreting Social Context	0.204	32%	0.177	33%
Serving the Value Chain	0.131	21%	0.121	22%
Articulating the Value Proposition	0.138	22%	0.113	21%
Leveraging Business Technology	0.164	26%	0.128	24%

By looking at importance across regions, we see a couple of interesting differences in Figure 8.7. First, the general pattern of importance depends on region. While it is true that in nearly all regions Interpreting Social Context was the highest impact factor, there are significant differences after that. For example:

- In Europe, Serving the Value Chain is almost as important as Interpreting Social Context. A more traditional view of business expectations may account for this, or it could be that Europeans have for years been immersed in a complex environment, including significant government regulation and cross-cultural business relationships, resulting in less differentiation for this factor. Certainly, European businesses have long led the movement toward social responsibility.
- China has some extremes for Interpreting Social Context and Leveraging Business Technology. Mark Huselid and his colleagues found that, paradoxically, HR has the greatest impact in organizations that have not invested as much in HR. Perhaps as China continues to invest more in HR practices, the business impact of HR will increase.
- In Australia and Asia Pacific, Interpreting Social Context accounts for 35% of the importance allotted to the Business Ally domain. This is higher than in the other regions, perhaps reflecting the multicultural reality of Australia's position in the dynamic Asia Pacific region.
- In Latin America, Leveraging Business Technology is a much bigger differentiator than in other regions. This could be a reflection of the rapid introduction and acceptance of information systems and other such tools in Latin America, whereas in more developed economies such technologies have a longer track record of use.

Figure 8.7. **Individual Performance by Region (associate raters only)**

	U.S.		Latin America		Europe		China		Australia/ Asia Pacific		India	
	R²	%	R²	%	R²	%	R²	%	R²	%	R²	%
Interpreting Social Context	0.142	31%	0.168	27%	0.132	31%	0.256	30%	0.231	35%	0.196	31%
Serving the Value Chain	0.105	23%	0.129	21%	0.118	28%	0.164	19%	0.136	21%	0.153	24%
Articulating the Value Proposition	0.107	23%	0.130	21%	0.081	19%	0.191	22%	0.130	20%	0.165	26%
Leveraging Business Technology	0.109	24%	0.197	32%	0.097	23%	0.243	28%	0.158	24%	0.113	18%

The data in Figure 8.8 also confirm the roles played by those working in each HR channel. Again, Interpreting Social Context is the big winner. Articulating the Value Proposition is most important for Embedded HR; more than their peers in others roles, they need to understand how the business makes money. To be seen as effective, those working in Service Centers must understand the social context, but also master business technology.

Figure 8.8. **Individual Performance by HR Channel (associate raters only)**

	Functional HR		Centers of Expertise		Embedded HR		Service Center		E-HR		Corporate HR	
	R²	%	R²	%	R²	%	R²	%	R²	%	R²	%
Interpreting Social Context	0.223	31%	0.208	32%	0.138	32%	0.152	36%	0.350	29%	0.195	31%
Serving the Value Chain	0.160	22%	0.145	22%	0.093	21%	0.052	12%	0.284	24%	0.139	22%
Articulating the Value Proposition	0.139	19%	0.141	22%	0.103	24%	0.062	15%	0.246	21%	0.126	20%
Leveraging Business Technology	0.199	28%	0.156	24%	0.100	23%	0.151	36%	0.307	26%	0.170	27%

Looking at importance to individual performance across size of business in Figure 8.9, Interpreting Social Context remains the most important, but is particularly acute in very small companies (39% of impact). Understanding the global environment will position HR professionals to demonstrate true business leadership within these small enterprises.

For smaller companies (0 to 5,000 employees), Leveraging Business Technology also is significant; in larger firms, it has less impact and in fact becomes less important than either Serving the Value Chain or Articulating the Value Proposition (for companies with more than 25,000 employees).

Figure 8.9. **Individual Performance by Business Size (associate raters only)**

	0 to 99		100 to 499		500 to 999		1,000 to 4,999		5,000 to 9,999		10,000 to 24,999		25,000+	
	R^2	%	R^2	%	R^2	%	R^2	%	R^2	%	R^2	%	R^2	%
Interpreting Social Context	0.237	39%	0.246	30%	0.203	29%	0.159	35%	0.194	31%	0.127	28%	0.163	34%
Serving the Value Chain	0.098	16%	0.162	20%	0.152	22%	0.090	20%	0.170	27%	0.110	24%	0.104	22%
Articulating the Value Proposition	0.126	21%	0.159	19%	0.144	21%	0.098	21%	0.125	20%	0.108	24%	0.109	23%
Leveraging Business Technology	0.150	25%	0.248	30%	0.189	27%	0.112	24%	0.139	22%	0.107	24%	0.102	21%

Correlations to Business Performance

HR associates have a slightly different opinion than non-HR raters regarding the impact of these factors on business performance, according to Figure 8.10. The correlations for HR associates showed greater impact for Serving the Value Chain (30%) than for Interpreting Social Context (26%), whereas non-HR raters placed the most importance on Interpreting Social Context (40%), followed by Leveraging Business Technology (22%). Interestingly, HR people viewed Leveraging Business Technology as the least important of the factors to business performance.

While this ranking could be due to point of view—HR professionals are more conscious of internal issues (Serving the Value Chain and Articulating the Value Proposition), while non-HR associates are more conscious of external issues (Interpreting the Social Context and Leveraging Business Technology)—it is clear that a disconnect exists within Business Ally. HR professionals may want to take a look at this discrepancy and determine which of these items truly contributes to business performance for their company.

Figure 8.10. **Business Performance by HR vs. Non HR (associate raters only)**

	HR		Non-HR	
N	329		361	
	R^2	%	R^2	%
Interpreting Social Context	0.082	26%	0.057	40%
Serving the Value Chain	0.096	30%	0.028	20%
Articulating the Value Proposition	0.075	23%	0.024	17%
Leveraging Business Technology	0.068	21%	0.031	22%

Another interesting cut of the data was by gender, as shown in Figure 8.11. The impact of gender on individual performance within these factors was minimal (see Figure 8.6). This is not the case for business performance. Respondents saw greater impact for men from Serving the Value Chain, followed by Interpreting Social Context. For women, the highest-impact factor was Leveraging Business Technology, followed by Interpreting Social Context. This perhaps reflects the stereotype that women are less avid users of technology than men, and hence its use is a greater differentiator for women than for men.

Figure 8.11. **Business Performance by Gender (associate raters only)**

	Male		Female	
N	295		311	
	R^2	%	R^2	%
Interpreting Social Context	0.064	28%	0.068	28%
Serving the Value Chain	0.069	31%	0.051	21%
Articulating the Value Proposition	0.057	25%	0.043	18%
Leveraging Business Technology	0.036	16%	0.079	33%

By looking at importance to business performance by business size in Figure 8.12, we see that in very small companies, Serving the Value Chain does not seem to be particularly important. This may be due to the fact that in smaller companies, the value chain is less complex than in larger ones.

Figure 8.12. **Business Performance by Business Size (associate raters only)**

	0 to 99		100 to 499		500 to 999		1,000 to 4,999		5,000 to 9,999		10,000 to 24,999		25,000+	
N	38		85		65		99		35		28		35	
	R^2	%	R^2	%	R^2	%	R^2	%	R^2	%	R^2	%	R^2	%
Interpreting Social Context	0.120	38%	0.194	27%	0.079	36%	0.047	25%	0.102	19%	0.251	24%	0.422	31%
Serving the Value Chain	0.024	8%	0.160	23%	0.088	41%	0.027	14%	0.193	36%	0.342	33%	0.268	19%
Articulating the Value Proposition	0.085	27%	0.177	25%	0.019	9%	0.073	39%	0.110	20%	0.261	25%	0.382	28%
Leveraging Business Technology	0.087	28%	0.176	25%	0.032	15%	0.042	22%	0.133	25%	0.185	18%	0.308	22%

Figure 8.13 shows quite dramatic differences across the HR channels:

- 50% of the impact of these factors on business performance is attributed to Serving the Value Chain for HR professionals working in a Service Center. The purpose of a Service Center is to leverage the ability to serve the value chain, so this makes sense.
- Those in Embedded HR could benefit from focusing more on Interpreting Social Context, and less on Serving the Value Chain. They also should be able to understand and Articulate the Value Proposition, and Leverage Business Technology. The nature of Embedded HR roles requires them to understand the business and the environment where it is operating, to have a good idea of how resources are organized to compete, and to know how to take advantage of emerging business technology in order to help the business compete.
- Functional HR, much like those in Service Centers, needs to focus on Serving the Value Chain. Additionally, an HR professional in a functional role should have an understanding of business technology and be able to leverage it to automate some of the more transactional portions of her job.

Figure 8.13. **Business Performance by Channel (associate raters only)**

	Functional HR		Centers of Expertise		Embedded HR		Service Center		Corporate HR	
N	190		165		187		70		126	
	R^2	%	R^2	%	R^2	%	R^2	%	R^2	%
Interpreting Social Context	0.064	23%	0.086	25%	0.031	42%	0.039	29%	0.064	21%
Serving the Value Chain	0.080	28%	0.049	14%	0.002	3%	0.066	50%	0.099	33%
Articulating the Value Proposition	0.065	23%	0.067	20%	0.021	28%	0.014	11%	0.090	30%
Leveraging Business Technology	0.072	26%	0.140	41%	0.019	26%	0.013	10%	0.051	17%

Conclusion

In summary, the time has come for HR professionals to focus on being business *people* rather than business *partners*. A good example of a company that fosters the development of Business Allies is Cardinal Health. A key part of Cardinal Health's growth strategy in the past has been to acquire medical supply companies and leave them alone. This strategy has evolved over the years, and now Cardinal Health finds itself trying to integrate the companies it acquires. From the onset, HR is heavily involved in an acquisition. The leadership team (of which HR is a part) looks to HR to assess the top-level people within the organization, devise ways to retain the top performers, determine what promises the parent company can make to Wall Street, and identify synergies that can be leveraged.

None of this would be possible if HR professionals at Cardinal Health were not Business Allies. To be able to strategically contribute during these acquisitions, Cardinal Health HR needs competency in all four factors mentioned above. They must understand:
- The social context of the business—what is happening and how the company's actions will affect overall stock price and competitive position.
- The value chain of the parent as well as the acquired companies—opportunities to leverage synergies, eliminate redundancies, integrate leadership teams, etc.

- The value proposition of the acquisition—why are they acquiring this company (efficiencies, distribution channel, etc.) and how resources need to be reallocated to make sure that this acquisition is effective.
- Business technology of both companies—what will need to be changed, what can be leveraged from the acquisition company, what will need to be adopted from Cardinal Health.

Thus, the strategic role that HR at Cardinal Health plays is based on a solid understanding of the business that they serve.

The benefits of executing on the four factors of the Business Ally domain are clear:

- Business savvy builds the credibility of the HR professional as well as the HR function within the organization. When HR professionals speak intelligently about a balance sheet or make recommendations based on market conditions, their credibility increases. This credibility allows them opportunities to participate in increasingly more strategic discussions at all levels of the organization.
- Business skill provides a foundation for more strategic types of work. As we mentioned earlier, being a Business Ally will not create a competitive advantage for either the HR professional or the business. However, understanding the ins and outs of the business and its environment provides a foundation upon which to build, as HR creates systems and processes that truly foster a competitive advantage.
- Understanding the business and the environment in which it operates is important to helping the organization respond. For example, if you rely heavily on engineering talent and are unfamiliar with the needs of your competitors, the expectations of the engineers whom you will hire, and your company's financial standing, you will almost certainly fail at crafting an effective recruiting program.

We began this chapter by examining the predicament of John Smith, Acme's vice president of HR. His new CEO was clear: John needed to be a business leader first and an HR specialist second. This is the essence of the Business Ally domain. True Business Allies are not distinguishable from other business leaders. A top HR person recently told us that she knew she was effectively playing the Business Ally role when an outside observer watched her in a management team meeting and didn't know that she was the head of HR. She actively participated in business debates. When needed, her HR expertise came to the forefront, but the dividing line between business leader and support staff manager was all but erased.

Becoming a Business Ally

Becoming a Business Ally first and foremost requires a change of perspective. This is difficult, but necessary. Instead of looking at the organization in compartments—marketing, finance, purchasing, operations, HR, etc.—start looking at the organization as a whole. By viewing the organization instead of any one department within that organization, interactions between the organizations and how they perform become more relevant to your job. The more relevant they become, the more apt you are to pay attention to them.

A quick and dirty way to assess your capability and awareness in the Business Ally domains is by answering the following questions:
- Who is our largest customer and why do they buy from us?
- Who is our largest competitor and why do people buy from them?
- What is our stock price?
- What is our P/E ratio?
- What was the profit and revenue of our division/company last year?
- Who sits on the board of directors?
- What is our market share?
- Is our market segment growing or shrinking?
- What are the emerging technology trends facing our industry?
- What are the top two or three priorities for our business leaders this year?
- What social and political trends might be disruptive to our industry?

This quick business literacy test gauges not only knowledge but awareness. Being a Business Ally is not about memorizing the financials of a company (although it definitely cannot hurt), but rather about being aware of what is going on around you. While you don't have direct responsibility for the budget (except for yours), understanding where your company stands on the budget helps you to make better decisions within your sphere of influence. Likewise, being aware of who your major competitors are and why people buy from them helps you build a culture that is better able to compete.

Of the four factors, Interpreting Social Context is clearly the highest impact, with Leveraging Business Technology a distant second. Using our Developmental Priority Index, however, brings Leveraging Business Technology higher on the priority list, since HR professionals are less proficient in this factor (see Figure 8.14). None of these factors scores above the average DPI, however. (For a reminder of the way we calculate the DPI, refer to endnote #4 in Chapter 3.)

Figure 8.14. **Development Priority Index Values for Business Ally Factors**

Competency Factor	Impact %	5.0-Proficiency	DPI
Interpreting Social Context	3.78%	1.30	4.91
Serving the Value Chain	2.55%	1.48	3.77
Articulating the Value Proposition	2.47%	1.56	3.84
Leveraging Business Technology	2.89%	1.57	4.54

= Value above the average DPI for all 21 factors (5.64)

Developmental Actions for the Business Ally

The following items are on-the-job ideas for increasing your proficiency in each of the four factors for Business Ally:

Factor: Interpreting Social Context
- Search the internet for Dr. Geert Hofstede and his cultural assessments. Research cultures where you currently do (or will do) business in the near future.
- Prepare a three-page memo on the context of the industry and culture in which your business primarily operates. Take into account all stakeholders: investors, customers, communities, employees, and line managers.
- Prepare a presentation on the demographic trends that will affect how your department crafts HR practices within your business.

Factor: Serving the Value Chain
- Interview leading thinkers from each component of the value chain.
- Lead a focus group whose task is to identify common interests and agendas that might improve quality, reduce costs or time, or create more effective processes, products, or services.
- Develop a process for identifying and transferring internal best practices across departments or businesses within your company.
- Identify which aspect of the value chain of your company is most critical with respect to its wealth-creating abilities, and establish a study plan for becoming more knowledgeable in that area.

- Conduct a competitive study that includes a value chain analysis of your major competitors. On which aspects of the value chain does your company outperform your competitors and vice versa? On which aspects of the value chain is it most important for your company to outperform the competition?

Factor: Articulating the Value Proposition

- Interview an investment analyst who is a specialist in your company's industry about the factors that constitute wealth creation in your industry.
- Be involved in a task force to determine the outsourcing criteria for your company and the activities of your firm that should be outsourced.
- Lead a discussion with a diagonal cross section of informed people in your company on the topic of wealth-creation activities. Determine what percentage of your employees create 90% of the wealth and what they do.
- Work with your company's investment officer to identify the buy, hold, or sell criteria of some of your dominant shareholders.
- Lead a task force that identifies the ethical principles of your firm. Discuss how to enhance the firm's ethical behavior and how to communicate its ethical position to the financial community.

Factor: Leveraging Business Technology

- Brainstorm ways to improve the current IT systems so that they better serve your customers.
- Evaluate your business's current use of technology. Benchmark your competitors to determine whether improvements can be made.
- Assess what changes will need to be made to current people, systems, and processes in order to implement.
- Educate yourself on current developments in the information technology field. Develop a cost/benefit analysis for a proposed technological improvement within your company.

Building an HR Department

We often hear comments such as, "I like my doctor, but I don't like the medical system." "I like my child's teacher, but I don't like educators." "I like my lawyer, but I don't like attorneys." "I like my Congressman; but I don't like Congress." And, in HR, we often hear, "I like my HR person, but I don't like the HR department."[1] The previous chapters have shown how HR professionals contribute as *individuals* to help themselves and their business to be successful. This chapter focuses on the HR *department* more than the individual HR professionals.

An HR department should operate as a business within a business. This means that it has a clear strategy and purpose and an organization structure to deliver on that purpose. The research in this chapter is based on the premise that having talented HR professionals is not enough; these professionals need to work together as an HR department for the business to get all it can from HR services. All-star teams of isolated and disconnected individuals generally would not beat high-performing teams who make the whole more than the sum of the individual parts. HR departments that successfully bring together the individual skills of HR professionals can have a positive impact on business performance.

In a company meeting, HR professionals examined the competencies required to be effective and then worked to create personal action plans for linking strategy and HR practices. Recently, they had implemented an e-HR delivery system for the transaction work in their organization structure and were very frustrated that too many mistakes were occurring. In a discussion with the head of shared services, people pointed fingers and blamed him for not doing his job and demanded that he improve.

Blaming the weak link in an HR organization is misguided and far too common. When one part of an HR department is broken or not operating well, it is easy to blame another part of HR and distance oneself from it. This is a false hope. Those outside HR who use HR are not interested in who is to blame and the subtleties of which HR delivery mechanism is not working. They want "HR" to work—when one part does not work, nothing works. Rather than finger pointing, it would have been more helpful for HR colleagues in other areas to figure out how to identify and solve the problems in the service center so that the entire function could move forward as one.

Learning to think about the HR department as more than the sum of the isolated individuals became a focus of this study by addressing four questions:

- How important is the HR department in helping the business perform better?
- Which stakeholders should the HR department serve to increase business performance?
- Where should an HR department focus to increase business performance?
- What HR practices should get priority for an HR department to increase business performance?

To answer these questions, we asked HR participants and HR associates questions about the HR department. Their scores were averaged to the organization level so we have multiple respondents' (vs. key informant) data on the department questions we asked. Likewise, the business performance measure is the aggregate of scores for business performance on four dimensions of business performance aggregated for all respondents within a business. (See Chapter 2.)

How Important Is the HR Department in Helping the Business Perform Better?

When we tried to understand the extent to which an HR department could impact business performance, we selected three ways to characterize an HR department: stakeholders, focus, and HR practices.

Stakeholders. Stakeholders are the groups of people that HR departments serve. We have argued elsewhere that the value of a transaction is defined by the receiver more than the giver,[2] so we identified stakeholders, or receivers of the work done by HR departments. HR departments can work to deliver value to those inside the organization (employees or line managers) or those outside the organization (customers, investors, or communities).

Focus. Those leading an HR department can focus the department's attention on an array of activities. These foci are often the priorities of the HR department and reflect how resources (budget, people, and time) are dedicated.

HR practices. There are a host of HR practices that the HR department may design and deliver. We wanted to know the extent to which these practices delivered value to the organization.

We also wanted to determine the department's capability for each of these three dimensions. For example, we wanted to find out the extent to which the department was capable of meeting the needs of each of the five stakeholders.

In Chapter 1, we made the distinction between individual *competence*, which encompasses the knowledge, skill and values of individuals (HR professionals, in this case), and department *capability*, which is the department's ability to serve stakeholders, focus attention, and create value through their HR practices. In Chapters 2 through 8, we examined the extent to which individual competencies in six domains affected individual performance and organizational performance. When we shifted to the department level of analysis, we want to determine how the department's capabilities related to the performance of the business.

With data on the three dimensions of the HR department, we could calculate the extent to which the department affected business performance. As with the individual competencies, we used a regression analysis showing the extent to which each of the three dimensions of the department explained business performance. Figure 9.1 shows the overall results of the three dimensions of the department on business performance and compares these results to the impact of HR competencies on business performance.

This table shows that the six competency domains explain 20.7% of the performance of the business. (Figure 2.23 details these six domains and their impact on performance.) Figure 9.1 also shows that

Figure 9.1. **Relative Impact of Department Dimensions on Organizational Performance**	
Department Dimension	R^{2*}
Stakeholders	.224
HR Focus	.239
HR Practices	.291
Note: Multiple Regression, all HR professional competency domains	.207

each of the dimensions of the HR department explains more about business performance than the competencies of the individual HR professionals. The average of the three dimensions is 25%. This means that the HR department explains 25% of business performance, while the competencies of the HR professionals explain 20%. The HR department is about 25% more important (20% vs. 25%) than the individual skills of HR professionals in predicting business performance.

The adage "I like my HR professional, but I don't like HR," may no longer be valid. If the department explains more about business performance than the competencies of individual HR professionals, then more attention should be paid to HR departments and how they can add value.

There are a number of implications of this finding. First, while it is important to hire, train, and reward individual HR professionals, it is equally, if not more, important to make sure that the HR department serves stakeholders, focuses attention on the right issues, and delivers value-added HR practices. Individual training of people in HR may not be sufficient. Ensuring that individual HR professionals join together around the right issues also affects business performance.

Second, many have done individual competency audits to determine their HR professionals' skill level. We would now argue that HR department audits should also be conducted to determine the extent that the HR department is delivering on its promises. These HR department audits identify the extent to which the HR department is serving stakeholders, focusing attention, and delivering value-added HR practices.

Third, HR executives who lead an HR department need to be thoughtful on creating both an HR strategy so that the department has a clear focus and an HR structure so that the different roles and responsibilities in the department work well together. The HR department's strategy and structure must evolve to operate as a business within a business.[3]

Which Stakeholders Should the HR Department Serve to Increase Business Performance?

As suggested above, HR departments create value as determined by their receivers. When we meet with HR professionals, we often ask who the customers of HR are. Their answer is "the employees of the company." We believe this is incomplete. We believe that HR departments have the potential to add value to the following five stakeholders: employees, line managers, external customers, community and investors.

- **Employees:** An HR department helps employees have both competence to do their work and the commitment to do it well.
- **Line managers:** An HR department helps line managers accomplish their goals, which generally translates into building organization capabilities that help deliver business strategies.
- **External customers:** An HR department may connect its work to a firm's external customers, thereby building bonds with those external customers that will result in greater customer share.
- **Community:** An HR department may help shape a firm's reputation and identity in the community through socially responsible policies and programs.
- **Investors:** An HR department may help analysts and investors have confidence in an organization's ability to produce future earnings as measured in intangibles.

Traditionally, we believe that HR departments have focused attention on employees and line managers inside the organization. We collected data on the extent to which the HR department had the capability to add value to each of the five stakeholders. When we did a regression to determine the relative impact of the HR department's capability, we found in Figure 9.2 that the five stakeholders were equally important in predicting organizational performance.

Figure 9.2. **Relative Impact of the Five Stakeholders on Business Performance**

Stakeholder	Mean Scores	R^2	%
External customers	3.38	0.164	20%
Investors	3.27	0.180	22%
Communities	3.26	0.179	21%
Line managers	3.68	0.151	18%
Employees	3.66	0.159	19%
Stakeholder Multiple Regression		.224	

Figure 9.2 shows that successful HR departments should serve all stakeholders equally. Figure 9.1 pictorially captures these results. Traditional HR departments focus primarily on internal stakeholders (employees and line managers) but, in our research, high-performing HR departments serve all five stakeholders equally. The shift from serving primarily internal stakeholders to serving inside and outside stakeholders comes as organizations operate in a more boundary-less world where customer expectations should translate into employee behaviors.

Figure 9.3. **Traditional vs. Ideal Emphasis HR Puts on Stakeholder Groups**

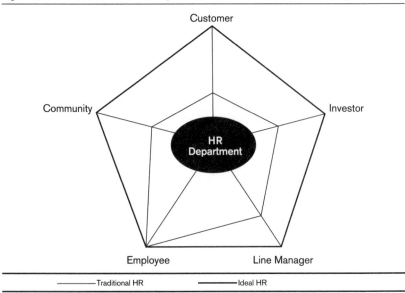

When HR departments integrate internal organization practices with external customer (and investor and community) stakeholders, they help organizations perform better. In staffing, it is no longer enough to be the "employer of choice," but the employer of choice of employees that customers would choose. If customers could be involved in an organization's hiring process by setting standards, conducting interviews, and helping to make hiring decisions, it is more likely that the right employees will be hired.

In training, customers may participate in designing, attending, and presenting material to make sure that the content taught meets customer expectations. General Electric's renowned Crotonville often hosts teams with GE employees and customers. Together, they learn how to solve problems, increase quality, and serve each other.

When a telecommunications company held its senior management conference, HR decided that, instead of planning an afternoon outing during the conference, it would invite a panel of former customers. These former customers spoke honestly about why they stopped doing business with the firm. This candid conversation led to insight and reflection and the "training" event become very real for attendees.

In performance appraisals, targeted customers may be asked to examine an appraisal form and respond whether or not the outcomes and behaviors on the form match the customer's expectations. Some hotels have placed a short survey on their guests' beds, which becomes part of the performance appraisal of employees who serve these guests. By seeking customer input, employees know that their service to guests becomes a part of their performance review.

In communication, customers may participate in giving and receiving messages. Medtronic, a medical device company, frequently invites customers to talk to employee groups. Its customers are in better health because of Medtronic's products. When these customers express their heartfelt thanks, they effectively communicate the impact of Medtronic employees' work.

In building task forces or teams to solve organization problems, customers may participate as team members to ensure their point of view is considered in making choices. When an appliance company found a problem with its compressor, it invited customers to attend quality improvement workshops.

At first, company representatives were nervous about sharing mistakes in their compressors with customers, but they soon realized that customers already knew the mistakes. The company wanted customer feedback to learn how it could address and overcome these mistakes.

In all of these cases, customers (or investors or community members) may participate in doing HR work. Engaging external stakeholders into HR work helps HR departments deliver value. Figures 9.2 and 9.3 show that organizational performance improves when external stakeholders are involved.

To further understand how to work with the five stakeholders, it is necessary to ask: To what extent is the stakeholder *considered* in building HR practices? To what extent is the stakeholder *involved* in building HR practices?

Building means the stakeholder requirements are considered in crafting HR practices. This means that the *essence* of the stakeholder exists as HR goes about its work. *Involving* is the extent to which the stakeholder participates in shaping the HR practices. This implies the stakeholders' presence in actively participating in doing HR work. Both the essence and the presence of stakeholders are fundamental to how the HR department operates.

Figure 9.4 shows that in building HR practices, it is important to consider investors, communities, and employees. This means that these stakeholders set criteria for how HR should be practiced. Investor criteria include factors that build intangible value, such as confidence in leadership, speed to market, customer service, innovation, and culture. Community criteria might include social responsibility and sustainability as defined by desired community expectations. Employee criteria might include investing in HR in ways that allow employees to meet their needs through the organization. These three stakeholders may be used to set the criteria on which HR investments are made.

Figure 9.4. **The Relative Impact of Stakeholders in Building Value through HR**

Build Items	Beta	%
Build HR practices that add value to external customers	0.045	16%
Build organization capabilities that investors value (or those who provide capital)	0.133	48%
Build HR practices that add value to the communities	0.125	45%
Build organization capabilities that help line managers turn strategy into action	0.016	6%
Build an employee value proposition that lays out what is expected from employees and what they get in return	0.93	33%
Stakeholder Multiple Regression		*0.223*

Figure 9.5 shows that involving customers and line managers can lead to higher performance. While criteria of investors, communities, and employees may be considered, the data suggest that customers and line managers should participate in defining and delivering HR practices. As suggested above, customers may participate in staffing, training, performance appraisal, communication, or organization design efforts. Likewise, when line managers participate in these activities, their results can lead to higher organizational performance.

Figure 9.5. **The Relative Impact of *Involving* Stakeholders in Creating Value through HR**

Involve Items	Beta	%
Involve customers in the design and delivery of HR practices	0.094	25%
Involve investors (or those who provide capital) in the design and delivery of HR practices that create value for them	0.023	6%
Involve communities in the design and delivery of HR practices	0.059	16%
Involve line managers in the design and delivery of HR practices	0.148	39%
Involve employees in design and delivery of HR practices that increase their abilities	0.053	14%
Stakeholder Multiple Regression		*0.172*

Conclusions

HR people matter, but the HR department matters more in predicting business performance. HR departments impact business more when they serve both internal and external stakeholders. Investors, communities, and employees set criteria for how HR should operate, and customers and line managers should actively participate in shaping HR activities.

Where Should an HR Department Focus to Increase Business Performance?

A checklist should be prepared to determine if an HR department is focusing on the right things. This checklist would determine whether the HR department has a strategy to take it where it is headed and how it fits with the business, a structure to allocate resources and determine roles and responsibilities for getting work done, a scorecard to measure success, and so forth. Based on characteristics of high-performing HR departments, we identified 11 characteristics of a high-performing HR department.

Figure 9.6 shows the extent to which these statements are true of the participant's HR department. The mean scores in the right-hand column simply indicate the extent to which each of the 11 characteristics exist within the HR departments. These mean scores indicate that issues related to strategy are truer than issues related to measurement. In the last decade, many HR departments have worked to make sure that their HR work aligns with business strategy. This strategic HR work helps translate business strategy into HR priorities and increases confidence in executing the strategy. HR departments have also done HR strategy, which is setting a vision or mission for the HR department. While attention to measurement has increased in recent years,[4] it is not yet embedded in HR departments.

Figure 9.6 also shows the relative impact of each of these HR activities on business performance. The two HR activities with the most impact on business performance both relate to the structure of the HR organization (each getting 13% of the 25% of explained business performance). Evidently, the ways in which the HR department is organized ensures that the HR department creates value for business performance. This is likely true because the organization can focus HR resources on the priorities that are the most important for business results.

Figure 9.6. **Mean and Percent of Impact on Business of HR Focus**

Item	% Impact	Mean
Ensure that HR strategy turns business goals into HR priorities	9%	3.75
Have an HR strategy that links HR practices to business strategy	10%	3.72
Ensure that organization structure of HR is consistent with the business strategy	13%	3.75
Align organization structure of HR with the organization structure of the business	13%	3.77
Measure the impact of HR practices on business results	10%	3.41
Use empirical research to identify best HR practices	7%	3.38
Create a workforce scorecard	5%	3.25
Track employee engagement	6%	3.50
Manage external vendors of outsourced HR activities	5%	3.42
Ensure that HR is a cultural role model for the rest of the organization	6%	3.60
Build the capability of the HR department to add greater value	8%	3.65
Invest in training and development of HR professionals	7%	3.64
Focus Multiple Regression	.235	

To find patterns or themes in these results, we performed a factor analysis on these 11 items. They factored, or clustered, into three groups as shown in Figure 9.7. The first factor (HR strategy and structure) explained 41% of the 25% of business performance explained by the focus of the HR department. The data suggest that when HR departments align their strategy with the business strategy and their organization with the business organization, they help the business perform better. An HR department should have a strategy and a structure that reflects the business in which it operates. If the business is trying to compete through efficiency, the HR strategy should also be driven by efficiency. If the business is trying to compete through product innovation, the HR strategy should also encourage product innovation through HR. If the business is organized as a holding company with decentralized decision making, the HR department should push authority and decision making into the business units. If the business is organized more centrally with a single business focus, the HR department should be functionally organized to serve the business. If the business is an allied/diversified business, the HR department should follow suit.

Figure 9.7 also suggests that HR departments should pay moderate attention to measures of the HR processes and employee engagement. There has been an increasing demand for HR departments to be accountable through measurement rigor. This research suggests that the measurement rigor should follow strategic and organization clarity. Getting the strategy and structure aligned with business requirements will likely lead to measuring the right things rather than what is easy to measure. Finally, Figure 9.7 suggests that when HR departments focus internally on themselves, they are not creating the best value that they could be creating. Training HR professionals to do HR work is less important than training HR professionals to do HR work that delivers business results. When HR focuses on HR for the sake of HR, the department does not contribute as much as it could.

Figure 9.7. **Factor Analysis and Relative Impact of HR Focus**

Factor	R^2	%
Strategy and Structure • Ensure that HR strategy turns business goals into HR priorities • Have an HR strategy that links HR practices to business strategy • Ensure that organization structure of HR is consistent with the business strategy • Align organization structure of HR with the organization structure of the business	.225	41%
Measures • Measure impact of HR practices on business results • Use empirical research to identify best HR practices • Create a workforce scorecard • Track employee engagement	.178	33%
Capability of Department • Manage external vendors of outsourced HR activities • Ensure that HR is a cultural role model for the rest of the organization • Build the capability of the HR department to add greater value • Invest in training and development of HR professionals	.142	26%
Focus Multiple Regression		.235

Conclusions

The implications of these findings help direct how an HR leader should focus his or her attention. Getting the HR strategy aligned with the business strategy, and then getting the HR organization aligned with the business organization should be priorities for heads of HR. While it may be seductive to build elegant and powerful measurement systems or focus on getting one's HR house in order, the priority should be ensuring that the HR department aligns with business goals.

Hallstein Moerck is the head of HR for Nokia. Nokia has continued to reinvent itself. The company began as a forest products company and dabbled in cable, rubber, and electronics before becoming known for cellular phones and networks. In more recent years, Nokia is working to reinvent itself to prepare for a more web-based future. It wants to compete in the Web 2.0 space where it is not merely a cellular phone company, but an internet company. This business and cultural change has required Hallstein to rethink and reexamine how HR contributes. When he holds annual meetings to set HR priorities, he works to make sure the HR priorities will deliver on Nokia's strategies. In one recent offsite meeting to define priorities, he included three of Nokia's targeted accounts. As the HR group identified what it considered a priority for the company, it asked these customers to confirm if these were the right priorities. By involving external customers in setting its HR strategy, the HR group focused on the right things.

What HR Practices Should Get Priority for an HR Department to Increase Business Performance?

One of an HR department's primary tasks is to invest in HR practices that will permeate the company. HR practices are the policies or programs designed by HR to manage both people and organization. People-related HR practices include staffing, talent assessment, training, and performance appraisal that directly affect how people enter an organization, how they are prepared to do their work, and what incentives shape their behavior. Organization practices include adapting the organization structure, workplace design, and communication that affects the capabilities that might exist within the organization. There are long lists of HR practices,[5] but we highlighted 11 of the most common and important HR practices from our research. We focused on the extent to which each of these 11 practices adds value to the business.

Figure 9.8 reports the means and percent of impact on business performance of these 11 practices. The right-hand column indicates that staffing, performance appraisal, and training seem to be the practices that deliver the most value to the business. These practices help an organization have a flow of talented people into and through the organization. Work process design and HR technology are less viable HR practices at this point. This may be because the HR technology and work process design are newer HR practices and their value may not be as evident.

Figure 9.8 also reports the relative impact of each of these HR practices on business performance (HR practices explained 27.9% of business performance). The middle column in Figure 9.8 indicates that organization structure (13%), talent assessment (12%), performance appraisal (12%), and coaching (12%) are the most critical HR practices in predicting business performance. It is interesting to note that while coaching is not a prevalent practice (lower mean score), it has higher impact (12%), and while training is more prevalent, it has lower impact (6%). A shift that others have documented from developing people through training vs. coaching has started to occur.[6]

To further understand patterns and trends in these HR practice data, we ran a factor analysis, which breaks the 11 items into three factors: Organization, Talent, and Administration.

Factor: Organization

HR departments may be involved in designing and delivering HR practices that focus on the organization. This work includes organization structure, communication, work process design, and rewards. These HR practices help define and shape an organization's capabilities.

Figure 9.8. **Mean and Percent of Impact of HR Practices**

Item	% Impact	Mean
Talent assessment	12%	3.74
Staffing	9%	3.90
Training and development	6%	3.86
Performance appraisal	12%	3.88
Rewards	6%	3.69
Internal communication	9%	3.70
Organization structure	13%	3.70
HR technology	8%	3.50
Workplace policies	9%	3.85
Coaching	12%	3.56
Work process design	4%	3.45
HR practice Multiple Regression	.291	

Factor: Talent Practices

HR departments may be involved in designing and delivering HR practices that improve an organization's quality of talent. These practices include talent assessment, staffing, and performance appraisal.

Factor: Administrative Practices

HR departments may be involved in designing and delivering HR practices that facilitate the administrative work within a company. These practices include technology and workplace policies.

Figure 9.9 shows that HR departments are most effective when they focus on both organization and talent HR practices. This finding about HR practices is consistent with the findings in this chapter that the HR department (organization) accounts for more of business performance than the individual HR professionals (talent). Likewise, HR professionals need to be knowledgeable in designing and delivering HR practices that shape the organization and engage the individuals.

Figure 9.9. **Factor Analysis and Relative Impact of HR Practices**

Factor		R^2	%
Organization Practices	• Rewards • Internal communication • Organization structure • Coaching • Work process design	.252	44%
Talent Practices	• Talent assessment • Staffing • Training and development • Performance appraisal	.197	33%
Administrative Practices	• HR technology • Workplace policies	.152	24%
HR Practice Multiple Regression			.291%

The implications of these findings are that HR departments need to build a mix of HR practices. It is not enough to design and deliver HR practices focused on the organization's talent. HR departments must also design and deliver HR practices that shape and build organization capabilities. HR departments should be repositories of knowledge about crafting a set of practices that permeate the organization. Knowing that some of these practices focus mostly on the individuals and their talent, and other practices focus on the organization, will help direct how to invest in HR practices. Another interesting finding is that in managing talent and organization, HR departments cannot forget the administrative work that has to be done. It affects 24% of the 27.9% of business performance accounted for by HR practices.

Implications for the HR Department

The findings in this chapter are quite compelling, as we have answered the four questions posed at the beginning of the chapter.

Figure 9.10. **Four research questions answered by HRCS**

Question	Research-based Answers
Question 1: How important is the HR department in helping business perform better?	The HR department explains 25% more of business performance than the competencies of the individual HR professionals.
Question 2: Which stakeholders should the HR department serve to increase business performance?	• All five stakeholders need attention to increase business performance. • Investors, communities, and employees set the criteria for HR work. • Customers and line managers should participate actively in designing and delivering HR work.
Question 3: Where should an HR department focus to increase business performance?	• HR strategy needs to be aligned with business strategy. • HR organization needs to be aligned with the business organization.
Question 4: What HR practices should get priority for an HR department to increase business performance?	• HR practices related to organization have more impact of business performance than those related to talent or administrative systems. • HR departments need to manage both talent and organization to fully impact business performance.

The HR department needs to be thought of as a business within the business. The overall capabilities of the HR department are 25% more important in predicting business performance than the competencies of the individual HR professionals. It is not enough to like my HR person and discount the HR department.

These findings suggest that HR leaders need to insist on creating a value-added HR department. Here are the steps for building an HR transformation plan, which may be as important as upgrading the quality of HR professionals:
• Diagnose business strategy and organization.
• Align HR and business organization structures.
• Audit the HR department.
• Create a project team.
• Blueprint the transformation.
• Monitor progress.

Diagnose Strategy

The HR strategy and organization should align with the business organization and strategy. So, the first step is to make sure there is clear understanding of the business strategy and structure. The strategy side has two components: corporate and business. Corporate strategy is about portfolio decisions and answers to questions such as: Are you a single-purpose business, a diversified business, or a holding company? On the business strategy side, HR professionals should know how the business makes money, how the business plans to grow in the future, and how the business differentiates itself from competitors.

Align Organization

Value comes when the HR organization aligns with the business organization. Single-purpose businesses require Functional HR; holding companies require dedicated HR; diversified companies require shared services HR. Setting the overall direction of the HR reorganization shows you what elements to put in place. The majority of businesses are allied/diversified, so the majority of HR departments are organized in a similar manner with five roles and responsibilities within the department. The following five roles and responsibilities should be delineated and defined with clear accountabilities and outcomes.

Shared services: E-HR, Service Center, or outsourcing vendors who manage the administrative transactions related to HR.

Corporate HR: The corporate level role that oversees the entire corporation, sponsors corporate-wide initiatives (e.g., firm reputation), services the top 1% to 3% of employees, and coordinates the HR department work.

Centers of Expertise: Specialists who design menus of choices on policies that might be adopted by the business units.

Embedded HR: Generalists who are like account managers, relationship managers or business partners who work with organization unit leaders to shape and implement strategy.

Operational HR: HR solution providers who help execute HR strategies and deliver HR practices within the business.

Audit the HR Department

Transforming an HR department requires baseline data on the department's performance. Based on research reported in this chapter, we proposed the HR audit in Figure 9.11 at the end of this chapter. This assessment may be given to those inside the department and to those outside the department. It draws on this chapter's key findings and can be a guide for benchmarking how the HR department is performing.

Project Team

Set up a project team, including key stakeholders—line managers, HR professionals from corporate, business unit, and specialist staffs—plus external consultants if needed, and charge it with creating the business case for HR transformation. Once that is done, tell the team to lay out the road map for transformation, define roles and responsibilities in the new organization, implement the project, and measure success.

Blueprint the Transformation

As the transformation team begins working, it creates a blueprint for how to transform the HR department. There are milestones along the way to ensure the transformation is progressing.

Milestone 1: Getting started

Imagine meeting with a large portion of the HR community 90 days into the HR transformation. The meeting agenda should include:

- An understanding of the business: a presentation that increases business literacy of the HR community. This presentation could be drawn from existing presentations about the business that might be made to the board of directors, senior managers, or industry groups. It grounds the HR transformation in the business.
- A vision for the HR department. A vision statement has three elements:
  - Who we are: words that capture the desired identity of the HR professionals (e.g., coaches, architects, partners, players).
  - What we do: images that capture the essential work of HR (e.g., build individual abilities and organization capabilities).
  - Why we do it: statements of the value of HR (e.g., to build competitiveness, to reach financial goals).

Goals for the HR Department

The goals for the HR department are likely to be the outcomes of good HR work, which may also be defined as the capabilities the organization requires to succeed. These capabilities may be defined in behavioral terms with clear measures and accountabilities stated to deliver them.

Milestone 2: Making investments

The HR transformation can now make investments to do HR for HR and ensure that the goals are delivered.

- HR practices: What HR practices can be designed and delivered to help deliver the goals within the business, and within the HR department? Often departments are the last to receive state-of-the-art tools in staffing, training, and rewards.
- HR structure: It is important to make sure that the HR organization is put in place with each of the five roles described above delineated and staffed with those competent to do the work.
- HR professionals: It is critical to upgrade the quality of HR professionals.

Monitor Progress

Measures of success should include HR costs, which can be tracked from HR staff ratios, and HR budgets. But measures of success should also include satisfaction with HR services as tracked by employees and line managers, and the perception of the firm by investors (as measured in intangibles) and customers (as measured by share of targeted customers).

Figure 9.11. **Audit of the HR Department**

To what extent does my HR department...	Low 1 to 5 high
1. Build HR practices that add value to and involve external customers?	
2. Build HR practices that add value to and involve line managers?	
3. Build HR practices that add value to and meet the criteria of investors ?	
4. Build HR practices that add value to and meet the criteria of communities?	
5. Build HR practices that add value to and meet the criteria of employees?	
6. Have an HR strategy that links HR practices to business strategy?	
7. Align organization structure of HR with the organization structure of the business?	
8. Ensure that HR strategy turns business goals into HR priorities?	
9. Ensure that organization structure of HR is consistent with the business strategy?	
10. Design and deliver organization structure practices that add value to the business?	
11. Design and deliver talent assessment practices that add value to the business?	
12. Design and deliver performance appraisal practices that add value to the business?	
13. Design and deliver coaching practices that add value to the business?	
14. Design and deliver staffing practices that add value to the business?	
15. Have a process for managing HR transformation?	

Scores:

65 to 75	Your HR department is in great shape. It is probably a source of competitive advantage.	
50 to 64	You have a very good HR department, but there are probably a few areas of weakness. Identify the lower scores and work to improve them.	
35 to 49	Your HR department is OK, but not great. You may want to pick one or two average scores and work to increase them and then try to get most of the other scores to average.	
20 to 34	Your HR department is struggling. Find one or two areas where you are good and work to become great in those areas.	
Below 19	Your HR department is in trouble. It is time to call for significant help.	

CHAPTER 10

Summary and Implications

D ata without insight is incomplete, like food without taste, driving without a direction, or going to college without a major. Our research was designed to discover the competencies required of HR professionals and the capabilities needed by HR departments to deliver value. The previous chapters highlight the data and findings. This chapter focuses on the implications of these findings for each of the five audiences of HR outlined in Chapter 1: HR professionals, HR departments, HR practices, HR profession, and the management of people and organization.

We will base these implications on the data, but we are not bound by it. We will take the liberty of also drawing on our personal experiences and our aspirations for the HR profession. Our hope in this chapter is to project what can and should be for the future of the HR journey.

Implications for HR Professionals

The primary focus of our research has been to figure out the competencies that will help HR professionals have greater impact. Our research suggests nine specific things HR professionals can do to make this happen.

Replace Self-Doubt with Self-Confidence

Generally, we are who we think we are. For too many years, HR professionals have lamented their image and role as administrators, policy police, and bureaucrats. They wanted to be at the table where key business decisions were made. HR professionals can definitely be *at the table* if they demonstrate the right competencies. Those who lament not being included in key decisions are, in effect, blaming others for their own lack of what it takes to contribute. Feeling victimized is a waste of energy; better to direct their efforts toward mastering the competencies we have identified and get on with growing their contribution.

We found that non-HR associates see enormous value in their HR professionals. The six competency domains of HR professionals explain about 20% of the performance of a business as seen by non-HR associates (see Figure 2.23). In particular, when HR professionals become Credible Activists, they are seen as personally effective and they help their businesses become more competitive (see Figures 2.16 and 2.23). The Development Priority Index pinpoints the competency factors where HR professionals stand to gain the greatest "bang for the buck." We summarize this work in Figures 10.1 and 10.2. The graph represents visually what we have reported in Chapters 3 through 8, plotting the performance impact of each of the 21 factors vs. the average proficiency demonstrated by the HR professionals in our study. The table gives the details. This yields a

Figure 10.1. **Summary of Development Priority Index**

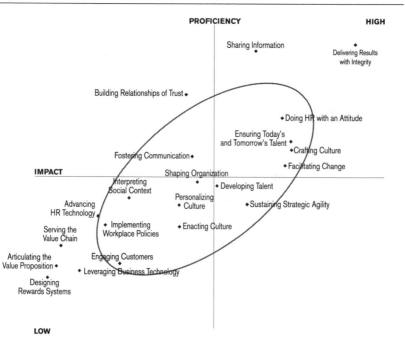

view of the competency factors that have the greatest effect on performance and, at the same time, the most room for improvement. These are the competencies that deserve the most attention for the profession overall. Figures 10.1 and 10.2 show that many of these high-priority factors relate to culture and strategy.

Figure 10.2. **Summary of Factor DPI scores. (Average score is 5.64)**

Factor	Percentage	DPI
Sustaining Strategic Agility	5.91%	7.82
Facilitating Change	6.59%	7.76
Crafting Culture	6.70%	7.51
Ensuring Today's and Tomorrow's Talent	6.69%	7.28
Developing Talent	5.37%	6.74
Enacting Culture	4.70%	6.61
Doing HR with an Attitude	6.53%	6.55
Shaping Organization	5.02%	6.22
Personalizing Culture	4.68%	6.21
Delivering Results with Integrity	7.85%	5.71
Fostering Communication	4.92%	5.64
Engaging Customers	3.62%	5.59
Interpreting Social Context	3.78%	4.91
Implementing Workplace Policies	3.35%	4.70
Sharing Information	6.06%	4.56
Leveraging Business Technology	2.89%	4.54
Advancing HR Technology	3.22%	4.41
Building Relationships of Trust	4.81%	4.40
Articulating the Value Proposition	2.47%	3.84
Serving the Value Chain	2.55%	3.77
Designing Rewards Systems	2.31%	3.69

Knowing what to do is very different from actually doing it, however. This research removes most of the mystery surrounding what HR professionals must do to be effective. Perhaps the greatest remaining barrier for HR professionals is their own self-doubt. Too often, HR professionals under-appreciate, undervalue, and under-apply their own competencies. A negative self-image can create a vicious circle of underperformance leading to incompetence. We hope that our data offer an affirmation of sorts, marking a path from self-doubt to self-confidence.

Self-confidence comes when HR professionals not only know what is expected (the competencies we have identified), but act on them. Often, HR professionals ask us, "Where should I start if I want to be more effective?" Our answer is to begin with the mindset and understanding that HR contributes to business performance. With this assurance, HR professionals are more likely to have conversations with their business leader where the focus is on the business requirements, not the HR practices. Determine the business issues facing your business, then think seriously about how to make HR investments that address the business challenges. A new self-image comes from doing little things that culminate in big things.

Develop an Inside and Outside View

HR professionals need to have a broader definition of how they add value. Value is defined by the receiver more than the giver, and too often the only perceived "receivers" of HR are employees and line managers inside the organization. As mentioned in Chapter 8, we often ask groups of HR professionals, "Who are your customers?" All too frequently, the answer is, "Employees throughout the company." True, but not complete. We found that the best HR departments focused equally on those inside the company (employees and line managers) and those outside the company (customers, investors, and communities) (see Figures 9.2 and 9.1). HR professionals can and should bring investor and customer data (see Figure 6.1) to strategy discussions, according to Figures 9.4 and 9.5. They can link their programs and activities with those outside the firm as well as those inside the firm. They are not just the designers and developers of HR policies and practices that affect employees, but business people whose practices affect all stakeholders. As we look to the future, those stakeholders will increasingly include investors, customers, communities, and partners (joint venture alliances) where HR professionals connect what happens inside their organizations with stakeholders outside.

For HR professionals, the change might be as simple as looking at their calendars and scheduling time to go on sales calls, attend investor presentations, or meet with community leaders. Such external exposure will help them align internal HR practices with external customer and investor expectations. In addition, HR professionals can apply their knowledge of how to "manage people" to customers outside the company. For example, HR professionals who are good at designing communication protocols that enlist employees can also do so for customers. Bringing the customer voice into the organization is a primary area for future HR development. (See Chapter 6 on the Strategy Architect domain).

Share Accountability for People and Organization with Line Managers

We found that for the most part HR professionals and non-HR respondents had similar views of HR excellence—with a couple of major exceptions. First, non-HR respondents included rewards in the equation for Talent Manager/Organization Designer; HR professionals did not include rewards in this equation. We side with the non-HR respondents. Performance measures, rewards, and benefits should not be excluded from other talent and organization-design practices. Hiring and training people on one set of criteria, then paying them on another, only creates confusion. The second area where non-HR associates differed somewhat from HR participants is the use of customer information. Non-HR associates tended to see HR professionals needing to be more aligned with external customers.

We strongly believe that managing people and organization is a team sport. HR professionals apply a body of knowledge and are able to turn that knowledge into processes that create and sustain strong organizations. Other staff groups (marketing, finance, IT, and so forth) do the same. General managers are ultimately responsible for the integration of these disparate functions into a business focus. HR professionals should be excellent in their functional expertise, but able to support line managers in delivering overall business results as well.

HR professionals often sit in the shadows when difficult decisions are made, allowing others to make things happen. Instead, they need to get involved, making sure that the right things happen for the business relative to people and organization and the business. As Strategy Architects (Chapter 6) they play a large part in clarifying strategy, designing HR practices to make strategy happen, specifying leadership behaviors consistent with strategy, including the customer point of view in strategy, and facilitating strategy processes. HR professionals should be able to envision not only what will (or may) happen, but translate this future state into present talent and organizational choices. In envisioning the future, HR professionals should not only understand economic, technological, demographic, and global trends, but shape today's HR practices in such a way as to anticipate and respond to them. They should be activists with a point of view, based on theory, experience, and data. They should engage in a debate with line managers and colleagues. And if they make bad choices, the only remedy is to admit it, learn, and move on.

Focus on Individuals and Organizations (not one or the other)

The data in this round of the study support what we have long known intuitively: Great individual talent without a strong organization will not endure. It is tempting to make HR professionals solely the guardians of talent. Terms like human capital, competencies, intellectual capital, talentship, workforce planning, and people processes all focus on talent. Much of the theory and logic of HR comes from psychology, where the focus is on the individual. Some HR people say they went into HR because they "care about people." Of course, those in HR should care about people. People are important, and talent, human capital, and workforce planning are essential for the success of any company. But if the talent within an organization doesn't embody and perpetuate the right organization capabilities, HR professionals have not done their job. All-star teams could seldom beat well-organized teams—and the game of business is mostly a team sport. HR professionals need to manage teams in all their forms: committees, problem solving groups, councils, forums, task forces, project teams, work teams, executive teams, and so forth. And, HR professionals need to learn to build organization capabilities such as learning, collaboration, speed, innovation, service, and efficiency.

It is significant that, in this round of our research, talent management and organization development factored statistically into the same competency domain (Chapter 5). The message is clear: It is not enough to worry about people without understanding how people work together in organizations. Theories from economics (how does the organization deliver financial value), sociology (how do people work together), and anthropology (how do we build a culture in the organization) help HR professionals understand not only people, but also organizations. To master these disciplines, HR professionals need to master the language of the business (strategy, finance, and marketing), the processes of collective behavior, and a sense of culture.

HR professionals can and should be doing a series of audits to inform and guide their work. Intangibles audits help find out what investors value. These audits rely on meeting and/or knowing investors and analysts who follow your industry, finding out how they perceive your firm, and determining how you can differentiate your firm from your competitors. Talent audits determine the extent to which an organization has the people resources to deliver on its goals. Talent audits begin with a theory of competencies required for business results, assess the extent to which those competencies exist, and invest in ways to build competencies. Organization audits focus on the capabilities required to deliver business strategies. Talent and organization audits may be done formally with a definitive methodology and deliverable report, or informally in conversations and discussions in the course of business. HR professional audits help identify the strengths and weaknesses of HR professionals. These audits may include personal 360-degree feedback based on the competencies we have identified in this research.

Serve People and Deliver on Business Results

Figure 2.8, the synthesis of our research, suggests that if/when HR professionals become masters on the people axis, but not on the business axis, they have a skewed and flawed view of their world. They care about people more than business. HR professionals need to understand business and make business results happen. To contribute to business, HR professionals must become Business Allies, as discussed in Chapter 8. HR professionals who want to contribute must speak the language of their respective businesses.

It is not enough to be credible, it requires being an activist and having a point of view, as discussed in Chapter 3. A business point of view is only credible when it is rooted in the language and requirements of the business. HR professionals who cannot pass the business literacy test will not be able to participate in ongoing business dialogues. (See test at the end of Chapter 8.)

We are quite disappointed that over the past 20 years, business literacy for HR professionals has not increased dramatically. For decades, HR professionals have been advised to learn finance, strategy, marketing, and other business concepts. But it is not happening fast enough to keep up with rising expectations. Linking people and the business means putting business terms on people issues and people issues into business discussions. Tracking people issues in business terms through productivity and performance analytics helps bring business discipline to people management; and making sure that business goals for innovation, growth, and financial performance are what drive HR practices puts people into business contexts.

Figure 2.8. **The Round 5 HR Competency Model**

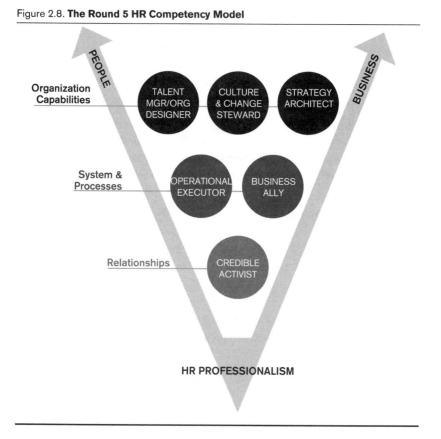

HR professionals who want to serve people and deliver on business results start by learning the language of both people and business. In the field of HR there is a body of knowledge that needs to be understood. Certification programs such as HRCI Certification ensure a minimal competence in the HR theory and research that has framed this profession. In the field of business, any HR professional needs to know how to read a balance sheet, income statement, strategic plan, and marketing analysis. An HR professional should understand and be able to present the state of the business to a board of directors, senior management team, or group of employees.

Accomplish Both Transactional and Transformational Work
In Figure 9.9, we showed that HR departments have more impact on the business when they manage three areas of HR: organization, talent, and admin-

istration. While organization and talent have a higher correlation to business results in our research, the administrative work also matters. In Chapter 7 on the Operational Executor domain, we found that HR professionals need to ensure that technology and HR policies are executed flawlessly. HR professionals need to be able to deliver on day-to-day plans while also configuring long-term strategies. But getting work done well and doing work well are two different things. Doing the work well is as critical as getting the work done. It is not as critical to do the work as to ensure that it is done well.

HR departments are more important in predicting business results than are the competencies of individual HR professionals within that department, as discussed in Chapter 9. This implies that while no individual HR professional has to master both transactional and transformational work, the collection of HR professionals in an organization should be excellent at both. Anyone outside the HR department should be able to trust the department to deliver both transactional and transformational work. For an individual HR professional, this implies that a career may evolve in a variety of ways. Some HR professionals may choose to become excellent in transaction work; others may focus on mastering how to transform organizations through Centers of Expertise and/or Embedded HR roles. Regardless of the specific area where an HR professional works, it is important to respect and support those doing other types of work.

Shift from Politics to Collaboration

At the heart of the Credible Activist domain is the ability to perform work with integrity, as explained in Chapter 3. Integrity means having and living against a personal standard of ethics. It also means building trust and credibility into each interaction. Too often, differences of opinion among people or departments lead to political infighting either among those in HR or between different departments within an organization. HR professionals need to model how to work as peers with other staff groups. The distinction between line and staff should blur. Likewise, different staff groups need to learn to work together to create organizations that win. While HR can offer any staff group insights on its talent and capability, it can partner with certain staff groups in specific ways. For example: With marketing, HR can help turn a firm brand into an organization culture; with finance, HR can help define the intangibles that investors value in specific and measurable ways; with IT, HR can make sure that enterprise-wide systems are implemented and that data is used for decision making.

Inward focus and infighting saps energy and attention. When HR professionals stay focused on how each individual and/or department contributes to collective success in the marketplace, internal political bickering gets replaced by a desire to achieve a common goal. Having a common enemy (competitor), goal (financial investors), or target (customer or community) may make internal differences secondary to the primary goals of serving stakeholders.

HR professionals collaborate by engaging others in a common cause, by sharing experiences, and by learning together. When HR professionals learn to work together and share challenges and opportunities, they cooperate with other staff and with line managers to deliver value. A colleague once taught us that one of HR's sources of power was, ironically, its lack of political power. Because none of the traditional power bases in an organization felt threatened by HR (e.g., engineering, marketing, sales, manufacturing), our HR colleague said he could call meetings and ask people to cooperate without pressuring anyone. HR professionals also remain apolitical by treating information with confidentiality and building relationships of trust (Chapter 3).

Support Others and Have a Point of View

In the movie *The Candidate*, a long shot won the election and became senator. Then, with a frightened look on his face, he asked, "Now what do we do?" Getting invited to participate in strategic decision making is easier than contributing to it. HR professionals need to come to meetings informed and able to engage in the give-and-take of decision making. They need to stop playing the stereotypical role of "speaking only when spoken to" or offering observations only on narrowly defined HR topics.

Ideally, if an outsider were observing the management team, it would not be immediately apparent who the HR professional is. At the same time, when HR issues arise, the HR professional needs to not only provide informed input to the team, but define alternative courses of action and make and defend reasoned recommendations. In the Credible Activist domain, we found that Doing HR with an Attitude is critical to successful HR, according to Figure 3.6.

Doing HR with an Attitude means having a point of view about what the business needs to succeed. This means that HR professionals should be active participants in discussions about customers, competitors, investors, communities, and other business issues. In the Strategy Architect domain discussed in

Chapter 6, we learned that successful HR professionals have a point of view about building strategic agility and incorporating external customer views into strategy conversations. When HR professionals make recommendations on how to formulate and execute strategy, they are more effective.

HR professionals also need to support others in their work. HR is an enabler. People and organizations are means to accomplish other goals. Financial performance may be tied to productivity and the quality of the workforce. Customer service scores may be tied to experience, skills, and affinity with the sales representatives who are selected and trained by HR. Manufacturing excellence comes when the socio-technical systems combine to implement lean and other efficiency based processes. When HR professionals connect their knowledge to the goals and outcomes of those they work with, they support by enabling. HR professionals support by coaching, facilitating, and architecting HR practices to align to business results.

Invest in Personal Growth

Finally, HR professionals who succeed will be constantly learning and growing. Over our 20 years of studying HR, competencies have evolved. For example, in this round of the study, change and culture have combined. According to Chapter 4, HR professionals not only have to make change happen as an event, but they have to build cultures or patterns. Increasingly, HR professionals need to understand the global social conditions that affect firms (see Figure 8.5). They need to be global thinkers as they seek best practices anywhere in the world.

HR professionals are often the cobbler's children who lack good shoes. While designing training and development experiences for others, HR professionals often under-invest in themselves. In each chapter, we suggest ways that HR professionals can invest in themselves to be more successful.

At BAE Systems, the HR professionals worked to improve their personal competencies through an intense training experience over eight weeks. The first week was how HR professionals could contribute to business success. Then each attendee was asked to do a personal development project and to work on some corporate-wide issues. Six weeks later, they attended a second program where they learned some of the innovations in HR practices and how to make change happen.

Investing in HR delivers value that can be measured. When BAE tracked the impact of this development, it saw remarkable results:

- HR's influence on business decisions and strategy increased 120%.
- HR's provision of innovative business solutions increased 85%.
- HR's understanding of key performance indicators increased 68%.
- HR's provision of good general HR advice and support increased 67%.
- HR's understanding of the business and its needs increased 45%.

In managing change and continuing to learn, HR professionals need to be resilient. Not everything works all of the time. Resilience stems from the ability to reflect on what did and did not work. HR professionals need to be resilient, which includes patience and persistence, as they work to get things done. We hope that our research on HR competencies will help focus practitioners on the areas where their professional growth and development will yield the greatest results.

Implications for HR Departments

HR departments need to operate like a business within a business. To be successful, a business needs a strategy, a structure, and ways of operating. Likewise, HR departments need a purpose, ways of delivering their expertise, and operating principles. Often, HR departments measure their effectiveness in overly simplistic ways, e.g., ratio of total employees per HR professional. These gross measures are useful to compare a department over time, but offer no insight about what is right and what is wrong. In general, this ratio has shifted from somewhere around 50:1 to 75:1 to about 100:1. Some companies have gone into the 300:1 range, thinking that fewer HR professionals is better. The risk with these companies is that when there are not enough HR professionals to do HR work, shadow staff emerge (called administrative assistants or staff in other areas). With doubtless the best intentions, such adjunct staff lack the professional training or competencies to do HR work properly.

When HR departments operate as a business within a business, they become service providers for those inside and outside the company. Here are five specific implications of our research for HR departments:

Serve all Stakeholders

HR departments spend too much time justifying their existence through inwardly-focused metrics, e.g., employee engagement or satisfaction. Our research shows that HR departments should deliver value to those inside *and* outside the organization. This means that in HR department meetings, agendas should include customer report-outs: What is our firm's market share? Customer share of key customers? Customer service ratings? Key wins or losses and lessons learned?

HR practices should be aligned with external expectations. New employees should be hired based on how well they demonstrate the skills and abilities that customers expect. Employee performance measures should be consistent with what customers would value. If a customer could look at your organization's performance standards and evaluation criteria, would he or she confirm or challenge the performance management system? If customers do not see the relevance or value of the standards used by employees, the standards need to be adjusted.

Training programs for employees should reflect customer expectations by offering content consistent with why customers chose to do business with the firm. Ideally, customers would be involved in the design and delivery of many training activities. When HR practices align internal employee actions with external customer expectations, the HR department serves multiple stakeholders.

Have a Clear HR Strategy

HR departments, like any business, need a clear strategy. An HR strategy should be created for any organization unit that has a business strategy that defines the financial and customer goals of the business unit. We have found that HR strategies can often begin with a synthesis of the business strategy. This synthesis may come from presentations made to the senior management team or information shared at meetings of the board of directors. When HR professionals grasp the business realities, they can then build a stronger HR strategy.

An HR strategy defines where the HR department unit is headed and starts with a vision. For an HR department, this vision answers three questions:

- Who are we?
- What do we do?
- Why do we do it?

The answers to these simple questions help define an HR vision. The head of HR and or a team of senior HR professionals may answer these questions and shape the HR vision.

This vision then needs to be turned into outcomes, goals, or objectives. For HR, these outcomes become the deliverables of the HR department. They ought to be the capabilities that the organization requires to succeed, or the intangibles that investors value. The deliverables or capabilities may be identified through an organization audit, then expressed in measurable terms. Visions that lay out where an HR department is headed and outcomes that specify goals and deliverables become the foundation of a good HR strategy. Visions inspire; deliverables operationalize.

Align HR Structure with the Organization Structure

Once an HR strategy is defined, an HR structure can be created to deliver against the strategy. If the organization is primarily a single-product business, a central HR department is likely to be organized functionally (i.e., staffing, training, compensation, benefits, labor relations, communications) reporting to the senior HR leader and designing and deploying policies throughout the organization. If the organization is a holding company (such as Berkshire Hathaway—a large collection of totally autonomous businesses), then each business should have its own separate HR department. If the organization is a collection of allied business (such as General Electric, where business as diverse as aircraft engines and broadcasting share executive talent and have some HR practices in common), then HR needs to centralize some services (Centers of Expertise, HR Service Centers, etc.) and "embed" others in the businesses. Figure 10.3 summarizes this discussion.

Figure 10.3. **Business Structure Affects the Structure of the HR Department**

	Holding Company	A separate HR plan for each unit; none at corporate
	Heavily Diversified	An HR plan for corporate and business unit
	Slightly Diversified	An HR plan for corporate and business unit
	Single-Project Company	An HR plan only for the corporation

Ensure Collaboration within the HR Community

As mentioned above, HR departments account for a greater percentage of business performance than do the competencies of individual HR professionals. Review Chapter 9 for more details. When the different roles within the HR department operate with friction and contention, stakeholders discount HR. Conflict between what a Center of Expertise wants to "push" into the business and what Embedded HR wants to tailor should not become contentious. Differences of opinion, when talked about, negotiated, and discussed, can be healthy tensions, not contentions. Sometimes, the "community" of HR goes across organizational boundaries. Some organizations, for example, have learning operations separate from staffing or compensation. While we advocate that these people- and organization-related areas should be combined structurally, we also appreciate that there may be cases where they will stay separate. In these cases, the HR community becomes more important than the HR department, as each area that touches people and organization should be integrated to make the whole better than the parts.

Create HR Measures and Scorecards that Track the Right Stuff

Too often, we measure what is easy rather than what is important. Easy measures of HR have pervaded the profession: % trained, attitude (1 to 5 scale) about training, number hired, time to hire, % with variable pay, % on flexible benefits, ratio of HR staff to total employee FTE population, and so forth. The right measures should be less activity-focused and more value-driven. Value-driven HR scorecards look at the outcomes of the activities. Many of these outcomes are the capabilities we delineated in Chapter 1. When HR does its work well, organizations have the ability to respond to change, innovate, serve customers, collaborate, learn, create leadership brand, and so forth. HR scorecards that focus on the outcomes more than the activities will have more impact on business results.

Implications for HR Practices

This study has not focused on specific HR practices and their impact on business performance. Rather than detail innovations in any one particular HR practice (e.g., how to retain talented employees), we can recommend three ways of thinking about the set of HR practices. In our work, we have clustered the myriad HR practices into four areas: people, performance, information, and work.

People. Many HR practices relate to the flow of people in, through, and out of an organization, including sourcing, recruiting, securing, orienting, training, developing, and outplacing people.

Performance. HR practices also relate to setting standards, having measures for behaviors and outcomes, and financial and non-financial rewards. Performance-based HR practices ensure that people know what is expected of them, have accountability for delivering results, and receive positive and negative consequences for meeting or missing standards.

Information. Increasingly we see the array of communication practices linked to HR. These communication practices may be from the inside out (sharing company information with those outside), outside in (bringing customer data into the organization), top to bottom (sharing information from executives to front-line workers), side to side (making sure that ideas are shared across boundaries inside the organization), and bottom up (helping employees have a voice in directing the affairs of their organization).

Work. The ways to coordinate work through teams, processes, and organization structures also fall into the bailiwick of HR practices.

HR professionals should understand and use these four flows of HR practices in three ways: align with business strategy, integrate HR practices, and innovate and upgrade continually.

Align with Business Strategy

These four HR flows of HR practices should align with business strategy. Alignment implies that the HR practices are consistent with where the business is headed. A business may focus on product, customer, or geography to expand and grow; HR practices should be designed and delivered to make the product, customer, or geographic strategy happen. For example, compensation systems would differ by strategy to help focus attention on the behaviors and outcomes consistent with that strategy. HR professionals help align HR practices when they focus on the strategy and make sure that each HR practice will create and sustain the strategy.

Integrate HR Practices

HR practices need to be connected. If people are hired for skills A, B, and C, then they should be developed for A, B, and C, paid for A, B, and C, given information about the importance of A, B, and C, and ensure that work processes reinforce A, B, and C. Too often, each HR practice is driven by a different set of criteria. HR professionals integrate HR practices when they cooperate with each other and are aware of the consistencies and inconsistencies across the array of HR practices. This means that Centers of Expertise for compensation or rewards, for example, should be aware of how other centers are creating HR practices for recruiting, development, organization design, or communication.

Innovate and Upgrade Continually

HR professionals should be constantly aware of emerging or best practices. Each of the areas of HR practices is constantly evolving as companies experiment to learn new ways to do things. HR professionals can learn about updating HR practices through active participation in HR conferences, joining HR communities of practice, and being current in the literature of HR.

Implications for the HR Profession

Our research was sponsored and facilitated by a variety of HR professional societies around the world. Clearly, they have a keen interest in implications of our research for the HR profession overall. We will focus on the following eight implications:

Keep Updating the Body of Knowledge that Makes HR HR

A common critique of HR is that it is just "common sense." Sometimes good research confirms what we know, sometimes it offers insight we did not anticipate. There is a growing body of knowledge through academic researchers and consulting firms that should inform the profession. Some of that knowledge offers relatively clear and consistent direction for how to do HR; other ideas are nascent and emerging.[1] Regardless, the profession must continue to invest in learning.

In other work, we defined learning as the ability *to generate, then generalize ideas with impact*. Doing the research to generate new ideas is not enough. These research-based ideas need to be put in language HR professionals can use, then disseminated and adapted. The widening gap between pure academic research and practice may hurt both. The best and most enduring academic work is generally grounded in an interesting phenomenon, and best practices need to be confirmed with good research.

Be Careful about Becoming a "Female" Profession

The dramatic increase in the percentage of women in HR over the past 20 years may have made HR a comfortable professional home for women. Gender should not be a basis for hiring, nor should it define the profession. Our data show that women and men bring somewhat different competencies to their HR work. Moving to a primarily female profession might neglect other points of view.

Work Across the Sub-Specialties Among the HR Practices

With more specialized knowledge, there is a danger of increasingly divergent sub-specialties within HR. Already, compensation (especially executive compensation) has been largely separated from other HR practices. We see this tendency as professional associations grow with increasingly narrow scopes: WorldatWork, HRPS, ASTD, SIOP, OD Network, etc. HR practices have the greatest impact on business results when they are not only aligned with the strategy, but integrated with each other. While there are technical aspects of each sub-specialty that require more focus, the profession needs to stay allied and unified to have impact. This might mean shared conferences of professional associations, making sure that HR teams inside a company have well-rounded technical experts whose knowledge extends into many of the HR specialty areas.

Ensure the Quality of the Next Generation of HR Professionals

A profession reinvents itself through the quality of the next generation. SHRM's initiatives with education and curriculum are a good example. One of HR's core domains is succession planning, and many HR professionals have helped their organizations create intricate and rigorous leadership pipelines. But are we doing so for the profession? We hope our research points not only to the content of the skills for the future, but a process to get there. Before this research, many companies created their own HR competency models based on the unique needs of their company. While useful to the firm, these isolated models did not build the profession. Building the next generation of HR talent may take a concerted effort across industries, universities, and professional associations to generate longitudinal and global research projects that shape the profession of the future.

Offer Ongoing Education to HR Professionals

Groups like SHRM, CIPD, AHRI, etc., who hold regular conferences and meetings need to continually look at the content and process of those meetings to make sure that they are at or ahead of the curve. In other professions with high standards, those who are certified need to earn continuing education credits by attending conferences or seminars. We believe that HR professionals need to continue to learn and upgrade their skills by being attuned to the latest trends and emerging practices. Professional development is ultimately the responsibility of the individual professional, but it also should become an expectation of the profession.

Transfer Knowledge Worldwide
We found that many of the competencies required of HR professionals are the same around the world. We also found, however, that some emerging markets focus more on the administrative side of HR than the strategic side. While there are clearly cultural differences in assumptions about life, labor policies, and HR practices, there are many common principles and practices that could be shared globally.

Look Forward
The profession needs to anticipate societal trends that may shift how people and organizations work. For example, partly because of advances in broadband technology, 60% of IBM's workforce has no physical office. This saves a great deal of money in physical plant, but it also raises many questions about to organize people to get work done. Technology also has human implications for the depersonalization of work (text messaging may allow next generation employees to communicate, but not connect). Demographic trends can be anticipated in raw numbers of people entering the workforce, but also social demographics in terms of education, gender, ethnicity, expectations, and other characteristics of the workforce of the future. The HR profession has spent a bit too much time looking back and wanting to leave the past rather than looking forward and helping shape a future.

Have a Voice in Public Policy
In a recent meeting with governmental officials in an emerging economy, these heads of government department shared the following about their economy:
- 40% illiteracy.
- 40% of the population under age 14. This is a huge resource compared to many countries that have declining birth rates, but they don't know how to leverage this advantage, partly because of the low literacy rates.
- 3.7% of college-age students in college.

- An agrarian economy that is not equipped to compete in the modern age. For example, there are far more "cows and plows" than tractors. We asked about modernization, but were told, "If we upgrade technology in farming, what will farmers do? Our farmers are some of the least productive in the world, but if we switch to large-scale farming, then they will have high unemployment and our unemployment is already too high."
- Some manufacturing, but at the low end of the value chain. "Developed countries are putting factories in our country to reduce costs," they told us, "but we end up doing the low-skilled production while other countries do the engineering, design, and service." Desire to be a service economy, but there is not enough demand for services.
- Periodic government instability, which leads to societal instability and the unwillingness of other countries to invest.
- Brain drain: Many of the educated people leave as soon as they can—or they get advanced degrees in other countries, then take jobs in those countries.
- Playing catch-up. They know that they need to compete in the knowledge economy, but neighboring countries are way ahead (India, Singapore, Malaysia, etc.).

They then turned to us and commented, "Obviously, these national issues have HR implications. What would you suggest we do?" We had not fully considered how HR can and should play a role in emerging markets. But also in established markets, the HR professional voice should be heard. We need to have a collective voice on employee rights, organizational requirements, managerial ethics, and management processes. We need to find ways to build alliances across government, industry, and academia where each serves the other and helps the others succeed.

Implications for People and Organizations

Our work has focused on the elements of HR as HR professionals, HR departments, HR practices, and the HR profession. But we know that the management of people and organization are central to the success of any company and fall within the accountability and stewardship of every line manager. At a generic level, HR refers to how all managers identify and manage people and organization. In this broader context, the following two implications flow from our research:

Make Line Managers Accountable and Responsible for People and Organization

It is easy to delegate HR to HR. This means that when a company wants to hire someone, the HR department takes the lead and makes it happen. The HR department designs and delivers training, compensation, and other HR systems. We believe that HR should not be done solely by HR. In fact, as knowledge work becomes more critical to an organization's success, line managers become even more central to the design and implementation of HR issues. In organizations where talent is critical, line managers take the lead in sourcing and managing talent. Movie producers hire the actors and actresses who perform in their movies; coaches and general managers select athletes who will be on their teams; department chairs and deans select faculty. In these and other organization settings, line managers realize that talent is the key to the success of the unit; line managers who want their unit to perform well become the guardians of people and organization. In these knowledge-driven organizations, HR professionals contribute real value by developing the competencies we have identified. (For reference, Figure 2.11 shows the importance of HR competencies by industry.)

Line managers are accountable and responsible for people and organization when they have clear measures and standards. Increasingly, we have seen managers being accountable for the balanced scorecard, where they have to meet financial and customer expectations, but also organization and people expectations. HR professionals may help define analytics that can be used to hold general managers accountable for people and organizational performance.

Have Line Managers Hold HR Managers Accountable to a Higher Standard

Rather than complain about weaknesses in HR professionals, line managers should challenge their HR professionals to live to a higher standard. Line managers should spend time learning what HR professionals can and should contribute to their business. When HR professionals lack the requisite skills, line managers stand to gain by investing in the HR professional's development. If the HR professional continues to fall short, line managers should be empowered to replace them.

Conclusion

We began this book with vignettes of HR professionals who are attempting to become more professional. Robert, age 52, has been promoted from a specialist role to a generalist HR position. Judy, the psychologist, has taken on organization development and change initiatives. Harvey is a new head of HR, moving into the role from a career in line management. Helen is a line manager worried about transforming the culture of her department. Daniel is the head of HR for a small and growing bank in India.

This book is written to each of these, and the other million HR professionals who are at various points along their respective HR journeys. The research we have done offers a clear and current statement of what HR professionals should know and master. We also have offered guidelines on how to go forward to develop these competencies.

Reinventing, transforming, revitalizing HR—all of these are worthy goals, but too often they are pursued without theory and data to guide choices. This book defines the competencies for HR professionals and the foci for HR departments that will help the HR profession move forward in a powerful way. For many individuals and departments, this work raises the bar on the way to do HR work, with specific implications for HR's ability to deliver on its opportunities. We hope that when applied, this research will in some small way help transform the field of HR.

History of HRCS Models

Over the past 20 years, the HR Competency Study (HRCS) has striven to develop these three areas of HR. We have seen consistencies in areas of HR that continue to be important as HR evolves. We have also seen differences that are very intriguing. The following is a brief history of the HR competency models developed through the years.

1987

HR professionals had a unique set of competencies that could be tracked around the world (prior to this work, models were within a company or a small set of firms). This was the first truly global and comprehensive data set. To be viewed as high-performers, HR professionals needed the following three competencies regardless of position, industry, or geography:

- **Business Knowledge.** Understanding how the business made money and how resources needed to be organized to add to the bottom line has been an important competency needed by HR professionals from the beginning of the HRCS.

- **HR Delivery.** HR professionals are responsible for taking care of the company's human capital. They need to know who to hire, who to promote, and how to train; make sure that systems are in place to pay; administer benefits; etc.

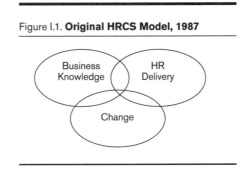

Figure I.1. **Original HRCS Model, 1987**

- **Change.** HR professionals' ability to manage change within an organization has demonstrated itself to be the most important set of competencies
by far.

1992

In 1992, the second round of
the HRCS was conducted with
several returning companies, as
well as a number of new participants. In addition to the three
competencies identified in the
first round, the model evolved
to include a fourth competency called Personal Credibility,
which includes being able to set
and meet expectations, and earn-
ing the trust of their constituents.

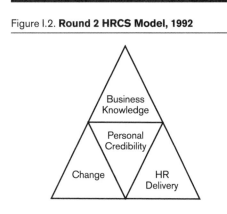

Figure I.2. **Round 2 HRCS Model, 1992**

This study also found that
businesses experiencing low rates of change and that invested in HR had a
significant impact on business performance.

1997

The third round of the HRCS
was conducted in 1997. As with
the two previous rounds, the
new model added another competency domain: Culture. Data
showed that the ability to manage culture was an important
factor in the overall view of HR.

This round also found that
Business Knowledge and HR
Delivery had lower impact on
HR professionals' individual
competency. In interviews and
follow-up, we found that these

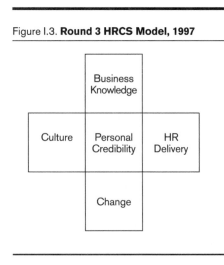

Figure I.3. **Round 3 HRCS Model, 1997**

competencies were assumed or expected and, therefore, did not act as differentiators for HR professionals.

2002

When the fourth round of the study was conducted in 2002, the research team focused not only on how competencies affected individual performance of the HR professional, but the performance of the business as well.

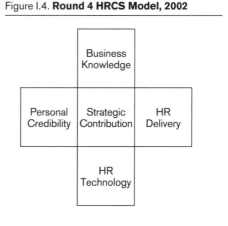

Figure I.4. **Round 4 HRCS Model, 2002**

The competencies Business Knowledge, HR Delivery and Personal Credibility remained important to the performance of HR professionals as well as the business. Culture and Change were rolled into a new competency domain called Strategic Contribution. This new competency included HR professionals' ability to link HR practices to external customers, which was referred to in that round as market-driven connectivity. Finally, a new factor called HR Technology emerged, encompassing the need for HR professionals to understand technology solutions related to the more transactional portions of their work.

This round found that Personal Credibility was still a primary predictor of individual performance and a secondary predictor of business performance. Together, Personal Credibility and Strategic Contribution explained 60% to 70% of both individual and business performance.

2007

In 2007, the HRCS research team continued to focus on the importance of competencies as they related to individual and company performance. Due to the changes in the past five years in HR, this model is more dynamic. HR professionals are expected to fulfill the roles of each of the six competency domains. Each factor under these domains is an action that makes that role effective. Major highlights from this round include:

- 20% of a business's success can be attributed to HR professionals.

- Credible Activist emerged as the most impactful competency for both the individual and the business.
- Talent Manager/Organization Designer, Culture & Change Steward, and Strategy Architect showed up as second tier in importance. With these competencies, HR professionals are able to develop organization capabilities that create competitive advantage.
- Operational Executor and Business Ally are table stakes—they do not differentiate a company or an individual, but knowledge and competency in these areas is necessary to play.

Figure I.5. **Round 5 Competency Model, 2007**

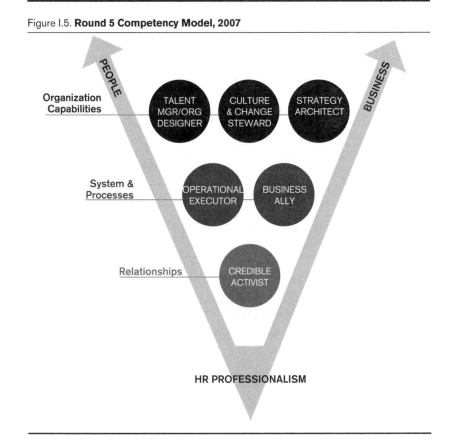

Research Methodology

O ver the last 20 years, we have collected five rounds of data on the competencies required by HR professionals. While the methodology has evolved, it has relied on the same basic premises in terms of sample procedure, participants, and survey questions.

Sampling Procedure

One of the major purposes of the original HRCS study was to understand the HR competencies and practices of leading American firms, biasing the research toward large companies in the United States. In subsequent rounds, the sample became global and focused on a broader distribution of small, medium, and large firms.

Two methods were used to involve companies in the competency study. The first method was used in the 1988 round in which 250 companies were invited to participate in the study drawn from the:

- 100 most admired firms in the United States as identified by *Fortune* magazine in 1988.
- 50 largest firms in the United States in terms of total number of employees as listed in *Human Resource Executive*, 1988.
- Firms with which research team members had research or consulting contacts.

Of the 250 invited companies, 91 chose to be involved in the 1988 study. Similar methodologies were used in the 1992 and 1997 rounds of the competency study. In Round 4 of HRCS, we worked to gain a more global sample by including partners from different geographic areas. We continued with this partnership methodology in 2007 and grew to 441 participating companies worldwide.

Respondents

To gather the data from this large number of companies, we relied on a 360 methodology that allowed us to look at expected competencies of HR professionals from multiple perspectives. At times, what is expected of HR professionals might best be understood by those outside HR who use their services (e.g., line managers, staff colleagues in finance, marketing, etc.). At other times, only HR professionals can understand what is expected of other HR professionals.

As an analogy, assume we were trying to figure out the competencies of a good parent through a 360 methodology. At times, it is useful to look at data from those outside the family (e.g., neighbors, teachers, friends) to find out how the parent fulfills his or her role. At other times, it is useful to look at data from those in the family (children, spouse, and grandparents). At other times, it is useful to do a self report. With the 360 data we collected in 2007, we were able to examine the competencies of HR professionals from multiple perspectives.

To do this research, we sent survey invitations to HR participants. These participants filled out their own survey (participant) and sent it to their peers, subordinates, supervisors, and clients (associates), some of whom were in HR and some were not. Most of the data were collected on-line. As a result of this methodology, there are different ways to look at the data set:

- Overall respondents. Everyone who filled out the survey.
- Participants: The HR participants who distributed the associate surveys.
- Total associates: The total number of associate respondents.
  - HR associates: Associates who work in the HR function.
  - Non-HR associates: Associates who do not work in the HR function.
- Businesses: We aggregated respondents into businesses. Sometimes this was the participant and his/her associates and sometimes it was multiple participants who worked in a single business. A business was the organization unit in which the HR participant worked. In small companies, the business was the corporation; in larger companies, the business might be a geographic, product, or functional unit.

Survey Questions

In the first round of the HRCS in 1988, the competencies and practices included on the survey were identified through a three-step process:

First, the research team examined the literature on HR practices and competencies to identify the domains into which these practices and competencies might be organized.

Second, the research team interviewed more than 150 HR professionals and conducted a focus group of industrial psychologists. The interviews and focus group identified the practices, skills, knowledge, abilities, and experiences that support the previously identified domains.

Third, a questionnaire was developed and pilot-tested with 23 HR professionals and 190 associates. A cross section of the HR professionals provided feedback on the questionnaire, modifications were made, and the final survey design was completed. This resulted in the identification of three major domains of HR competencies: business knowledge, HR delivery, and change management.

Appendix I shows the evolution of the study results. In each ensuing round of the survey, we looked at the questions and identified which ones did or did not explain the performance of HR professionals. We focused on questions that explained HR performance. We also examined trends in the profession and added questions that reflected current HR challenges while keeping a core set of questions.

As mentioned in Chapter 2, we began the research and data collection process for Round 5 by having a meeting with our global partners:
* Society for Human Resource Management.
* IAE School of Business.
* Irish Management Institute.
* Tsinghua University.
* Australian Human Resource Institute.
* National HRD Network.

We spent significant time revamping the survey—deleting questions that were outdated and no longer relevant, and adding questions that portrayed challenges or situations facing businesses today. From this process, about

50% of the old questions were replaced by new questions. We did this to maintain historical data while making the new survey more relevant.

Factor Analysis

The figure below reports the factor analysis scores for the items in the survey. They are grouped into the six domains that emerged from this factor analysis. The numbers in each column indicate the relative weight (or "loading" in factor analysis terms) of this item on the identified domain. We report all weights (or loadings) over .4. As is evident from this figure, most items only load on one factor or domain, which makes this validates and confirms the selection of six domains. If an item has a higher score the .4 on two domains, we included it in the domain where it scored the highest.

Factor analysis was performed to factor out the new domains using an exploratory method. We looked at several options for numbers of factors, etc., and chose the one that made the most sense. We performed this factor analysis in two steps:

- **Domain factor analysis:** We examined 130 items pertaining to the competency of individual HR professionals and performed a massive factor analysis to determine how many major groups would be defined in the new model.
- **Factor factor analysis:** We performed factor analysis on items within each of the domains described above to define a deeper level of granularity in the model.

Domain Factor Analysis

To perform this factor analysis, we used the following settings:
- Show values for factor loading >.4 for all items (rule of thumb).
- Criteria factors (6) iterate (25) (final version—we tried this with as few as 3 and as many as 12).
- Varimax with Kaiser Normalization.
- Extraction Method: Principal Component Analysis.

Incidentally, we ran several subsets of this data set to take a look at the differences in the data. These differences influenced our model and will be discussed as the need arises.

Only Exploratory Factor Analysis was performed for both domain and factor factor analysis. Confirmatory Factor Analysis (CFA) was not performed.

Some items have multiple factor loadings across domains. We selected the highest loading items for each factor list. More rigorous structural equation modeling and CFA may be needed to confirm these domain (and factor assignments).

For items that factored in more than one component, the highest factor loading score was used (precedent from past rounds of the study). For items where there was little or no difference, the item was not used.

Figure II.1. **Domain Level Factor Analysis**

All Respondents, N=10,063						
	1	2	3	4	5	6
Use challenging and valuable work to motivate and retain key talent	0.5983					
Strategic level: Human resource practices that focus on linking human resource activities to long-term business success	0.4048					
HR best practices	0.4742					
Establish standards for required talent	0.6427					
Assess key talent	0.6526					
Attract appropriate people	0.5886					
Promote appropriate people	0.6575					
Retain appropriate people	0.6220					
Remove people from the organization when appropriate	0.5848					
Manage workforce diversity	0.5541					
Facilitate establishment of clear performance standards	0.6196					
Offer training programs	0.5226					
Design development initiatives that facilitate change	0.5879					
Design developmental work experiences	0.5729					
Develop people management skills in leaders and managers	0.6390					
Set expectations for leadership behaviors	0.6311					
Follow up and reinforce personal change	0.5647					

Figure II.1. **Domain Level Factor Analysis continued**

All Respondents, N=10,063						
	1	2	3	4	5	6
Organization design	0.4865					
Design measurement systems that distinguish high-performing individuals from low-performing individuals	0.6052					
Facilitate the design of internal communication processes	0.4204					
Work with managers to send clear and consistent messages	0.4420					
Develop a comprehensive internal communication strategy and plan	0.4403					
Help establish reporting relationships	0.4756					
Facilitate the design of organization structure	0.4957					
Know when and how to leverage teams	0.4802					
Perform organizational diagnosis and audits	0.4206					
Provide accurate and candid feedback	0.5552					
Design feedback processes	0.5886					
Encourage others to make change happen fast		0.4129				
Help employees to understand the behavioral implications of the desired culture for them personally		0.6401				
Frame culture in a way that engages employees		0.6630				
Encourage executives to behave consistently with the desired culture		0.5656				
Translate culture into management practices (e.g., staffing, resource allocation, compensation)		0.5438				
Communicate desired culture inside the organization		0.6578				
Measure the influence of culture on firm performance		0.5777				
Make the whole organization more than the sum of its parts		0.5961				
Identify the culture required to meet the business strategy of your business		0.6045				

Figure II.1. **Domain Level Factor Analysis continued**

All Respondents, N=10,063	1	2	3	4	5	6
Align individual behavior and organizational goals		0.4989				
Help people understand why change is important		0.5079				
Identify and engage people who make change happen		0.4905				
Sustain change through HR practices		0.4729				
Have a clear concept of the culture that is required for your business to succeed		0.4949				
Design and deliver HR practices that create and maintain the desired culture		0.5443				
Share knowledge across organizational boundaries		0.5173				
Make culture management a business priority		0.6331				
Focus the internal culture on meeting the needs of external customers		0.5992				
Help employees find purpose and meaning in their work		0.5541				
Ensure that the culture of your business is recognized in the mind of external stakeholders (i.e., customers and shareholders)		0.5674				
Manage work-life balance within the organization		0.4929				
Encourage innovation in your business		0.4930				
Articulate outcomes of change		0.4222				
Build commitment to strategic direction		0.4337			0.4190	
Facilitate change processes		0.4662				
Monitor progress of change processes		0.4592				
Adapt learnings about change to new change initiatives		0.4740				
Help create the need for change		0.4795			0.4386	
Meet commitments			0.6816			

Figure II.1. **Domain Level Factor Analysis continued**

All Respondents, N=10,063						
	1	2	3	4	5	6
Have track record of results			0.6575			
Demonstrate high integrity			0.6983			
Have earned trust			0.7493			
Perform accurate (error-free) work			0.6610			
Work well with management team			0.7099			
Am a role model of organization			0.6986			
Respond quickly to internal constituents			0.6758			
Express effective written communication			0.6298			
Express effective verbal communication			0.6519			
Have effective interpersonal skills			0.6716			
Have "chemistry" with key internal constituents			0.6654			
Have "chemistry" with key external stakeholders			0.4830			
Take appropriate risks			0.4646			
Provide candid observations			0.5483			
Influence others			0.5887			
Your business HR practices	0.4401		0.4476			
Globalization of business				0.5503		
External political environment				0.5608		
Social issues that impact your business				0.4959		
Demographic trends that influence your business				0.5832		
Design of work processes				0.4377		
Government regulation				0.4442		0.3994
Competitor analysis				0.6713		
Requirements of external customers				0.6671		
Managing customer relationships				0.5976		
Marketing and sales				0.6437		
Managing supplier relationships				0.6437		

Figure II.1. **Domain Level Factor Analysis continued**

All Respondents, N=10,063						
	1	2	3	4	5	6
How your business makes money (who, where, how)				0.5566		
Mergers and acquisitions				0.5939		
Financial statements (balance sheet, income statement, cash flow)				0.6487		
Market capitalization valuation and intangibles				0.6746		
Requirements of shareholders and owners				0.6663		
Computer information systems				0.5588		
New emerging technologies				0.5358		
E-commerce				0.6457		
Research and development				0.6146		
Production or manufacturing processes				0.5609		
Help establish the business strategy					0.6357	
Engage in constructive problem solving with client					0.4389	
Forecast potential obstacles to success					0.5339	
Have a vision of the future for your business					0.5171	
Bring intellectual rigor to business decision making					0.5993	
Identify problems central to business strategy					0.6413	
Set the direction of change					0.6281	
Recognize business trends and their impact on your business					0.5814	
Frame complex ideas in useful ways					0.5514	
Provide alternative insights on business issues					0.6123	
Are proactive in contributing to business decisions					0.6000	
Translate business strategy into annual business initiatives					0.6376	

Figure II.1. **Domain Level Factor Analysis continued**

All Respondents, N=10,063	1	2	3	4	5	6
Work with business leader to articulate purpose and meaning for the organization					0.5562	
Ensure the availability of resources (money, information, people) that make change happen fast					0.4269	
Ensure that key leaders are aligned around major change initiatives		0.4362			0.4347	
Facilitate the integration of different business functions					0.4065	
Design performance-based compensation systems	0.4192					0.5500
Design non-financial rewards systems	0.4416					0.5222
Design appropriate benefits systems						0.6757
Labor legislation						0.4346
Contribute to the design and allocation of physical space						0.6318
Manage labor policies and procedures						0.5747
Design flexible work schedules						0.5291
Manage the arrangement of physical space and workplace environment						0.5952
Manage pension programs						0.7130
Leverage information technology for HR practices						0.4853
Use technology to facilitate organizational transformation						0.4543
Leverage HR information systems to make better decisions						0.4400
Transactional level: HR practices that focus on efficient delivery of HR transactions such as payroll, benefits, etc.						0.5744
Extraction Method: Principal Component Analysis.						
Rotation Method: Varimax with Kaiser Normalization.						

Factor Analysis

Once domains were identified, factor analysis was performed within each domain as well to determine sub-domains, or factors, that represent behaviors or competencies needed by HR professionals.

To perform this factor analysis, we used the following settings:
* Show values for factor loading > .4 for all items (rule of thumb).
* Some items have multiple factor loadings across domains. We selected the highest loading factor items for each factor list.
* Criteria factors (6) iterate (25) (final version—we tried this with as few as three and as many as 12).
* Varimax with Kaiser Normalization.
* Extraction Method: Principal Component Analysis.

Incidentally, we ran several subsets of this data set to take a look at the differences in the data. These differences influenced our model and will be discussed as the need arises.

Only Exploratory Factor Analysis was performed. CFA was not performed. Some items have multiple factor loadings across domains. We selected the highest loading items for each factor list. More rigorous structural equation modeling and CFA may be needed to confirm these domain (and factor assignments).

Domain 1: **Credible Activist**

Domain Central Tendency:	• Mean: 4.188 • SD: .589
Reliability Coefficients for all Domain 1 Items:	• N of Cases: 8,356 • N of Items: 16 • Alpha: .949

Factor Name	# of Items in Factor	Mean	Standard Deviation	Cronbach's Alpha
Factor 1 Delivering Results with Integrity	8	4.275	0.607	0.921
Factor 2 Sharing Information	3	4.242	0.668	0.847
Factor 3 Building Relationships of Trust	2	4.071	0.776	0.750
Factor 4 Doing HR with an Attitude	3	3.997	0.703	0.788

Factor Loadings for Items within the Credible Activist Domain

Credible Activist	1	2	3	4
Delivering Results with Integrity				
Meet commitments	0.7627			
Have track record of results	0.6895			
Demonstrate high integrity	0.7243			
Have earned trust	0.6500		0.4257	
Perform accurate, error-free work	0.6506			
Work well with management team	0.5721		0.4190	
Am a role model of organization	0.5972			
Respond quickly to internal constituents	0.6083			
Sharing Information				
Express effective written communication		0.7754		
Express effective verbal communication		0.8092		
Have effective interpersonal skills		0.6063	0.4877	
Building Relationships of Trust				
Have "chemistry" with key internal constituents	0.4060		0.7289	
Have "chemistry" with key external stakeholders			0.7640	
Doing HR with an Attitude				
Take appropriate risks				0.7711
Provide candid observations				0.6642
Influence others		0.4492		0.5058

Domain 2: **Culture & Change Steward**

Domain Central Tendency:	• Mean: 3.796 • SD: .684
Reliability Coefficients for all Domain 2 Items:	• N of Cases: 7,806 • N of Items: 28 • Alpha: .974

Factor Name	# of Items in Factor	Mean	Standard Deviation	Cronbach's Alpha
Factor 1 Facilitating Change	10	3.831	0.722	0.949
Factor 2 Crafting Culture	11	3.888	0.713	0.947
Factor 3 Valuing Culture	4	3.574	0.816	0.862
Factor 4 Personalizing Culture	3	3.681	0.804	0.796

Factor Loadings for Items within Culture and Change Steward Domain

Culture & Change Steward	1	2	3	4
Facilitating Change				
Encourage others to make change happen fast	0.6892			
Help people understand why change is important	0.7101			
Identify and engage people who make change happen	0.7113			
Sustain change through HR practices	0.6701			
Articulate outcomes of change	0.6765			
Build commitment to strategic direction	0.6653			
Facilitate change processes	0.7610			
Monitor progress of change processes	0.7456			
Adapt learnings about change to new change initiatives	0.7218			
Help create the need for change	0.7182			
Crafting Culture				
Align individual behavior and organizational goals	0.4432	0.5028		0.4017
Identify the culture required to meet the business strategy of your business		0.4337	0.4260	0.4297
Help employees to understand the behavioral implications of the desired culture for them personally		0.5979		
Frame culture in a way that engages employees		0.5412	0.4245	
Encourage executives to behave consistently with the desired culture		0.5695		
Translate culture into management practices (e.g., staffing, resource allocation, compensation)		0.5196		
Communicate desired culture inside the organization		0.5699		
Have a clear concept of the culture that is required for your business to succeed		0.7584		
Design and deliver HR practices that create and maintain the desired culture		0.6934		
Share knowledge across organizational boundaries		0.6419		

Make culture management a business priority		0.5856	0.4913	

Valuing Culture

Measure the influence of culture on firm performance			0.6256	
Make the whole organization more than the sum of its parts			0.4569	0.4391
Focus the internal culture on meeting the needs of external customers			0.6634	
Ensure that the culture of your business is recognized in the mind of external stakeholders (i.e., customers and shareholders)			0.7625	

Personalizing Culture

Help employees find purpose and meaning in their work				0.6712
Manage work-life balance within the organization				0.7755
Encourage innovation in your business	0.4311			0.4527

Domain 3: **Talent Manager/Organization Designer**

Domain Central Tendency:
- Mean: 3.78
- SD: .673

Reliability Coefficients for all Domain 3 Items:
- N of Cases: 6,462
- N of Items: 29
- Alpha: .965

Factor Name	# of Items in Factor	Mean	Standard Deviation	Cronbach's Alpha
Factor 1 Ensuring Today's and Tomorrow's Talent	11	3.920	0.702	
Factor 2 Developing Talent	6	3.743	0.809	
Factor 3 Shaping Organization	5	3.759	0.758	
Factor 4 Fostering Communication	3	3.859	0.839	
Factor 5 Designing Rewards Systems	4	3.364	0.963	

Factor scores for items within the Talent Manager/Organization Designer Domain

Ensuring Today's and Tomorrow's Talent				
Provide accurate and candid feedback	0.4756			0.4473
Use challenging and valuable work to motivate and retain key talent	0.4701			

HR best practices	0.4577		
Establish standards for required talent	0.6512		
Assess key talent	0.6749		
Attract appropriate people	0.7583		
Promote appropriate people	0.7895		
Retain appropriate people	0.7755		
Remove people from the organization when appropriate	0.7066		
Manage workforce diversity	0.6557		
Facilitate establishment of clear performance standards	0.4878		
Developing Talent			
Offer training programs		0.7516	
Design development initiatives that facilitate change		0.7869	
Design developmental work experiences		0.7700	
Develop people management skills in leaders and managers		0.6889	
Set expectations for leadership behaviors	0.4503	0.5042	
Design feedback processes		0.4287	0.4151
Shaping Organization			
Organization design			0.5707
Help establish reporting relationships			0.7378
Facilitate the design of organization structure			0.8053
Know when and how to leverage teams			0.6312
Perform organizational diagnosis and audits			0.6820
Fostering Communication			
Facilitate the design of internal communication processes			0.7745
Work with managers to send clear and consistent messages			0.7412
Develop a comprehensive internal communication strategy and plan			0.7464

Designing Rewards Systems				
Design performance-based compensation systems				0.8399
Design non-financial rewards systems				0.7754
Design appropriate benefits systems				0.8292
Manage pension programs				0.7069

Domain 4: Strategy Architect

Domain Central Tendency:
- Mean: 3.596
- SD: .711

Reliability Coefficients for all Domain 4 Items:
- N of Cases: 7,201
- N of Items: 19
- Alpha: .958

Factor Name	# of Items in Factor	Mean	Standard Deviation	Cronbach's Alpha
Factor 1 Sustaining Strategic Agility	15	3.647	0.735	
Factor 2 Engaging Customers	4	3.435	0.799	

Factor Loadings for Items within the Strategy Architect Domain

Sustaining Strategic Agility				
Help establish the business strategy	0.7082			
Engage in constructive problem solving with client	0.6650			
Forecast potential obstacles to success	0.7587			
Have a vision of the future for your business	0.7148			
Bring intellectual rigor to business decision making	0.7882			
Identify problems central to business strategy	0.7968			
Set the direction of change	0.7445			
Recognize business trends and their impact on your business	0.7117			
Frame complex ideas in useful ways	0.7584			
Provide alternative insights on business issues	0.7787			
Am proactive in contributing to business decisions	0.7668			
Translate business strategy into annual business initiatives	0.7327			

Work with business leader to articulate purpose and meaning for the organization	0.7164			
Ensure the availability of resources (money, information, people) that make change happen fast	0.5468	0.4287		
Ensure that key leaders are aligned around major change initiatives	0.6602			
Engaging Customers**				
Facilitate dissemination of customer information		0.8109		
Contribute to building the brand of the company with customers, shareholders, and employees		0.8199		
Facilitate the integration of different business functions		0.7325		
Remove low value-added work		0.6440		

**This factor did not show up when using the entire data set; it did, however, show up when using the non-HR respondents. Note that a couple of the items making up this factor did not factor at all in the overall database but have been added under the factor Engaging Customers for the final version of the model.

Domain 5: **Operational Executor**

Domain Central Tendency:	• Mean: 3.577 • SD: .742
Reliability Coefficients for all Domain 5 Items:	• N of Cases: 7,388 • N of Items: 8 • Alpha: .872

Factor Name	# of Items in Factor	Mean	Standard Deviation	Cronbach's Alpha
Factor 1 Implementing Workplace Policies	5	3.5779	0.739	0.834
Factor 2 Advancing HR Technology	3	3.6072	0.892	0.912

Implementing Workplace Policies				
Labor legislation	0.5178			
Contribute to the design and allocation of physical space	0.8063			
Manage labor policies and procedures	0.7534			
Design flexible work schedules	0.6965			
Manage the arrangement of physical space and workplace environment	0.7438			

Advancing HR Technology				
Leverage information technology for HR practices			0.8771	
Use technology to facilitate organizational transformation			0.8464	
Leverage HR information systems to make better decisions			0.8861	

Domain 6: **Business Ally**

Domain Central Tendency:	• Mean: 3.498 • SD: .661
Reliability Coefficients for all Domain 6 Items:	• N of Cases1: 6,139 • N of Items: 21 • Alpha: .945

Factor Name	# of Items in Factor	Mean	Standard Deviation	Cronbach's Alpha
Factor 1 Serving the Value Chain	5	3.501	0.806	0.875
Factor 2 Interpreting Social Context	5	3.681	0.707	0.811
Factor 3 Articulating the Value Proposition	5	3.421	0.807	0.866
Factor 4 Leveraging Business Technology	6	3.401	0.712	0.825
Serving the Value Chain				
Competitor analysis	0.5803			
Requirements of external customers	0.7511			
Managing customer relationships	0.7783			
Marketing and sales	0.6764			
Managing supplier relationships	0.6279			0.4525
Interpreting Social Context				
Globalization of business		0.6210		
External political environment		0.7392		
Social issues that impact your business		0.7802		
Demographic trends that influence your business		0.5345		
Government regulation		0.4607		
Articulating the Value Proposition				
How your business makes money (who, where, how)		0.4597	0.4961	

Mergers and acquisitions			0.6043	
Financial statements (balance sheet, income statement, cash flow)			0.7398	
Market capitalization valuation and intangibles			0.7503	
Requirements of shareholders and owners			0.6634	
Leveraging Business Technology				
Computer information systems				0.7079
New emerging technologies		0.4312		0.5684
E-commerce			0.4512	0.6340
Research and development	0.4614			0.5427
Production or manufacturing processes				0.5405
Design of work processes				0.4413

Once factor analyses for both domains and factors were accomplished, the following items were dropped for the following reasons:

Figure II.2.

Follow up and reinforce personal change	Factored in three of the five sub-factors under Talent Manager/Organization Designer, and in none of them very strongly
Design measurement systems that distinguish high-performing individuals from low-performing individuals	Did not factor in the sub-factor Talent Manager/Organization Designer
Your business HR practices	Factored under Talent Manager/Organization Designer and Credible Activist, in neither very strongly; was disregarded before doing the factor level factor analysis
Help ensure privacy of personal data	Did not factor in the domain factor analysis
Focus on how to get decisions made quickly	Did not factor in the domain factor analysis
Understand and manage the global implications of HR practices	Did not factor in the domain factor analysis
Transactional level: HR practices that focus on efficient delivery of HR transactions such as payroll, benefits, etc.	Did not factor in the domain factor analysis; also does not belong
Operational level: HR practices that focus on day-to-day delivery and administration of HR practices, policies, and procedures	Did not factor in the domain factor analysis; also does not belong
Strategic level: HR practices that focus on linking HR activities to long-term business success	Did not factor in the domain factor analysis; also does not belong

Domain and Factor Scores

Once the domains and factors were defined, domain and factor scores were created. The rules and guidelines used for creation of these scores are as follows:

- Domain scores were generated as the average of all items within a domain.
- Factor scores were generated as the average of all items within a factor.
- Domain and factor scores are generated for each case (respondent, whether HR participant, HR or non-HR associate rater, and regardless of missing data).

Regression Analysis

The rules and guidelines that were used in calculating the regression scores for the 2007 data set of the HRCS are as follows:

- **Missing data.** While domain and factor scores were generated for all cases (10,711), we used a 60% missing data rule (missing data is comprised at N/A answers as well as unanswered items). This eliminated cases with more than 91 missing variables. The number of cases considered for regression analysis is N=10,063.
- **Multiple vs. bivariate regression.** Because of a challenge with multicollinearity, multiple regression to find the amount of effect one domain or factor has on the dependent variables was not as useful as we would have hoped. For example, regressing all six domains against the dependent variable of Individual Performance yields the following betas. Percentages have been added to further demonstrate the point.

The variance in the model is absorbed by the first and most dominant variable in the model—in this case, Credible Activist. Because of the multicollinearity of the data set and resulting model, the usefulness of this type of analysis (multiple regression) is limited.

Figure II.3.

Domain	Beta	%
Credible Activist	2.01	62%
Culture & Change Steward	.57	18%
Talent Manager/ Organization Designer	.08	3%
Strategy Architect	.69	21%
Operational Executor	-.19	-6%
Business Ally	.07	2%

To illustrate the point further, we used a different process. Each of the six independent variables is added into SPSS as a different block. This allows us to control which of the variables is considered first. This process was repeated 6 times, each entering in a different independent variable (domain) first. The R squares were then normalized to produce the following chart:

Figure II.4. **Domain Listed First in Multiple Regression**

	Credible Activist	Culture & Change Steward	Talent Manager/ Organization Designer	Strategy Architect	Operational Executor	Business Ally
Credible Activist	93%	16%	20%	30%	47%	53%
Culture & Change Steward	6%	79%	1%	2%	4%	4%
Talent Manager/ Organization Designer	1%	4%	76%	1%	1%	1%
Strategy Architect	0%	0%	4%	66%	0%	0%
Operational Executor	0%	0%	0%	1%	37%	0%
Business Ally	0%	0%	0%	0%	11%	42%

Due to this multicollinearity, multiple regressions provide little insight into the model. For this purpose, the following rules were used in regression analysis for this round:

- Bivariate regressions were performed for each domain and each factor using the 60% rule.
- The resulting R squares were then normalized to provide a basis for comparison of domains and factors. This was done by totaling the R squares and then dividing the R square for each domain and factor by the total to provide a percentage.
- Multiple regressions for entire domains or factors are provided for comparison purposes.

Individual Performance Regression

Regression analysis of each of the domains discussed above was performed to determine relative importance of each on individual performance. The dependent variable used was the answer to the following question:

Overall, how does this participant compare to other HR professionals you have known? Respondents to this question used the following scale:

1 = Bottom or Lowest 5%	6 = 25% to 29%	11 = 50% to 54%	16 = 75% to 79%
2 = 5% to 9%	7 = 30% to 34%	12 = 55% to 59%	17 = 80% to 84%
3 = 10% to 14%	8 = 35% to 39%	13 = 60% to 64%	18 = 85% to 89%
4 = 15% to 19%	9 = 40% to 44%	14 = 65% to 69%	19 = 90% to 94%
5 = 20% to 24%	10 = 45% to 49%	15 = 70% to 74%	20 = Top 5%

Two models were considered for use in the calculations of regressions for the individual performance. Model 1 used raw data from all associate raters (N~8400) for domains and individual performance scores to perform regressions. Model 2 aggregated (averaged) all rater scores to the participant level and ran this average score per participant against the average individual performance scores (N~1750).

Results are provided below for a means of comparison across the different domains.

Figure II.5.

	No Aggregation			Aggregation to Participant Level		
	All Associates	HR Associates	Non-HR Associates	All Associates	HR Associates	Non-HR Associates
Credible Activist	.407 | 24%	.383 | 24%	.440 | 23%	.518 | 23%	.429 | 23%	.509 | 24%
Culture & Change Steward	.348 | 20%	.318 | 20%	.386 | 20%	.464 | 20%	.362 | 20%	.439 | 20%
Talent Manager/ Organization Designer	.333 | 19%	.308 | 19%	.371 | 19%	.444 | 19%	.347 | 19%	.405 | 19%
Strategy Architect	.284 | 17%	.272 | 17%	.315 | 16%	.371 | 16%	.313 | 17%	.348 | 16%
Operational Executor	.164 | 10%	.142 | 9%	.214 | 11%	.238 | 10%	.177 | 10%	.241 | 11%
Business Ally	.184 | 11%	.171 | 11%	.202 | 10%	.247 | 11%	.199 | 11%	.219 | 10%
Multiple Regression R²	.441	.419	.473	.562	.479	.538

While the patterns are the same, the numbers associated with the data sets aggregated to the participant level are higher than those with no aggregation.

Business Performance Regression

Regression analysis of each of the domains discussed above was performed to determine relative importance of each on business performance. For the dependent variable we created a variable called business performance mean, which was an average score on a 5-point scale (1 being low and 5 being high) of the following items:

- Meeting customer requirements.
- Meeting owner/shareholder requirements.
- Being competitive.
- Financial management.

The business measure in and of itself presents problems of bias, since it is not based on quantitative data, but rather on the opinions of those who completed the survey on their company's performance. We did a couple of things to minimize this bias:

- Used an aggregate of four business measures instead of the overall business score.
- Aggregated all respondents to the business unit level to get an overall average for the company (N~400).
- This business measure was constant, meaning that regardless of which subset we were looking at (non-HR, associate raters only, etc.) the same business score was always used.

In looking at business performance, we also considered different subsets of the data.

In order to look at domain scores by HR raters only or non-HR raters only, a new database was created using the following steps:

- Selected desired subset of data (all HR, all non-HR, all participant, by gender, whatever) and eliminated other cases.
- Aggregated this selected subset to the business-unit level and created a new database with only the desired variables. In most cases, this consisted of the domain and factor scores.
- Imported the business performance variable, discussed above, to be included in the data set being analyzed.

Business Performance regressions based on the above rules are shown below.

Figure II.6.

	All Respondents		HR Raters		Non-HR Raters	
Credible Activist	0.183	22%	0.152	22%	0.179	19%
Culture & Change Steward	0.162	20%	0.128	18%	0.188	19%
Talent Manager/ Organization Designer	0.158	19%	0.102	15%	0.168	17%
Strategy Architect	0.102	12%	0.119	17%	0.170	18%
Operational Executor	0.111	13%	0.085	12%	0.126	13%
Business Ally	0.111	13%	0.106	15%	0.133	14%
Multiple Regression R^2	.208		.207		.207	

Chapter Endnotes

Chapter 1 Endnotes

[1] John Boudreau and Peter Ramstad, *Beyond HR: The New Science of Human Capital.* (Boston: Harvard Business Press, 2007).

[2] Others have made lists of these HR practices.
Anne Tsui and Luis Gomez-Meija, "Evaluating human resource effectiveness," *Human Resource Management: Evolving Roles and Responsibilities.* (Washington, DC: BNA Books, 1988).
B. E. Becker and Mark Huselid, "High-Performance Work Systems and Firm Performance: A Synthesis of Research and Managerial Implications." *Research in Personnel and Human Resources Journal, 16*(1), pp. 53-101. 1998.
Randall Schuler and Stuart Youngblood, *Effective Personnel Management.* (Minneapolis: West, 1999).

[3] Mark Huselid, "The impact of human resource management practices on turnover, productivity, and corporate financial performance." Academy of Management Journal, 38, pp. 635-672. 1995.
Mark Huselid and B. E. Becker, "The strategic impact of high-performance work systems." Paper presented at the 1995 Academy of Management annual meetings, Vancouver, BC.
Mark Huselid and B. E. Becker, "Methodological issues in cross-sectional and panel estimates of the HR-firm performance link." *Industrial Relations, 35,* pp. 400-422. 1995.
Mark Huselid and B. E. Becker, "The Impact of High-Performance Work

Systems, Implementation Effectiveness, and Alignment with Strategy on Shareholder Wealth." Presented at the annual meeting of the Academy of Management, Boston, Mass.

⁴ Those who have studied business trends include:
Gary Hamel, *The Future of Management*. (Boston: Harvard Business Press, 2007).
Adrian Slywotsky and Karl Webber, *The Upside: The 7 Strategies for Turning Big Threats into Growth Breakthroughs*. (New York: Crown Business, 2007).
Thomas Davenport and Jeanne Harris. *Competing on Analytics: The New Science of Winning*. (Boston: Harvard Business Press, 2007).

⁵ Dave Ulrich, Jon Younger, and Wayne Brockbank. Under review: "The next evolution in HR organization." *Human Resource Management Journal*.

Chapter 2 Endnotes

¹ P. McLagan and D. Bedrick, "Models for excellence: The results of the ASTD training and development study." *Training and Development Journal*, 37(6), pp. 10-20. (1983)
See also P. McLagan and D. Suhadolnik, *Models for HRD Practice: The Research Report*. (Alexandria: American Society for Training and Development) and P. McLagan, "Competency Models," *Training and Development*, 50, pp. 60-64.

² We should note that in the 2007 study, we had 9 categories for education and we combined them to match previous rounds of the study.

³ We are grateful for Monika Ulrich pointing out these gender insights.

⁴ Dalton & Thompson, Novations: *Strategies for Career Management*, Scott Foresman, 1986.

⁵ Some may not be aware of the statistical program called factor analysis. Factor analysis is a statistical procedure that identifies patterns of relationships among groups of variables (survey questions) and identifies the closeness of variables that coexist within a specific pattern. Essentially, it groups survey items that essentially have common underpinnings together. For example, factor analysis might statistically group together in

the same factor the perceptions of an HR participant's tendency to "have a vision for the future of the company" and an HR participant's tendency to "bring intellectual rigor to business decision making." In reality, HR participants who do one will also be likely to do the other. Thus, factor analysis reduces large complex numbers of questions into more useable groups of data.

6 Regression analysis (or more technically, linear regression analysis) is a statistical technique by which it can be determined what percent of changes one variable (e.g. an individual question or an individual factor) is accounted for by changes in another variable. Sometimes regressions are bivariate where one variable predicts another. At other times, several variables might be used to predict the changes in another single variable which is called multiple regression.

7 We should review the logic we used in doing regressions. Multiple regression equations will show how much of a dependent variable is predicted by a set of independent variables. In this work there are two primary dependent variables: an individual's HR performance and the business performance. The six domains make up the independent variables. By running a multiple regression with the six competency domains on each dependent variable, we can determine the overall extent to which we can explain individual and business performance by HR competence. But, when we try to partition the relative impact of each of the six competency domains on individual performance, we ran into a multi-collinearity problem. The six domains overlapped. When someone is good in one, they are good in another. While these domains showed up in discrete factors, they still correlate highly with each other. So, to partition the impact of the competency domains on performance, we used bivariate regressions to determine the percent of each of the six competency domains on the outcome. This allowed us to then scale these regression scores to 100 points to determine the relative impact of each of the six domains on individual and business performance.

8 Dave Ulrich and Robert Eichinger, "Delivering HR with an Attitude." *HR Magazine*, June 1998, pp.154-160.

9 Many have talked about the importance of "human" in human resources. Michael Losey, "Remember the human in human resources," and Dave Ulrich, Michael Losey, and Gerry Lake (editors), *Tomorrow's HR*

Management: 48 Thought Leaders Call for Change. (New York: Wiley: 1997).

[10] When looking at India data, it is important to recall that this is a smaller sample size than the other regions, thus the results may not be as easily generalized.

[11] We did this by first calculating the bivariate regression of each domain separately on the individual performance outcome, then summing the resulting R-squares for the six domains, and finally creating a percent of this total for each individual domain.

[12] The idea that competencies may be divided into core vs. differentiators is not unique to the data. In his work on high-performing teams, Richard Hackman divided results into essential elements of a high-performing team (real team, compelling direction, right people) and enablers of high-performing teams (sound structure, supportive context, team coaching). In our work on leadership, we separated leadership competencies into leadership code and differentiators. We believe that this data set on HR competencies highlights the code or basics endemic to all HR professionals. There may be differentiators depending on the unique position and context of the individual HR professional.

[13] Anita McGahan and Michael Porter, "How Much Does Industry Matter, Really?" *Strategic Management Journal, 18* (Summer special issue): pp. 15-30, 1997.
Rumelt, Richard. "How Much Does Industry Matter?" *Strategic Management Journal, 12*(3), pp. 167-185, 1991.

[14] This 20% is the R^2 that comes from the regression of the six competency domains on business performance.

Chapter 3 Endnotes
[1] Tony Blair, "What I've Learned." *The Economist*, May 31, 2007.

[2] Dave Ulrich and Dick Beatty, "From Partners to Players: Extending the HR Playing Field." *Human Resource Management*, 40:4, pp. 293-308. 2001.

³ Gene W. Dalton and Paul Thompson, *Novations: Strategies for Career Management*. (Chicago: Scott Foresman, 1986).

⁴ The percent of impact is the R^2 value for each factor, converted to a percentage of the sum of all 21 R^2 values. The reason we subtract the proficiency score from 5.0 is to quantify the idea of "proximity to perfection." If the HR profession scored a perfect 5.0 in one of the factors, then the difference (5.0 – 5.0) would be zero. When multiplied by the impact %, this would yield a product of zero, indicating a very low priority for development because the HR profession already does it so well. Thus, the higher the index number, the greater the developmental priority—a simple technique for "weighting" the findings.

Chapter 4 Endnotes

¹ *Harvard Business Review*, Feb 2007, p. 146.

² Culture from the outside in has been discussed in Dave Ulrich and Norm Smallwood, "Leadership Brand," *Harvard Business Review*, July-August 2007; and Dave Ulrich and Norm Smallwood, "Leadership Brand: Developing Customer-Focused Leaders to Drive Performance and Build Lasting Value," *Harvard Business School Press*, 2007.

³ Many books have focused on culture: Edgar Schein, *Organization Culture and Leadership*. (San Francisco: Jossey Bass, 2004); Lee Bolman and Terence Deal, *Reframing Organizations: Artistry, Choice and Leadership*. (San Francisco: Jossey Bass, 2003); Terrence Deal and Allan Kennedy, *Corporate Cultures*. (New York: Pereus Books Group); James Collins and Jerry Porras, *Built to Last: Successful Habits of Visionary Companies*. (New York: Collins).

⁴ Edgar Schein, *Organization Culture and Leadership*. (San Francisco: Jossey Bass, 2004).

⁵ Jody Hoffer Gittell, *The Southwest Airlines Way* (New York: McGraw Hill, 2005).

Chapter 5 Endnotes

[1] If we were to follow the current convention among professional athletes, this domain would be abbreviated to the somewhat funky-sounding label of "T-Mod."

[2] Ed Michaels, Helen Handfield-Jones, and Beth Axelrod, *The War for Talent* (Harvard Business School Press, 2001).

[3] R. Knight, "Fears for U.S. Public Sector as People Opt for Jobs Elsewhere," *Financial Times*, Feb. 5, 2007, p. 3.

[4] Dave Ulrich and Norm Smallwood, *Leadership Brand* (Harvard Business School Press, 2007).

[5] Dave Ulrich and Norm Smallwood, *How Leaders Build Value* (Wiley & Sons, 2004).

Chapter 6 Endnotes

[1] David Nadler, Michael Tushman, and Mark Nadler, *Competing by Design: The Power of Organizational Architecture* (London: Oxford University Press, 1997).
David Nadler, Marc Gerstein, and Robert Shaw, Organizational Architecture: Designs for Changing Organizations (San Francisco: Jossey Bass, 1992).

[2] Dave Ulrich and Norm Smallwood, *How Leaders Build Value* (Hoboken: Wiley & Sons, Inc., 2003).

[3] Research from Franklin Covey XQ survey.

[4] Robert S. Kaplan and David P. Norton, *The Strategy-Focused Organization: How Balanced Scorecard Companies Thrive in the New Business Environment* (Boston: Harvard Business School Press, 2000).

[5] Michael Beer and Russell Eisenstat, "The Silent Killers of Strategy Implementation and Learning," *MIT Sloan Management Review*, 41(4), Summer 2000.

Chapter 7 Endnotes

[1] Frederick Herzberg, Bernard Mausner, and Barbara Snyderman, *The Motivation to Work*, 2nd ed. (New York: John Wiley & Sons, 1959).

[2] We have worked to define how operational executors fit within the new HR organization.

[3] Dave Ulrich, Wayne Brockbank, and Jon Younger, "The next evolution in HR" (paper submitted to the *Human Resource Planning Journal*).

Chapter 8 Endnotes

[1] Brian Becker, Mark Huselid, and Dave Ulrich, *The HR Scorecard: Linking People, Strategy, and Performance* (Boston: Harvard Business Press, 2001).
Mark Huselid, Brian Becker, and Richard Beatty, *The Workforce Scorecard: Managing Human Capital to Execute Strategy* (Boston: Harvard University Press, 2005).

Chapter 9 Endnotes

[1] Even the now infamous article, "Why We Hate HR" talks about the author liking his HR person, but not HR as a whole. See K. Hammonds, "Why We Hate HR," *Fast Company*, August 2005, Issue 97, p. 40.

[2] Dave Ulrich and W. Brockbank, *The HR Value Proposition* (Harvard Business School Press, 2005).

[3] We have presented in some detail the evolution of the HR department. The organization of the HR department must align with the organization of the business to be effective. And, the emerging HR department may be dissected into five roles that each need to be managed independently, but also need to be managed collectively.

[4] HR measurement has received increased attention. See work:
J. T. Delaney and Mark Huselid, "The impact of human resource management practices on performance in for-profit and nonprofit organizations," *Academy of Management Journal*, 39, pp. 949-969, 1995.
B. E. Becker and Mark Huselid., P. Pickus and M. Spratt. "HR as a source of shareholder value: Research and recommendations." *Human Resource Management Journal*, pp. 39-47, 1997.

B. E. Becker and Mark Huselid, "Higher performance work systems and firm performance: A synthesis of Research and managerial implications," Research in *Personnel and Human Resources Journal*, 16, (10), pp. 53-101, 1998.

[5] For a list of HR practices, see:
A. Tsui, "Defining the activities and effectiveness of the Human Resource Department: A Multiple constituency approach," *Human Resource Management*, 26:35-69, 1987.
[6] M. Goldsmith and Mark Reiter, "What Got You Here Won't Get You There," January 2, 2007, Hyperion.
M. Goldsmith and L. S. Lyons, *Coaching for Leadership: The Practice of Leadership Coaching from the World's Greatest Coaches*, Pfeiffer 2nd edition, October 19, 2005.

Chapter 10 Endnotes
[1] Two books capture much of this HR knowledge:
Robert Eichinger, Michael Lombado, and Dave Ulrich, *100 Things You Need to Know: Best Practices for Managers and HR*. (Minneapolis: Lominger, 2002).
Robert Eichinger, Dave Ulrich, John Kules, and Ken DeMeuse, *50 More Things You Need to Know: The Science Behind Best People Practices for Managers and HR*. (Minneapolis: Lominger, 2007).
We have found that when we test HR professionals on the things we should know, they often fall short. Other professions (medicine, psychology, law) have requirements for continuing education; maybe it would be appropriate to require HR professionals to track their continuing education work.

Appendix II Endnotes
[1] N, or number of cases, refers to the number of listwise cases (cases without any missing data for the particular domain or factor—which includes anyone who marked an item N/A. Listwise is used for the reliability calculations only. In all other cases, pairwise elimination is used.

[2] Designing rewards systems factored with Operational Executor with all respondents and with Talent Manager/Organization Designer with only non-HR rater respondents. (See Appendix I). In the model creation and future discussion, these items appear with Talent Manager/Organization

Designer because we agree with the non-HR rater respondents: rewards systems can have a very large effect on talent management and organization design.

Index

factor analysis, 146, *243–44*
factors associated with, 146–47
    advancing HR technology, 147, 159
    implementing workplace policies,
        146–47, 158–59
    gender, 150–51, *151*, 152, *153*
    geographic distribution, 148, *149, 151*
    historical perspective on, 145–46
    HR channels, *149*, 151, *152, 154*
    individual performance, 150–52, *151,
        152*
    industry sector, *149*
    organizational implications, 156–57
    rewarding aspects of, 155–56
    size of business, *150, 152, 153*
    victimization problem, 154–55
Organization Designer. *See* Talent Manager/
    Organization Designer
organization factor, HR practices, 194–95,
    195, 208
organization structure, 103
organizational development (OD), 103
organizational response to business context,
    7, 8–14, *10*
owner distinguished from Strategy Architect,
    137

P

people/business vectors of HR, 36–38, *37*,
    207–8, *208*
personal growth of HR professionals, foster-
    ing, 211–12
personalizing culture, 82, 95
point of view and attitude, importance of,
    62–63, 210–11
policies, implementation of, 146–47, 158–59
practices, HR. *See* human resources (HR)
    practices
Procter & Gamble (P&G), 101, 116
profession of HR. *See* human resources (HR)
    profession
professional HR employees. *See* human
    resources (HR) professionals
public policy involvement of HR profession,
    219–20

Q

Qingdao refrigerator factory, China, 79

R

regional distribution. *See* geographic
    distribution
regression analysis, 246–50, *247–50*
    business performance, *249–50*
    defined, 253n5–6
    HR department and, 183
    in HRCS, 33, 45, 46
    individual performance, *248–49*

missing data rule, 246
multiple vs. bivariate, 246–48, *247*
rewards systems, designing, *105*, 105–6
Rucci, Tony, 104

S

Sears, 104
shared mindset, *10*, 11
sharing information, 60–61, 76–77
Sioli, Alejandro, 25
size of business
    Business Ally, *170*, 172–73, 173, 174,
        175
    business performance and competencies
        by, 54–55, *55*
        Business Ally, 174, *175*
        Credible Activist, *72*
        Culture & Change Steward, 91–92,
            92
        Operational Executor, *153*
        Strategy Architect, 135, *136*
        Talent Manager/Organization De-
            signer, 114–15, *115*
    Credible Activist, 66–67, *67, 69, 70, 72*
    Culture & Change Steward, *86*, 88–89,
        89, 91–92, *92*, 93
    HRCS participants by, 27, *30*, 31
    HRCS scoring and, 43–44, *44*
    individual HR professional performance
        by, *51*
        Business Ally, 172–73, *173*
        Credible Activist, 69, *70*
        Culture & Change Steward, 88–89,
            89
        Operational Executor, *152*
        Strategy Architect, 133, *134*
        Talent Manager/Organization De-
            signer, 112–13, 113
    Operational Executor, *150, 152, 153*
    Strategy Architect, 131, *132*, 133, *134*,
        135, *136*
    Talent Manager/Organization Designer,
        110, 112–15, *113*, 115
social context, interpreting, 164, 179
Society for Human Resource Management
    (SHRM), 25
speed in response to changing business
    context, 9–11, *10*
stakeholders, business performance, and HR
    department, 182–83, *184*, 185–90, *186,
    189, 196*, 212–13
Statoil, 103
strategic unity, *10*, 13–14, 216
Strategy Architect, 123–41
    business performance, *134–36*
    characteristics of, 136–40
    clarity, strategic, 137–38
    defined, 35, 124–26
    descriptive statistics, 128–32, *129–32*

About the Authors

Dave Ulrich is a professor of business at the University of Michigan and a co-founder of The RBL Group. He has published 13 books and more than 100 articles. Moreover, he has consulted and done research with more than half of the *Fortune* 200.

Wayne Brockbank is a professor at the Ross School of Business at the University of Michigan and a principal of The RBL Group. Brockbank has written award-winning papers on HR strategy and advises top global organizations.

Dani Johnson is a director of research for The RBL Group. She is responsible for the administration and statistical analysis of *The Human Resource Competency Study* and delivery of assessments and related educational tools and products.

Kurt Sandholtz is a consulting associate with The RBL Group who specializes in leadership development and executive education. He is pursuing a Ph.D. at Stanford University, where he continues to study the evolution of the HR profession.

Jon Younger is a principal of The RBL Group and leads the firm's Strategic HR practice. He advises HR leaders on HR strategy and organization, and HR leadership and professional development.

Learn More About The Human Resource Competency Study

For more information on assessments and learning surrounding *The Human Resource Competency Study*, please visit www.rbl.net/hrcs.

The HR Competency Suite includes tools that provide important feedback on how individuals and HR organizations measure up and identify areas where improvement will provide the greatest returns. The suite includes:
* Assessments against established HRCS global norms
* Feedback on HR competencies that matter most
* Comprehensive reporting and support for improvement planning
* Application and development tools to increase HR impact

Recommended SHRM
Published Books

The Practical HR Kit

Solving the Compensation Puzzle:
Putting Together A Complete Pay and
Performance System
By Sharon K. Koss, SPHR, CCP

Legal, Effective, References:
How to Give and Get Them
By Wendy Bliss, J.D., SPHR

Proving the Value of HR:
How and Why to Measure ROI
By Jack J. Phillips, Ph.D., and
Patricia Pulliam Phillips, Ph.D.

Investigating Workplace Harassment:
How to Be Fair, Thorough, and Legal
By Amy Oppenheimer, J.D., and
Craig Pratt, MWS, SPHR

The Source Book Kit

Employment Termination
Source Book
By Wendy Bliss, J.D., SPHR, and
Gene Thornton, Esq., PHR

Performance Appraisal Source Book
By Mike Deblieux

Hiring Source Book
By Cathy Fyock, CAP, SPHR

Trainer's Diversity Source Book
By Jonamay Lambert, M.A., and
Selma Myers, M.A.

HIPAA Privacy Source Book
By William S. Hubbartt, SPHR, CCP

To Order SHRM Books

SHRM offers a member discount on all books that it publishes or sells. Bulk
purchase discounts are also available for SHRM published books. To order this
or any other book published by SHRM, contact the SHRMStore.

Online:
www.shrm.org/shrmstore

By Phone:
800-444-5006 (option #1); or
770-42-8633 (ext. 362); or
TDD: 703-548-6999